Summer Madness

WITHDRAWN

Summer Madness

Inside the Wild, Wacky, Wonderful World Of The WNBA

Fran Harris

Authors Choice Press
San Jose New York Lincoln Shanghai

CALVIN T. RYAN LIBRARY
U. OF NEBRASKA AT KEARNEY

Summer Madness
Inside the Wild, Wacky, Wonderful World of the WNBA

All Rights Reserved © 2001 by Fran Harris

No part of this book may be reproduced or transmitted in any form or by any means, graphic, electronic, or mechanical, including photocopying, recording, taping, or by any information storage or retrieval system, without the permission in writing from the publisher.

Authors Choice Press
an imprint of iUniverse.com, Inc.

For information address:
iUniverse.com, Inc.
5220 S 16th, Ste. 200
Lincoln, NE 68512
www.iuniverse.com

All action photos with the exception of Fran Harris (NBA photos), and including cover shot of Tammy Jackson, were taken by Rebecca Hamm for SportsForWomen.com.

ISBN: 0-595-16030-1

Printed in the United States of America

CALVIN T. RYAN LIBRARY
U. OF NEBRASKA AT KEARNEY

DEDICATION

This book is dedicated to #10, Kim Perrot, for epitomizing the champion in all of us.

In memory
of my mother and
high school coach, Mike Stevenson.

ALSO BY FRAN HARRIS

About My Sister's Business: The Black Woman's Road Map To Successful Entrepreneurship (Simon & Schuster/Fireside, 1996)—available at booksellers nationwide.

In The Black: The African American Parent's Guide To Raising Financially Responsible Children (Simon & Schuster/Fireside, 1998)—available at booksellers nationwide.

The Dream Season: Inside the NCAA's first undefeated women's basketball team, The University of Texas at Austin (1991)—available at www.franharris.com.

Coming Winter 2001!!!

Houston By Morning, a novel set in the world of players, agents, broadcasters, and coaches in the WNBA.

Send email to franharrisbooks@aol.com to be placed on email notification list for book's release.

Or send address to:
Fran Harris
P.O. Box 5285
Austin, TX 78763

CONTENTS

FOREWORD

Do you ever reflect back on your life and think about the experiences that brought you to where you are today? Well, actually I do that quite often. In fact, where basketball is concerned, I find myself doing it a lot. Little girls always ask me about why I chose to play basketball. And I have to say that I don't really know. When I was younger, I don't think I had any idea at the time that basketball could lead me to a successful professional career. There was nothing out there to make me believe that.

I didn't even know whether I would play the game on a consistent basis. All I wanted to do was prove to a bunch of knuckleheaded boys that girls could play basketball too. And probably beat them. But the more I played ball, the more I liked it. And the more I liked it, the better I wanted to be at it. And the better I got at it, the farther I wanted to go with it.

It was during my senior year at USC in 1997 that I finally realized that there was a chance for me to continue to play the game that I love and also get paid to do it. It was an exciting thought. All of a sudden I found myself in a whirlwind of discussions about playing professionally right here in the United States.

There I was. Forty-eight hours before the first ever WNBA draft. My agent at the time, Jerome Stanley of Stanley and Associates, and I, had been involved in one conference call after another. Jerome went back and forth with the WNBA and the ABL in search of the best deal for me. The ABL was offering a larger salary for a conventional seven-month season but the WNBA, whose season was only three months long, appeared to offer more stability. Either way, it was evident that I had a real chance to play professional women's basketball in my own country—an opportunity a lot of women before me never had. I felt blessed.

At the time, I couldn't think of anything that could have been more exciting to me. Well, maybe an acceptance letter from the Harvard School of Law. But that was about it. I struggled to figure out which league to play in. Would I choose the longevity of the WNBA or the high salaries offered by the ABL?, which at the time were four to five times higher than the money being offered by the WNBA for marquee players. Put plainly, the ABL's six-figure deal sounded a lot sweeter than the WNBA's mid-range five-figure deal. And at 22, you just don't ignore dollar signs. But at the same time, because I was young, the WNBA's potential staying power would mean a long, financially secure future if I stayed healthy.

The big wigs from the ABL and WNBA came at me strong, which made my decision even more difficult. Since the WNBA's eight inaugural teams would be in established NBA cities, the ABL used that to their advantage by offering to strategically place me on one of their new expansion teams in the upcoming season. Long Beach was one of their new expansion teams and it was only about 25 minutes from where I grew up in Los Angeles. But the WNBA could play the location card too. Their franchise, the Los Angeles Sparks, held the third pick in the WNBA draft and they showed a lot of interest in having me play there as well. I tried not to get too excited because I knew that in professional sports, there were no guarantees. You could literally end up anywhere.

After hours of lobbying and negotiating, time was forcing me to make a decision. And although it was hard, I chose the WNBA at the last minute. Don't ask me why. It just felt right for me. So, to ratify the deal, several phone calls were made and numerous faxes sent. Then, in less than 24 hours I was on a red-eye flight to the NBA Entertainment offices located in Secaucus, New Jersey. In no time, I was receiving calls from WNBA coaches and general managers. Rhonda Windham, the GM for the Los Angeles Sparks, who had also played her college ball at USC, had shown tremendous interest in me, but now appeared annoyed because I had taken so long to decide which league I would play in.

I remember one of our last conversations in which she told me that her staff had been talking, and that they'd decided that if I didn't make a decision soon that they would have to explore other options. That was cool, because by now, I understood that basketball was a business, and Rhonda had to do what she felt was best for her franchise. I had no problem with that. But then she added, "Even if you do decide to play in the WNBA, there's no guarantee that we'll take you with our third pick anyway."

Her comment stung but I still felt that I needed to take my time. This was a decision that I'd have to live with for a few years at the least. And even though I had already pictured playing in the Great Western Forum on the court where my favorite basketball player, Earvin "Magic" Johnson had made history and won many championships, this was one decision that deserved much thought and consideration. Yes, it would have been great to play alongside my former college teammate Lisa Leslie and maybe even win a couple of WNBA championships in my hometown. At Southern Cal, Lisa and I had been an extremely powerful hi-low post tandem that teams had trouble defending. Who knows how dominant we could have been had I been chosen by the Sparks?

Like I said, a lot of things started happening right after I chose the WNBA. I received a call from a man by the name of Van Chancellor, who said he'd just been hired to coach the Houston Comets. He said that he was considering drafting me at number one. I have to admit that I didn't understand most of the conversation because of his Mississippi dialect but I did understand the words 'number one'. And although playing at home in Los Angeles would have been great, nothing was gonna beat being the top pick of the first WNBA draft.

The entire process was exciting but it was also eye opening. And a little intimidating. In New Jersey, I sat in a room with players who had more *professional* playing experience than I had playing experience. Folks like Nancy Lieberman-Cline and Pam McGee, pioneers in women's hoops. On the business side, I'd learned so much in just a short time. And I knew that I had made the right decision to choose the WNBA over the ABL. Jerome had done his job well. He'd tried to get me what he thought was the best deal based on my talent. But not everyone agreed with his assessment of me. One conversation sticks out in my mind. Jerome was pushing me as a high draft pick but the WNBA thought he was being a little unrealistic. One person in particular, Renee Brown, her title at the time, Director of Player Personnel, thought Jerome was crazy for saying that I was among the best in the college crop. She basically laughed and said that it was ridiculous to think that I would be a top five pick. Her words to Jerome, and I'll never forget them, were, 'Tina should just be grateful to play in the WNBA; if she makes it, it is a privilege, not a right'. She went on to imply that Jerome need not bring up the names of other players like Rebecca Lobo, Kate Starbird, Kara Wolters, and Jamila Wideman because I could not hold a candle to them. Can you believe that? Boy, did she supply me with ample motivation coming into my rookie season!

But I got through the draft and was chosen by the Comets as the first pick. I was thankful I had survived all of the negativism from the WNBA front office because now I was ready to get on the court and do my thing. Without any expectations of where I'd fit in with my teammates and coaching staff, I told myself to do the best I could and not to worry about the outcome. And that approach really helped me my first year because although few people knew it, I was incredibly nervous heading into the '97 training camp. And I was very homesick. Thank God for long distance telephone service!

So, it's the year 2000 and sometimes I can't believe my life so far. Houston, in many ways, has been a dream come true. Four championships in four years? Unbelievable. And although each season has brought me joy in its own unique way, that first season will always be the most special, probably because no one thought we'd win the championship that year. They thought the New York Liberty would. I guess you can't blame them. First, we lost our marquee player to maternity leave. Sheryl Swoopes was the player the folks in Houston were excited to see play. And yes, she was a great loss. But even without such a talented individual in the lineup, I knew that our team had tremendous potential and I also knew that we'd be a force to be reckoned with.

As soon as the '97 season tipped off we became known for our impressive pick and roll offense, similar to that of John Stockton and Karl Malone of the Utah Jazz. I don't think anyone had seen women exploit defenses the way we did. I'll go even farther and say that we revolutionized the pick and roll. Cynthia Cooper with her abilities to do so many things off the dribble—pulling up for the three-pointer, driving to the basket and passing to the open player when she was double-teamed. Me, slipping the screen and hitting a short jumper or deep three-pointer. Yep, the pick and roll offense was a catalyst for that first championship. The other ingredient was our stingy defense, which was led by our point guard, Kim Perrot, who I really feel should have won the Defensive Player of the Year award in 1998.

It also helps when you have a cast of very talented supporting players who are mature enough to accept their roles and do whatever we needed to help our team win. And we had lots of them. Players like Janeth Arcain, our silent but deadly assassin who'd been the MVP of the Brazilian league and who was the perfect compliment to Cynthia on the other wing. Another one of our unsung heroes was a woman who I'm told was one of the deadliest shooters in NCAA history, Fran Harris. She was Janeth's edgy backup who approached her work out on the court from an intelligent and aggressive angle. The list goes on and on. We had several players on that inaugural team who went underrecognized, but in our minds, they never underachieved.

I'm proud to have been a part of the league's first four championships because four championships in four years is an amazing accomplishment. But I'm even more proud that the WNBA continues to get stronger each season.

I wish I could describe what it feels like to be a player in the WNBA. To feel the electricity in WNBA arenas all summer long. To see the faces of girls and women who are so excited that our time has finally come. This is a day that women basketball players and their fans have dreamed about for so long. And I'm thankful that I've been able to see it all unfold. I'm grateful to have added to the WNBA's legacy.

Some people have asked me, what has been the best part of being a player in the WNBA. They think it's the championships. And yes, those have been great, really great. But without a doubt, it's the appreciation we all feel for the opportunity to perform on the ultimate sports stage. On a personal note, it's also been gratifying for me to have seen players like Cynthia Cooper, Jennifer Gillom, Lynette Woodard and Teresa Weatherspoon play, because they are the ones whose talent and efforts this league's foundation was built upon. They are our ambassadors. Our foremothers, if you will. And now they are passing the baton on to us. I only pray that my generation will nurture this great game as well as the veterans before us have. Because above all, it has brought each and every one of us unspeakable joy. Finally, I extend a very special thanks to Fran for her persistence in getting this book published (when's that WNBA novel comin' out, girl?). And I thank you, the fans, for your incredible support of the WNBA. We couldn't do it without you.

Tina Thompson

ACKNOWLEDGEMENTS

To God for giving me the gift of expression and the courage to speak my truth.
A book like this requires the support of so many people. Too many to name individually. First and foremost, I would like to acknowledge the women of the WNBA who continue to dedicate themselves to putting a great product on the floor each and every night. I appreciate your willingness to share your thoughts and personal stories so that this book would be authentic.

Props to the fans who show up to watch the players do their thing night in and night out. To the little girls whose eyes shine brighter now because they have an outlet for their blossoming talents and gifts. To the NBA for knowing a good thing when you saw it and then for putting your money where your mouth was.

For my family who continues to support me and encourage me in my many efforts, I love you and I thank God for giving us each other. Especially, you, Ron.

To Rebecca for her photographic contributions to MADNESS, Amin Momin at Photo Magic, and Lynsey "Comma Happy" Thomas for her editorial contributions. To screenwriter Bill Broyles for his kindness and for introducing me to Sheila Gallien, who's already helped me become a better screenwriter. And my agent, Jill Smoller of the Artists Management Group, for her belief in my talent.

To the Lifetime Television crew who made getting on a plane every Thursday for the past two years worth every second. Daniel Kron of SportsForWomen.com, thanks for giving me an outlet to discuss women's basketball in the written form. To my fantasy campers from coast to coast who continue to show love and get my back, thanks. And finally, to the women basketball pioneers and legends whose sweat and hard work helped make my dream of professional basketball in this country a reality, I'm eternally grateful.

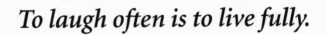

To laugh often is to live fully.

INTRODUCTION

I've never wanted to be a guy but that doesn't mean that I don't think it has its privileges. Had I been born one, I know exactly what I would've done after my junior year in college. I would have skipped my senior season, thanked the University of Texas at Austin for three glorious years of free room and board, packed up my deadly long-range jumper and defensive know-how and entered the NBA draft.

I would have played for fifteen years in the league, made multiple All-Star teams, and battled the Indiana Pacers' Reggie Miller for the league's Free Throw Shooting Champion award. I would have had a sneaker named in my honor, The Stroke Master, or something like that. Something that would let you know how automatic the jumper was back then. My agent would have secured hefty endorsement deals with McDonald's, Sprint and Gillette. In 2000, I would have retired to a multimillion-dollar broadcasting deal with NBC and smiled daily at my bulging bank account and hefty investment portfolio. But best of all, I would have had the whole wide world right in my capable little hands.

But I was born a girl and there was no WNBA when I graduated college in 1986. Nothing for elite women college players to get excited about. Our only option to continue playing was to travel 3,000 miles from home to a team where English was the third language and the women smoked cigarettes in the locker room during halftime. No cable? No shopping malls? No call waiting? No thank you. But I succumbed and left for Italy, as did most of my peers. And while the Italians treated me like the queen I was, I wanted to play on my own soil, in front of people who knew me.

I knew that a professional women's league would eventually launch, I just wasn't sure it would happen during my playing lifetime. But it did. And I was fortunate to be on the first championship team in Houston.

Now, here we are in our fourth season with sixteen teams, three national broadcasting contracts and millions of fans worldwide.

When I finally decided to sit down and write this book, I had no idea what the final work would look like. I knew that the journey for female basketball players had been turbulent at times but it was also thrilling and adventurous. I knew that it was a story that needed to be told. But when I took the idea to several publishers, I was surprised and disappointed that none of them felt the same way. I encountered editors who agreed that there should be a book about women's basketball but they just weren't willing to make a publishing commitment to the project. They all said that there wasn't a big enough buying market to warrant publishing a book. That women's sports titles had not done particularly well.

I disagreed and decided to find a way to get our story told so that millions could read about it. In my view, the legacies of the women in and around the WNBA deserved immortality. And unless you're a woman who played during a time when women's professional hoops was merely a fantasy, you can't truly appreciate just how special the WNBA is to us. You can't fathom what it's like to look for stories about us in print, on television or the big screen and find nothing. Zero. Zip.

Think for a second. How many times have you gone to a bookstore, browsed the sports section and seen shelves lined with books about people that mean absolutely nothing to you? If you're like me, more times than you'd like to admit. And if there's one book on football, there are 50. The same for baseball and men's basketball. But I can count on one hand the number of books on women's basketball there are on those shelves. And that is sad to me. Besides, I want my daughter or son to know what life for women players has been like. I want them to know about their mother and grandmother's history as athletes. I want the players coming out of college to know about our humble beginnings so that they can better appreciate the stage on which they now perform and showcase their amazing talents.

SUMMER MADNESS is the first book written about what really goes on in the WNBA. In practices, games, on the bench, in the huddles, in the stands and in television production meetings. It gives you a ringside seat into your favorite (or not so favorite) players and coaches. It's as much about celebrating where we are and where we've been as it is a spoof on the crazy things we endure in the name of putting that little round, orange leather thing through that nylon. It's about the long road from obscurity to national prominence. It's about little girls with big dreams. And it's about the love and joy we all have for this game that has meant so much to us. So, sit back and bask in the glow and goof ups of the WNBA as told by someone who's been there, got the soundtrack. It's been a great ride and I hope you're enjoying it. I know I am.

DID YOU KNOW?

In 1986, the 34-0 University of Texas Longhorns defeated the University of Southern California Women of Troy, 97-81, to become the NCAA's first undefeated women's champion?

<u>All Tournament Team</u>
Cynthia Cooper, USC
Clarissa Davis, Texas
Kamie Ethridge, Texas
Fran Harris, Texas
Lillie Mason, Western Kentucky

PROLOGUE

In the fall of 1982, at 17-years old, I left my hometown of Dallas, Texas and headed to The University of Texas at Austin on a full basketball scholarship. There had been several attempts at a women's professional league but none seemed to have the stamina to hang around for very long. I kept hearing that there wasn't enough interest in women's basketball and that's why the leagues continued to fold.

This baffled me because I'd played high school ball during a time when the stands were always full of fans. Furthermore, during my four years at UT, we were always among the nation's leaders in attendance, drawing close to 9,000 a night in the mid '80s. So when I would hear that women's basketball didn't have the fan base to warrant a pro league, I'd scratch my head. This just didn't compute, primarily because I was naïve enough to think that what was happening at UT in Austin, Texas, at The University of Tennessee in Knoxville, and at Louisiana Tech in Ruston, was happening all over the country. But I was wrong. Some college teams were barely drawing 100 spectators even when somebody's family was in town.

Still, despite the obvious challenges, I firmly believed that women's basketball would eventually have its day. I had faith that a women's league would start and last. I just wasn't sure I'd be around to see it, let alone play in it. Boy, this was one time I was really glad I had been wrong.

CHAPTER 1

The Wonder Years: From Retirement to the WNBA

You can't stop destiny. I believe that 100%. It was destiny that landed me in the WNBA in 1997. I had taken off eight years from competitive basketball and aside from my family and a few close friends, everyone else thought I was crazy for even trying to make a comeback. And I guess I can understand why. If someone had walked up to you and told you that they'd taken nearly a decade off from basketball, would you have believed that they would make a professional team? Probably not. But I'm glad I didn't listen to the people who had so little faith in the human spirit. I don't take it personally, though. I know that what we put out to others is really a reflection of how we feel about ourselves. But I'm thankful that I believed in myself or I wouldn't have pressed on and made it into the WNBA, which also means I wouldn't be writing this book.

Let's go back a few years. After I graduated college in 1986 I had high hopes and big dreams like most top basketball players. And because there was no professional league to set my sights on, my main goal was the 1988 Olympics. Going overseas to play didn't exactly knock my socks off and the only reason I was even considering it was so that I could stay in shape for the Olympic trials.

As a sophomore in college, I had been one of 27 finalists for the 1984 Olympic team that was headed to the Los Angeles Games, so I felt that my chances for the '88 team were sparkling. Two years after the '84 trials I had beaten out hundreds of women to land a spot on the USA national team that competed in the Goodwill Games and World Championships in Russia. The following year, 1987, I earned a starting spot on the Pan American team.

With the national team experiences in my arsenal, I was certain that I had put myself in a position to become one of the elite 12 players to represent the United States in Seoul, Korea in the '88 Olympic Games. But I knew that in order to solidify a spot on that Olympic squad that I would have to return to the trials in the spring of '88 in supreme physical condition. I also knew that whatever accolades I had earned in college and even in international competition wouldn't mean squat if I showed up at tryouts in Colorado Springs out of shape and a step slow.

The '87 Pan Am Games had been played in Indianapolis that year and we'd won the gold medal on August 22. That meant that I'd have eight months to stay sharp in preparation for the Olympic trials in April. So, I did what many other American players did after college—I packed an oversized bag of workout clothes, sneakers and an assortment of American goodies like peanut butter, oatmeal and Eggo waffles and I boarded a plane. Destination? Cesena, Italy.

I'll get into more details about the journey in Italy later on in the book but for eight months I played in the Italian professional league against the likes of players such as Teresa Edwards, Lynette Woodard, Paula McGee, Jennifer Gillom and the WNBA's two-time MVP, Cynthia Cooper. I played in places where a sellout crowd was 1,000 fanatical Italians. I played in places where my team had to be escorted from the locker room to the bus because the fans were too irate or were threatening to do us bodily harm. Mamma mia! That was life overseas for the best of the best up until about five years ago.

When I returned to the states in April 1988, I was leaner, stronger and in the best shape of my life. I felt sure I would land a spot on the Olympic team. After all, past Olympic teams had been comprised of players from the World Championship and Pan American teams—two teams I'd been a member of. Plus for good measure, I'd put in my time overseas.

Olympic trials back in the day were meat markets. Three to four hundred players would convene in Colorado Springs to duke it out for twelve spots. A committee of about 10-15 coaches would sit courtside and evaluate your play for 3, 4, sometimes 5 days. If that last day rolled around and your number was printed on that list that was plastered on the gym door, you felt extremely proud and honored. And most of all, very relieved.

As we all expected, our entire '87 Pan American and '86 World Championship/Goodwill Games team had survived the intense open tryouts in Colorado Springs, which meant that we'd reconvene in the early summer for training camp at a designated place, usually the stomping ground of the Olympic team head coach. The June training camp began with about 24 players. We assembled at North Carolina State in Raleigh and immediately began our two-a-days for almost two weeks with Coach Kay Yow and her staff. The first round of cuts was made and my three Texas teammates, Kamie Ethridge, Andrea Lloyd and Clarissa Davis and I were still in the hunt.

Rewind a second. In the spring of '88, right after I got back from Italy, I discovered that I had an ovarian cyst. And it had flared up right at the end of training camp in June, putting me in great pain for the last few practices. I saw a specialist who told me that it was nothing to worry about and then she suggested that I take birth control pills to dissolve it. I got the prescription and although they made me extremely sick, they worked. And it was a good thing they had worked, because I wasn't going to let anything get in the way of my Olympic dream. Not even my ovaries.

The first round of training camp ended and we were allowed to go home for a few days before the second session began in July. Weeks after we broke up camp, sixteen players arrived back in Myrtle Beach, South Carolina for the final leg of training camp. Sixteen players. For only 12 spots. Everything was going great. My cyst had dissolved and I was still playing well.

But then a funny thing happened right in the middle of training camp. The environment made a 360-degree change after several college coaches showed up to watch our games. Up until this point, I felt like it would take some fluke for me not to make that team. I had performed well in our scrimmages against the current and former NBA guys. I had not missed one practice because of my cyst. And the coaches had been very supportive. There were several media reports that quoted Coach Yow as saying that I was the best player in training camp behind Georgia's Teresa Edwards. I've still got those clippings. Being put in the same sentence as T had said it all. So when I was suddenly knocked out of the top seven or eight rotation during scrimmages, I knew something was up.

I got the call around 2:45 p.m. Coach Kay Yow was requesting my presence in her condominium in five minutes. I remember my heart doing a dance. Not one of those leaping-because-I'm-gleeful dances, either. But rather a dum duh-dum dum dance. If Coach Yow wanted to see you, it was usually not a good thing.

I entered the still of her chilly living area where she sat silently on the Aztec sofa with her hands clasped in front of her. Her eyes peering through my soul.

"How ya doin', Fran?" Those words hung in the air like a spider web. It was D-day. Or rather C-day, I should say. Because I knew I was about to be cut. My mind did a mini slide show of the last few days of training camp. The coaches had practically ignored me. I'd been one of the last players put into the recent exhibition game against Cuba. And spiritually things just didn't feel right.

I sat about two feet from her on the sofa and held my breath. Her eyes were already starting to water. "Well, Fran, it's looking like it's gonna be really difficult for you to make this team," she said. I thought that was an interesting way to put it.

Tears streamed down my face as I listened to her continue in her North Carolinian dialect. "See, you know, the European teams we're gonna face are much bigger at your position and we feel that we need someone with more size there." Size? Is this the best you can do? Is that really the best excuse you can come up with? The player who was competing with me for that spot was my height and maybe ten pounds heavier. You call that a substantial size difference? My heart ached as she poured on what I now call a healthy serving of politricks. I knew that the head coach never had 100% control over who made the national teams they were coaching but knowing that still didn't make me feel any better.

Like I said, there were four players in training camp from my college team. Kamie Ethridge had been the last person cut from the '84 Olympic team—she was gonna make that '88 squad and deservedly so. Then there was Andrea Lloyd, women's basketball answer to Larry Bird minus the jumper. She was gonna make the team too. Next there was my good friend, Clarissa Davis, young but talented. She was coming off a knee injury and had not had the greatest training camp. I wasn't surprised when she was waived but I also knew that she'd make the '92 Olympics for sure if she hung around. But me? Cutting me after the camp I've had? No way. It just didn't make sense. But this was USA basketball for you. Political to the bitter end. I finally understood why my weeklong plea for a smaller pair of game shorts had fallen on deaf ears.

I rose from the sofa not sure if I should stomp my feet like the four-year old I felt like or if I should rant and rave about the injustices of the system and how unfair it was that they wouldn't put three Texas players on the Olympic team. I felt that the main reason I wasn't making the team was because there was some unspoken rule that we had to have at least one Tennessee player on each Olympic team.

Instead, I stood and looked around the room. For what, I don't know. Then I hugged and wished Coach Yow good luck in Seoul and disappeared. No faster than you could say boo I was in the team van with our manager on my way to the airport. I was on my way back to Austin to an empty condominium. A home I had carefully emptied just a few weeks before because I wasn't planning on being there until after the Olympic Games were over.

When I got home, I walked around stunned for three days straight. What was I gonna do now? I didn't have a job and I didn't want one. I was supposed to be at the Games and I didn't wanna hear anything about going back overseas or trying out for the 1992 Olympic team, as Coach Yow had suggested after she broke the news to me. And after about a week of crying and cussing. And cussing and crying. I decided that the only way I could get over the hurt I was feeling was to leave behind the thing that had caused me this unbearable pain. So, I did the only thing I could do. I broke up with basketball. I threw away my sneakers. Gave my practice stuff and uniforms to friends and family. Packed up my Olympic memorabilia and walked away from it all.

That was late July 1988. Local and national media interviewed me asking me how I could just walk away from something I loved so dearly all because I'd been cut from the Olympic team. One reporter said, "You're one of the best players in the world and you give it up," she snapped her fingers. "Just like that?" I told her that when you give your life to something with the faith and quiet assurance that your commitment will pay off, it's devastating when it doesn't. And had I not clearly been one of the best players on that team, I could have accepted being cut. It would have still been disappointing but I could have accepted it and hung in there to make the '92 squad. But that wasn't the case. The way I saw it, I'd been screwed. And that's the way I'll always see that situation. Oh sure, time and maturity have healed the wound, but sometimes I still think about it and get mad. I think it'll always be that way.

So, there I was, done with basketball but still in love with it. Though not enough to go back overseas or tryout for another USA national team. I wasn't ready to jump back in the fire that soon. I needed to get as far away from basketball as I could. So I took up golf. And it was fun, I guess. Learning a new sport and all. But it wasn't basketball. I didn't feel the adrenaline flowing in my body like I did when I sank a jumper or stole the rock from someone. I continued to get offers from club teams in places like Germany, France and Italy but turned them all down.

Then in 1992, ironically an Olympic year, I got a call from Athletes in Action, a Christian organization that uses basketball to spread the good news of Christ. They were putting together a team to tour the United States to play against top college programs. I prayed about what to do. A few days later I decided to join the team in Dayton, Ohio. Slowly but surely I started falling in love all over again and I think I needed the spiritual approach to the game to sorta help me deal with how painful the whole Olympic ordeal had been for me. I wasn't ready to give my heart back to hoops yet but at least I was loving it again.

Hoop Dreaming

I don't remember where I was when the American Basketball League announced its plan to launch a professional league, but I know that I got excited. It didn't matter that I hadn't played organized ball in eight years. I'd won Outstanding Player awards in tournaments as well as a Hoop-It-Up national title in the mid '90s. I could still play and I knew it. I had just turned 31 years old and was actually peaking for the second

time in my short career. I say short career because I've had a weird basketball life. I didn't start playing until I was 15 years old. I quit when I
was 23 and here I was jump starting my game again at 31. It was strange
even for me, I have to admit. But I was going for it just the same.

The buzz was high. Not one but two organizations were thinking of
starting a new women's professional basketball league. Life didn't get
any better than that. I made plans to attend the ABL tryouts in Atlanta,
Georgia. I logged onto the Internet trying to find out as much as I could
about this new league that was touting itself as the league for women by
women. I found out that it was going to cost me $200 to try out plus air-
fare, food and lodging. I thought it was kinda strange to charge for a
tryout for a professional league but I was so excited about the opportunity that I quickly let the $200 fee become a distant memory. Next, I
sent in my $200 money order (they didn't accept checks) and started
getting ready to go to the tryouts, which I'd heard were going to feature
more than 200 players.

I spoke to the President of the ABL, Gary Cavalli, who informed me
that they were looking for the best players in the world to form this new
league. Good, I thought, surely I'm still somewhere in that number.

To ABL or WNBA? That Was The Question

They had placed all of the participants in one of three groups: A, B
and C. The A group was comprised of players who had either played at
lower level Division I colleges, Division II or NAIA schools. They were
the ballers who didn't have as much experience as the B and C players.
The B group was made up of players who had some experience overseas
or who'd perhaps come from top college programs but had been out of
the system for whatever reason. Some of the B players had been on USA
national teams back in the day. Players like Joyce Walker who was an
incredible scoring machine out of LSU in the early eighties. I was also in
the B group. The C group was made up of players who were currently
playing basketball, either overseas or in a semi-pro league in the States.

It was May 27, the day before the B group was to arrive and I'd talked to Nykeisha Henderson, who had just graduated from Texas and was one of my city league teammates. She had been placed in that infamous B group as well. I carefully packed enough clothes for three days because I promised myself that I would still be around on Saturday and Sunday when the elite C people got there.

That night I lay in bed looking at the ceiling, just wondering and pondering. I hadn't been to a tryout since the Olympic training camp in '88. Eight years earlier, I reminded myself. I lay there thinking about what an acquaintance of mine had said to a mutual friend when she found out I was trying out for the ABL. 'Isn't Fran a bit old for that?' Sometimes I get so ticked off when I hear people acting as if women are over the hill at 25. As far as I'm concerned, 25 is only old if you're a loaf of bread or a dog. Then you're old.

So, granted, I wasn't 25 anymore, but I was actually a much better player at 31 than I had been at 25 and that's what I kept in mind. Later that night I called my sister, Debra, because she was supposed to be meeting me in Atlanta the next day. After we spoke I was fired up. Deb had come to watch 99% of my home games at UT, and it had been a while since she'd seen me in real competition. I mean, she'd come to Austin on numerous occasions to see me kick booty in Hoop It Up but that was about it. So, I was as excited as she was about the tryouts and her getting to see me play. And I have to admit, now that I think about it, I was deeply, deeply touched by her suggestion to come to Atlanta in the first place. I needed that kind of support.

The flight to Atlanta was pretty uneventful and when I got there and looked around, but Deb was nowhere in sight. I shifted my backpack to the other side of my body and headed down the deserted airport. Before I could get farther than 30 yards, Deb and Becky, her roommate from college, were walking down the hallway when I turned the corner.

"You don't look a day over 17, Fran," Becky said, looking at the multi-colored headband on my round head. She continued on to my white

Carpe Diem T-shirt, black gym shorts and caramel colored hiking boots. "You look so young, girl." That was the kind of compliment I needed heading into a tryout with a bunch of Gerber Graduates.

The confirmation letter from the ABL had said that there would be people waiting to greet us at the airport, but when I arrived I saw no one. We were on the last 50 yards before we hit the door and then a teenage boy said, "You hoop?"

I said yeah and he waved for me to come back to where he stood. He looked for me on the list but I wasn't there for some reason. They handed me some information and we took off.

When I got to Becky's apartment, I got everything ready for the next day. First thing I needed was a blender for my breakfast…a smoothie. I would be too nervous the next morning to eat a traditional breakfast. I wanted to be fresh, rested and ready. I knew that the selection process was going to be political, just as the '88 Olympic team scenario had been, but I didn't care. I decided not to focus on the injustices of the system. I wasn't 21 anymore. I had learned a lot from my last minute slice from the '88 Olympic team. And I was not going to get bogged down in politics. Not this time. I was going to get to the gym, meditate and get down to business. I told myself, I'm going to be drafted by the ABL—politics and all.

At 5:15 a.m. my eyes popped wide open. I lay on the sofa with my mind racing faster than the cars in the Indy 500. Not much had changed since my college days. I could never sleep very well the night before a big game. I tried to go back to sleep but nothing happened at first. So, I got up and read. Around 6:00 Deb started stirring. I'd told her the night before that I wanted to leave by 6:30 because we had to be there by 7:30.

As soon as I got to Emory Gymnasium the adrenaline started pumpin'. The smell of leather, sweat and 20 different deodorants sailed through my nostrils as I got closer to the actual registration table right outside the gym door. I looked around and just as I'd suspected, I didn't recognize any of those women. Finally, a sister showed up with a clipboard.

"Are you here to register?" she asked.

"Yes, my name is Fran Harris and I'm in the B group."

She looked on the list and scratched through my name. "Here you go, you're number 264." She handed me the nylon navy jersey with big white numbers on the back and the letters ABL splashed on the front with a set of smaller numbers. I thanked her and walked inside the gym where the A group was just beginning their workouts. There must've been 100 players spread out over three courts. I remember thinking, how in the world are they going to find the hoopers in one day with all of these folks running around?

I went upstairs where Deb and the other spectators were sitting. "I can't get taped yet. They won't let us in until 30 minutes before we start practice," I told Deb.

When we finally got on the floor I realized that I still didn't know anybody except Keisha. I spotted her and walked over and asked how things were going with her and if she were ready. She asked about my Achilles. She knew that I had re-aggravated an old Achilles tendon injury and it killed me every time I got out of bed in the morning. I had tried to get some anti-inflammatories before I left Austin.

I walked down to get taped and that's when I finally saw a familiar face. It was Mara Cunningham, a forward from Vanderbilt. I had done some color analyst work for them two years before. We spoke but she looked surprised that I was there.

The trainer asked me a few questions about my Achilles and then proceeded to tape my foot so tight that I was sure it was going to explode as soon as I hit the floor. After I walked around on it about ten minutes it loosened up. Right before workout was to start about 50 women walked into the gymnasium. And maybe it was me, but they sure looked big. I always felt so small at trials. Six feet women are tall to most people. But not when you've got a 6'5", 220-pounder leaning on your frail body.

A few people in white golf shirts had filed in and stationed themselves around the perimeter of the gym. I assumed they were important people. I quickly discovered that they were the court coaches. And there were a lot of them. These were some of the people who were going to determine our fates.

A whistle sounded as a medium height, medium sized, brown-skinned African American woman with an authoritative 'let's go' called us to assemble at half court. She was Renee Brown, who'd been an assistant coach at Kansas and Stanford. She'd also worked with the '96 USA National team before she headed to Atlanta for the trials. She was obviously running the tryouts. She stood and told us what to expect for the next few days.

By now, another group of different important looking people had pulled chairs up to the endlines of each court. I assumed they were the coaches for the ABL franchises. I was right. Workout began and they divided us by position. As always there were ten million point guards and off guards. I decided to go to the small forward position, the 3 slot instead of the 2. But I also knew that once workouts started that the coaches would want to see me at the 2 spot as well. I figured that if there were a more versatile 3 player in those trials then I wanted to meet her. For the next 30 minutes we went through ball handling drills. As always everybody was so anxious to scrimmage. So ready to show their stuff. Eager to get their ball on.

I had been to enough trials in my day to know what kinds of things eliminate players. I knew what coaches looked for. I knew which sins they'd forgive and which ones they'd cut you for. Things like not hustling or not playing defense. Or being a hotdog or a showboat. According to the paperwork they'd given us at registration, they weren't going to waive any players until the following day. I was sure that they already had some idea of who they wanted from each group even though they weren't going to post a list until the next day at lunchtime. They knew. They always know. After workout, Deb and I headed to the hospital across the street for some grub. I'd had a decent workout. Not too bad for an old timer.

Here's the thing about trials. When the numbers get to be so astronomical you've gotta have something to make you stand out. Something that will make everybody in the gym notice you. So, I decided to wear my do-rag. I told myself, they might not remember your name but they'll remember the do-rag.

When we got back to Becky's that night I was Exhausted Incorporated. I mean, I was beat. I had bought two 5-pound bags of ice for my Achilles. I poured both bags of ice into the bathtub and added some cold water. A trainer at the '84 Olympic trials had recommended taking an ice whirlpool for sore, tired limbs. She said it worked wonders. And it did. When that torture was over, I sat around and talked to Deb, and Becky for about 30 minutes and then I headed for the shower.

The next day we arrived at the gym for the early workout. Me in my saggy number 264 jersey and a United States flag bandanna. Today though, three other people had decided to wear a do-rag as well. At the end of the second session on Friday, all of us sat at center court as Renee announced that they'd be posting *the* list in 30 minutes. Cavalli, a gentle, short, salt and pepper headed guy, spoke to us and thanked everybody for coming out. He said the usual, 'Everybody can't make the team but everybody's a winner' line. We'd all heard that before.

It was always so interesting to feel the energy at trials. I mean, when cuts are posted people get tense, me included. And even though I didn't think I was going to be cut, stranger things had happened. I grabbed my bag, took the elevator (yes, the elevator) up to the third floor, nudged Deb and told her let's go.

"But aren't they gonna post the names of the people who are supposed to come back tomorrow?" she asked.

"Yep," I said smiling slyly.

"Oh, so you're pretty confident, huh?" she asked laughing.

I smiled bigger this time. "Yep. Let's go."

On my way out a woman I'd played with in the afternoon scrimmage, Tara Davis, was hanging out near the door looking like a chicken on a farm around dinnertime. Girlfriend was very nervous.

"You out, man?" she asked.

"I'm gone, big baby," I told her as I straddled my shoulder with my black and hot pink Reebok bag strap. "Gotta get some sleep."

"You not coming back to look at the list?" she asked giving me an incredulous look.

"Nope. Would you mind calling me?…here's my number."

It was 9:00 at night and the last thing on my mind was somebody's list. I had food on my mind. I'd been too nervous to eat much during the day. So, Deb, Becky and I went to Applebee's for dinner and when we got home around 11:00, Tara had left a message. *Fran, it's Tara. I'm just calling to let you know that you made it, girl. But you already knew that. I made it too. Okay. So, I guess I'll just see you tomorrow. We go at 10. Peace.*

Deb and Becky stood in the doorway grinning and staring at me the way my mother use to when she wanted to know who was on the other end of the phone. I erased the message, hung up the phone and brushed by them on my way to the bathroom. "I'm gonna take a shower… tomorrow is the day, ya'll."

On Sunday there were about 120 of us sitting on the bleachers in Atlanta. And I was pleased to be a part of that group. For three days we had scratched and clawed our way through drills and scrimmages. And finally, they announced the finalists and told us that the draft would take place several weeks later. I knew that I had not been in my best shape, but I also knew that I'd done enough during those 72 hours to impress a few coaches. I could still play.

The announcement was made, and a few weeks later, I was drafted as an alternate by the Seattle Reign. Part one of my mission had been accomplished. Over the next week after the draft, I could never get clear communication with the coach and general manager in the Reign's organization. One day they wanted me to come there, the next day they wouldn't return my calls. They jockeyed around and basically didn't appear to have their ducks in a row. I was frustrated because I really wanted to play but the last thing I wanted to do was pack up my things and move to a place where there were lots of loose ends. So, I sat tight.

During the next few weeks, my faith was tested. I wanted to forge my way into the ABL, but I felt that the doors had been shut in my face because I hadn't played competitively since the Olympic trials. But I also had to keep in mind that I still had a while to get in shape for the WNBA. I spent a lot of time second-guessing my decision to quit playing. I'd say things like, 'If I'd only gone back to Italy or kept playing, I would have been a higher draft pick'. I've since learned that things are always just as they should be. It does no good to second guess and fret over things that you can't change anyway. You have to trust. Do the legwork and then just have faith.

Several Texas exes had also been drafted—Clarissa to the New England Blizzard, Edna Campbell and Vicki Hall to the Colorado Explosion. I was determined to get on a team, so Clarissa turned me on to her agent, Eric Fleischer, the guy who got Kevin Garnett that fat contract with the Minnesota Timberwolves. I spoke to him and he sounded genuinely interested in representing me. I told Eric that I'd also called Norm Nixon and Leonard Armato, two guys who repped some big names in the NBA. So big that neither one of them called me back.

But Eric was different. I could tell he genuinely wanted to help me out and I respected him for that. He listened empathetically to me and then broke it down for me. "I'm not gonna lie to ya, Fran. It's going to be tough for you to get into the WNBA because you haven't played in eight years." I told him that I could handle *tough*. Tough was not *impossible*. And that as long as there was a crack in the door, I'd find a way to squeeze in! Besides, by then I'd already decided that Swoopes' pregnancy was a sign that I was supposed to go the Houston Comets.

It was obvious Eric wasn't taking me on as a client for the money he was going to make. The lil' ol' money I would be paid the first year probably equaled his monthly mortgage. Still, he worked very hard for me. He was on the phone everyday with the WNBA trying to get some answers about how to get me back into basketball. A few weeks passed and Eric called with some news from the ABL. The San Jose Lasers had expressed some interest in my coming out to play for them. The coach, Jan Lowrey, telephoned, asked for game tape and said that they were very interested. Said she would be calling back within a week.

But when a week was knocking on my door and Jan still hadn't called, I decided to call her. I left her a voicemail message asking for an update. She called later that day and left me a message saying that the Lasers had decided to go with another player but that they'd keep my file active. I hung up disgusted. I felt that leaving me a voice mail was completely unprofessional but what could I do? So, that was the end of the San Jose Lasers and Jan Lowrey. At the end of the season she was fired.

My former teammate, Annette Smith-Knight, an assistant coach at Texas at the time, called me on the phone and spelled it out for me.

"Don't sign with the ABL even if they try to pick you up …the WNBA is getting ready to announce plans to start a league."

I listened carefully as I jotted down the specifics of what Annette was saying.

It was the end of September and the only thing we knew was that the WNBA had plans to launch its league in June. The coaches had not yet been named. They weren't that far along in the plans yet. I immediately started planning for tryouts by snooping around for playing venues to get me ready for the WNBA season.

After the ABL thing had fallen through, I was even more determined to make it to the WNBA, just to show the ABL what they'd missed out on. I also knew that being out of competitive basketball for eight years was somehow not going to work in my favor when it came time to get into the league, but I didn't care. I told myself that I was going to play in the WNBA…and that I was going to play in the inaugural season.

As fate would have it, shortly after Annette's call, I learned about this All-Star team this guy named Nick Mells was taking on the road to play against Division I teams in Kansas, Tennessee and Alabama. I got his number from a friend and called and asked if he had room on his team for another player. He said that he remembered me from my days at Texas and asked if I had any game left. I said 'is fried chicken greasy?' Then I gave him my information so he could make my flight arrangements.

This opportunity could not have come at a better time for me. The ABL thing had just fizzled and I was kinda bummed. To make matters worse, the ABL season had started and pretty soon I'd have the games to remind me of how awful it felt to be on the sidelines. I kept tabs on what was happening inside the ABL through friends. That's how I found out that they had started filling out their squads with local players who didn't have the credentials I had, and this really upset me. Boy, was I glad I'd hooked up with Nick and his All-Star team.

At 8:00 the next morning, I was on a plane to Nashville. We'd have three games in six days. No problem if you've got a full squad, but we only had only six players. Three guards, two forwards and one center who *thought* she was a guard. The good news was that this little tour would give me the ammunition I needed to get onto a pro team. By the time I'd get home from the tour, I'd have game statistics and a better idea of how I'd stack up against some of the players I'd be going up against in the WNBA tryouts. I didn't think I'd lost a whole lot by sitting out all of those years, and my performances in those three games proved me right. I scored 88 points and grabbed 37 rebounds in three games. I shot 54% from the field and 90% from the charity stripe. Needless to say I was pretty pleased. And if the ABL didn't want me, then I was willing to go to Europe to get ready for the WNBA.

The day after I got back from the tour, I slept in. And after I rolled out of bed around noon, I got another phone call from Annette telling me that an agent from the Bay Area had called looking for players to go play in Europe. She said that this guy needed to hear from someone immediately because he had a job for the right person. I hung up the phone thinking that even if they needed a 6'5" center, that I was still the right person. The agent's name was William and he was an attorney. We spoke briefly and he asked if I could fax over my athletic resume and statistics from the All-Star tour.

As soon as I faxed over that information, I called Eric to tell him that I had a good chance to go to Europe to play. I was sure that going overseas would improve my chances of getting into the WNBA. Eric listened to my enthusiasm and then he let me have the cough syrup. "I don't think it would matter too much in the WNBA's mind whether you went to Europe or not," he said. I was puzzled. He continued. "I spoke with Renee Brown, the WNBA player personnel director, and she says she saw you play at the ABL tryouts." I perked up.

Then there was that familiar pause between sentences that always tells you the worst is yet to come. The unwelcomed breath you hear when someone's calling you to tell you someone's died. The deafening silence when a doctor walks back into the examination room with the results of your Pap smear and there's a problem. "Anyway," he continued. "Now, she didn't say this, but I got the impression that she wasn't impressed with you from what she saw at that tryout." I laughed. Then I said, "Hell, Eric, there are days *I'm* not impressed with me, but you don't have the resume I have if you can't play." Eric said that he told Renee that you can't overlook a player with my background and experience, but apparently she wasn't buying it. According to Eric, I wasn't going get any help from the WNBA. I was on my own, no matter how good I'd been back in the day. According to Renee, there were certain players who deserved the league's consideration and I wasn't one of them.

After my conversation with Eric, I was deflated. I pulled up a chair to the pay phone and plopped down. He kept talking but I didn't hear one word he said. It was depressing. And it was starting to feel eerily like the Olympic thing. Eric remained positive about my chances and said that he thought I should just get into a local tryout and kick butt. "I know you can play. I've talked to some coaches and players about you and I know you belong in this league," he said. "It's going to be political. You know how this stuff works, you've been around long enough to know what you're up against. So, just go out there and show them."

Tryouts? The last tryout I'd attended, I'd played my butt off and still hadn't made the team. I couldn't imagine sitting around all winter long waiting. It would drive me crazy. I just couldn't do it. It wasn't going to work that way for me. I had to get to Europe. Even if Eric didn't think it would help. Even if the WNBA wasn't interested. I still had to go. I could not believe that after all I'd given to women's basketball that this was my payback. No, my song would not, could not end on this note. That's when I knew I was going to Europe.

A few days later, William called me back and said that the Swiss team was impressed with my resume and wanted to proceed as quickly as possible. Orlando, the President of Baden ABB, called me that day to say how excited they were that I was coming over to join their team. He was Italian and his English wasn't all that good. "We look forward to have you with our team. We have lots of young, but good, players here…we need a veteran with experience who has won a lot to come here."

The next morning I drove to Houston to get my passport renewed. It was finally starting to look like I'd get off the bench and back into the game. I telephoned William from Houston and left a message telling him I was packed and ready to go. But when I got home that night I was reminded of how crazy this business can be. William called the minute I walked through the door. I didn't even let him speak.

"This Swiss chocolate is ready to leave for the Alps," I shouted into the phone.

"I'm sorry, Fran, I hate to tell you this but there've been some new developments in Baden," he said slowly.

My heart sank. "What kind of developments?"

"They can't bring you over. They're gonna finish the season with the current American they have. I'm sorry, I know you're disappointed."

Disappointed couldn't even begin to describe what I was feeling in that moment. But desperate and helpless came to mind. "So, that's it?" I said. "That's all they said?"

"Yep. I'll keep looking for a job for you. Are you open to other countries? I think there's a team in Greece, Athens I think, that might be looking for a guard to play with Jennifer Gillom. You know her?"

I was depressed. "Yeah, yeah, I know Jent."

"I'll keep you posted. Don't worry, we'll get you on a team, okay?"

I hung up the phone and cried the rest of that day.

Thanksgiving had come and gone. Sleigh bells were ringing. And holly was everywhere. The historic buildings in downtown Austin were now lined with green and red holly but nobody from Europe had sent me any Yule tide greetings. I was still toiling daily on my part-time job and burning the midnight oil as I worked on IN THE BLACK, a book about raising financially responsible kids. I was having a pretty depressing holiday season. Holidays are hard for me anyway. My mother's absence always seems more obvious between Thanksgiving and New Year's Day.

I hadn't heard from William, so, I was still pretty depressed about everything. The ABL fiasco, the Switzerland screw up, the WNBA dissing me, everything. I was becoming more anxious because the WNBA had announced where the eight teams would be located: New York, Los Angeles, Cleveland, Charlotte, Phoenix, Sacramento, Utah and of course, Houston. Then the league announced television contracts with NBC, ESPN and Lifetime. That's when I knew the WNBA was going to happen. And in a big way.

Still no word from William, so I made my holiday plans which included going to Dallas to spend Christmas with my family. I called William to make sure he knew that I was interested in almost anything overseas and that I'd be back right after the holidays. When I'm expecting news I'm pretty obsessive about checking my voicemail. So, when I left Austin on December 24, I checked my messages three or four times from my Dad's house. We celebrated Christmas in normal fashion. Plenty of good food, thanksgiving and hearty conversation. I decided to give the phone a rest, and just enjoy the day.

The next day I took off to visit a friend in Mississippi and when I'd gotten about two hours from her home, I called to check my messages. Guess who'd called? William. The day before. Christmas day. The only day in the last month I hadn't checked my messages. He indicated that the team in Athens was indeed interested in taking a look at me. And that I'd be playing with Gillom.

He said he needed to speak with me on that day. And that tomorrow, the next day would be too late. I stood in the rain at an Exxon gas station in Lafayette, Louisiana, thinking that I'd just blown my one chance to go overseas. When I finally reached William, he confirmed my fears. I was too late. They wanted me to leave the next day, December 27, only I wasn't going to be home until the day after New Year's Day. I stood silently, listening to him chew me out for not telling him that I wasn't going to be able to leave before the beginning of the year.

I thought about telling him that we'd actually discussed an 'after the break' departure, which was how teams usually handled mid-season changes. But I didn't bother. It was pretty irrelevant at that point. The bottom line was that I couldn't leave on the 27th, period. We decided to talk after the first of the year and just play it all by ear. When I hung up the phone, for some reason, I was not as upset as I thought I might be. Maybe I knew something else would come along.

It was now the first week of January and I was still stateside, with no signs of Europe in my forecast. The only thing that kept me sane was writing in my daily journal about my return to the basketball. On Saturday, William called me before the sun came up.

"Can you leave for Zurich on Monday?"

I wiped the sleep out of my eyes, sat up and cleared my throat. "What? Who is this?"

"Can you be ready to go in three days? It's William. You do still wanna play, don't you?"

"Of course I do but I thought you said that they were gonna stick it out with the other American."

"Well, they changed their mind. They want you. Orlando said he really liked you."

"When did all of this happen? And what happened to make them change their mind?"

William laughed. "You know how it works, Fran. They lost a game and she had only 6 points." In case you've never heard, low point production from an American player is suicide in Europe, where we're often viewed as basketball playing machines who can turn it on as soon as the whistle is blown and the ball is tossed. If you don't bust 30 every night they're wondering if you're ill or homesick. And if you're not careful, your butt will be on the next flight to LaGuardia. I asked William about the specifics of the 'firing' but European clubs are best known for being evasive and sometimes outright lying to get what they want. I guess it's not fair to lump them all in the same boat because in Italy I didn't have one problem with my management.

The team, which was located in Baden, a tiny town about 20 minutes from Zurich, had lost a couple of games that they should have won. Apparently the American player, whose name had yet to be revealed, was not meeting their expectations.

The next day Orlando telephoned me again but I wasn't home. And instead of leaving a phone number for me to reach him like most people would, he said he'd try again later on. Later on turned out to be 2 o'clock the next morning. He asked if I were in shape and if I were available to come over immediately. Of course I said yes to both questions. He said that my statistics, and especially my resume, was very impressive. He couldn't stop talking about the national team experiences.

The conversation ended with him telling me that they needed someone who could score points and that the coach, a guy named Claudio, would be calling me soon. About two and half-hours later, the phone rang. Claudio. His English was a little bit better than Orlando's but basically he echoed the President. That they 'may' be making a change and needed an experienced player heading into the playoffs and cup play. "You are in shape?" he asked. Yep, I said again. He said that they would let me know in a couple of days. "Can you come that soon?" Again I said yes. I stumbled in the dark to find the receiver's place and laid my weary head back on my pillow. This time with a big old grin on my face. I'd never been to Switzerland.

The next day I quit my job and turned in all of my route and paper-work. The checkout procedure for the company was pretty painless. The employees all wished me well and told me to send them a postcard when I got to Switzerland. That was Wednesday. I spent Thursday paying bills and getting someone to agree to look after my apartment while I was away. That evening William called and asked if the club had contacted me. I told him that we'd had a short conversation and that basically they just wanted to make sure that I could run up and down the floor without a respirator.

He reemphasized how displeased they were with the American they had and suggested that I get packed and ready to go. He said that he'd have an answer, complete with flight information if they made a decent offer, by 7 o'clock the next morning.

Morning came and went, and nothing. No phone call from William. No call from the club. I went on about my day but something in my gut told me that something just wasn't right. William had said that he would call me when he heard something, so I didn't call him because I didn't wanna bug him. Around 4 o'clock that evening I decided to just go by Kinko's where I sometimes received faxes, to see if they had one for me.

I had a four-page fax. From William. The first page read, *Dear Fran, I'm sorry but the President of Baden called today. They will not be bringing you to Baden to play. I am away from my office, I will call you when I return.* I just stared at the hazy looking letters on the page. The next page was a copy of a letter from William's law firm to the club in Baden expressing his dissatisfaction with their unprofessionalism. I thought it ironic. Here he was slapping their wrist for making an offer and then reneging on it but here he was sending me, his client, a fax to let her know that she wasn't going to play pro ball overseas after all. I was devastated. Over not going, yes, but also because William didn't pick up the phone and call me to deliver news that he knew would disappoint me. I went to a restaurant across the street and cried in my pizza. How could they do this to me? And William? My own agent. How dare you? How dare you send me a *fax*? I couldn't wait to get him on the phone.

I was a wreck. I'd quit my job. I'd just told someone that they could move into my apartment for two months. I had told everyone I was going overseas. That evening I finally reached William. The first thing he said was, 'we need to talk about how we want to proceed. If you'd still like to go play there are a couple of teams that...' I didn't give a rip about his contract. I wanted to talk about our professional relationship and the infamous fax. "William," I said interrupting. "Before we do anything I wanna tell you how awful it felt to get that news from you in a fax. A fax! You couldn't even extend me the courtesy of a phone call?" He realized how upset I was and offered an apology but still stuck to the 'I was out of the office' excuse. To which I said, 'five minutes. Five minutes for that personal touch.'

We moved on. And he said that he'd try to find something else for me. He'd heard that a team in southern Italy was looking for a player but thought they wanted an inside player. My hopes were fading fast and those local WNBA tryouts were sounding better each day.

Forty-eight hours after the fax, William's associate, Bonnie, called and said that the team in Baden had reconsidered and wanted me to come after all. I needed to call her right away. I didn't know whether to get my hopes up or blow it off. I didn't appreciate Baden being so wishy-washy. But I didn't wanna blow them off in case this was my big chance. So I called her for the details. She said that they'd just called her and they wanted to make a deal. They wanted me to leave in two days.

When I got to the Zurich airport, there were three people standing at the baggage claim carousel looking like they were looking for someone they didn't know. So, I waved. I assumed that they were there for me. They waved back. I grabbed my bag and headed toward customs and on out the double glass doors.

"Fran?"

I extended my hand to the tall, curly-headed man. "Yes. Ciao."

I recognized Orlando's voice. "Ciao, come va?" he asked.

"Bene, tu?"

"Bene. Cuesta e Claudia Campanotta e Petra Necas, due giocatrice de la squadra feminile nationale B."

The two women, one tall with dark hair, the other short with dark hair were both basketball players on the team below the first team, the team I would be playing on. Orlando informed me that Claudia spoke German, Italian, English and a little French. Petra spoke English and German but no Italian. For the next 15 minutes we stood around and drank expressos and ate chocolate for about ten minutes then headed to the vehicle. Orlando's car radio glared with American rock tunes as we headed down the breezy highway laced with beautiful, rich grass and trees en route to Neuenhof, the city where I would be living for the next two months. We spoke of nothing of consequence other than the fact that the American they'd supposedly fired…was still in Neuenhof.

"Really?" I asked. "She's still here?"

Their eyes met each other. "Yes, is that a problem for you?" Orlando asked.

"Is what a problem for me?" I asked sarcastically.

He looked through his rear view mirror at Claudia. "That she's still here."

I looked out of the passenger window. "Why would that be a problem for me?"

"So, it's okay?" he asked, surprised by my response.

"Sure. I don't see why not." I knew I didn't have all the details and whatever they weren't telling me had all three of them on pins and needles the entire 20-minute ride from the airport.

I really like Europe. And it had been several years since I had stepped on foreign soil. Switzerland was lush and magnificent. And from what I could see at that point, the cleanest place in Europe I'd been to with the exception of maybe, Amsterdam. Petra and Claudia helped me take my bags to my flat, a compact little space nestled on a street right off of the main avenue in Neuenhof. Lagerstrasse 4 was my new home. It had a Fred Flintstone-size bed in it. The kitchen was one strip of floor with a stove, oven and refrigerator. The bathroom was tucked away between the bedroom and kitchen. In all, you could walk through my front door take five paces in either direction and be in my bedroom, bathroom or kitchen. Small, yes, but the emerald green view from my bedroom stole my breath each morning.

Petra and I made an appointment to go downtown to pickup some necessities. Toothpaste, cleanser, shower gel, stuff like that. We headed to the bus stop, but first I had to make a phone call to the states to let everyone know that I'd made it safely. As I stood in the phone booth, I spotted a black woman walking across the street. Of course, I waved. That's what you do when you see an American in a foreign country. Especially if you're a black woman who sees another black person. Man, you go crazy. Plus, she looked like someone I knew. She waved again, so I waved again.

When I hung up the phone and stepped outside the phone booth, I was shocked. I actually knew the woman who'd waved. It was Kim Evans, and I'd coached her on an AAU team the summer before her senior year in high school, maybe six years before. We hadn't seen each other since that summer. She was 17 and I was 25 at the time. It all started to click. Kim was the nameless American player that management was put out with. Kim was the player who hadn't met their expectations. Kim was the player that was supposed to have been on a jet plane heading back to the states before I got there. She walked over to me and I noticed the strange look on Petra's face. As Kim and I caught up, I noticed that Petra stood silently to the side. Saying very little. She was obviously uncomfortable. Kim said something about telling me all about it later, so Petra and I left to catch the bus.

"You know each other?" Petra asked rather nervously.

"Yeah, I coached her in a junior type tournament about five or six years ago."

Petra didn't utter a peep.

"I didn't know Kim was your American player," I said. Petra said nothing. "Interesting."

The bus had arrived so we boarded the crowded orange vehicle with a sign on the front, '2 Baden SBB'. I hadn't gotten a chance to tell what Neuenhof was really like, although I got the distinct impression that nothing much ever happened there. On the bus, Petra put a couple of coins in a machine and out popped a small yellow piece of paper. This was my bus pass. She explained that the time on the pass was the time that the pass would expire. I could ride on the ticket for one full hour from the time of purchase.

I looked around at the people on the bus. Young, old, mostly dressed in corduroys, jeans or trousers. The most noticeable things about the attire were the shoes. The women had on closed toe shoes with heels

twice the height and depth of the shoes we (well, my brother's generation) wore in the '70s. The thick, black soles on the shoes made everyone wearing them at least three inches taller. The men mostly wore
some form of hiking boots. And everyone seemed to have on layers and
layers of clothes. There I was looking like a straw in a glass of Coca-
Cola. I had on a T-shirt, a sweatshirt, some jeans, a leather jacket and
some Nike terrain boots. I now know that I looked very touristy. Petra
had on at least three shirts plus her jacket. Were we expecting a blizzard?

When we arrived downtown I wished I'd brought my camera with
me. I loved the architecture in Europe. The apartments on top of businesses. The flowers hanging from balconies on every corner. People,
many of them, elderly, riding around on bicycles. Parents and kids coming out of the bakeries with aromatic breads and pastries. Young men
and women debating over cappuccino at the local smoke-filled bars.
Mothers and daughters strolling arm in arm through the center of
town. I'd forgotten how much I loved being in this setting.

But the thing that struck me the most, was the sense of honesty that
pervaded the streets, restaurants and businesses. Downtown on the main
strip, where the street is maybe a half a mile long and 30 feet wide, there
were shops on either side. Stores with racks of clothes and bins of shoes
outside the doors in the walkway. All of this merchandise with no sign of
security guards. No security systems attached. No censors. No cameras.
Stores on corners even had merchandise around the corners. Unattended.
It was very strange. In the U.S. there's no way we'd ever leave merchandise
sitting outside a retail store without locks or chains attached.
Immediately I felt safe in Baden. Any country that had that much faith in
the human spirit was all right with me. I liked Switzerland already.

I had a great comeback in Switzerland. We finished the season in third place and I averaged nearly 30 points a game. I was feeling pretty good about my game heading back to the states in mid-March. In April, I learned that Houston had named its head coach, Van Chancellor from Ole Miss. I immediately called the Comets office and left a message for Van asking if he'd give me information about his local tryouts.

He returned my phone call that night and was very nice. We spoke of our 1986 regional final against his Rebel team that had Alisa Scott and Jennifer Gillom on it. We'd beaten them 66-63 to advance to our first Final Four tournament. That had been 11 years ago and I didn't know if he'd really remember who I was. Or more importantly, if I could play. I hadn't had the best game of my life against them that night. I was sorta praying he wouldn't remember that particular game. I was hoping that his mental tape recorder would fast forward to the Final Four weekend where I'd played great and made the all tournament team. That's what I was praying he would remember.

"Listen, Fran," he said. "I gotta have some players. What's Beverly Williams doing? Do you know a point guard?" He was talking so fast, he sounded like an auctioneer. I told him that Beverly was pretty much signed, sealed and delivered to the ABL for the 97-98 season. Like me, she'd felt pretty dissed by the WNBA. Van finally asked me what I'd been doing. I knew that every woman who'd ever picked up a basketball would be trying to land a spot in the league. He'd seen me working games as an ESPN broadcaster and he probably thought my basketball days were behind me. My best ones, anyway.

I told him that I'd just come back from Switzerland and that I was interested in attending his tryouts since I knew he was gonna be short at least one small forward with Swoopes out. He said he was in search of a 1, 2 and a 3. So, I grabbed a pen and began getting the tryouts essentials. He paused for what seemed like an eternity before he started spewing out the specifics. Then he said, "Fran? I hope you're not offended that

I'm asking you to come to tryouts. I know what a great player you were but I haven't seen any of ya'll play in so long."

"No, not at all. I understand," I said.

He said that tryouts would take place between May 5 and May 12, but that he'd call back once the dates and sites were confirmed. Good enough for me.

I hung up and called everybody in Texas! After looking frantically all spring long via the Internet for my name to come up on a WNBA invitee list, I'd finally nailed something I could sink my teeth into. A tryout. I don't ever remember being so excited about a tryout in my life. Van Chancellor didn't know it, but he had given me a new lease on my basketball life. And I was eternally grateful.

On May 7, I packed up my car and headed to Dallas. I was higher than a kite. And there was no doubt in my mind where I was going to spend the summer of 1997.

It was Mother's Day weekend. The smell of turnip greens, candied yams and other goodies sailed through my severely soul food deprived nostrils as I walked through my Dad's den into the kitchen. Daddy is an awesome cook and he's never met a stick of butter he didn't like.

The sound of Al Green's "Let's Stay Together" reminded me of how much I loved going home sometimes. My Dad had followed all of the ABL and WNBA hoopla and whenever I'd talk to him over the phone, he always seemed a bit edgy whenever I mentioned teammates who were playing in the ABL. So, after dinner I told him that I was gonna have to cut my trip to Dallas short because I'd have to pull out on Sunday morning to go to Houston. "What's in Houston?" he asked.

"WNBA tryouts," I answered. He started laughing. "Well, hell it's about time. You play as good as any of 'em," he said. " I been wondering whatchu been waitin' on." I appreciated my Dad's excitement. But he didn't really understand that I couldn't just call up the WNBA and say, 'Hey, I'm the cat's meow—put me on one of these teams.' But you know how parents are. They don't believe there's anything you can't do when you put your mind to it. And it felt good knowing that my Dad didn't care how long it had been since I last suited up. He knew I could still play. And his words were just the reinforcement I needed heading into Houston for the tryouts.

That night, I curled up in my brother's old bed watching reruns of Mary Tyler Moore, I Love Lucy, Bob Newhart and The Dick Van Dyke Show. My Dad's house is always either freezing or burning up hot. There's no in between. On this night, the night before the trials, I was freezing even though it didn't feel all that cold in the house. So, I got up and turned the air conditioner down. Then I began sneezing, sniffling and just having a coughing fit. My nose was out of control and I was starting to clear my throat every five seconds.

The next morning I woke up with eyes that looked like I'd tangled with Evander Holyfield. I couldn't breathe. And I had a cough that wouldn't quit. Great, I thought. How am I gonna have the tryout of my life feeling like I've been run over by a truck? My Dad was blaming himself and saying that if I didn't make the team it was his entire fault for having a meat locker for a house. I told him not to worry. That some way, somehow, I was gonna be playing in Houston in June.

I was supposed to be at the St. Thomas High School gymnasium by 2:00 on Mother's Day. When I rolled up into the parking lot, the nervous energy set in. I could hear the sounds of balls bouncing. Feet pounding. Coaches instructing. Players chatting.

Parked near the door was a candy apple red convertible Mercedes. Coop. I knew it was Coop's. I walked through the double doors and who walks out of the restroom? Coop. She grabbed me around the waist and lifted me off of the dusty floor. "Fran!!!" Girl, what are you doing here? I mean, I know whatchu doing here but I didn't even know you were still playing?"

"Yep, still at it, girl. Or trying to be anyway."

"We had a meeting this morning and I saw your name on the tryout list and I said, Fran Harris? Fran Harris is not here. I know Fran Harris. That's when they told me you were coming in later. I'm so glad to see you."

There are moments that Cynthia is as real as real gets. I have such genuine affection for that person. That's who gave me a bear hug that muggy afternoon at St. Thomas. Coop was the perfect welcoming committee I needed coming into that firing zone. She told me how crazy Houston had been in the last week alone and that she was ready for practice to start.

"Have you been in there?" she asked pointing to the gym floor. I hadn't. "Well, look." I stepped to the door and my mouth flung open. There were at least 100 players in the gym. Ten on the floor and the others gaping along the sidelines. I'd just called Peggy Gillom, one of the Comet's assistant coach the night before to find out how many people they were expecting for the three roster spots they had left. She'd answered an unconvincing 50 or 60. Cynthia went on to say that since I was trying out for one of the last spots on the team that the money wasn't anything to jump about. What she actually said and I'll never forget it is, 'Don't do it, Fran…the money's not worth it.' I was surprised by this response. Didn't she know that money was the last thing on my mind? I didn't respond to her comment.

"Is that yours?" I said pointing at the backside of the candy apple toy right outside. We exchanged those 10-year-old smiles. "Yeah, that's mine."

"They say they want a 1, 2 and a 3," Coop said to me as we headed to the sidelines to stretch.

Sounded good to me, since I could play both the 2 and 3 positions. I grabbed my shoes from my bag and began lacing them. She and I continued to catch up and talk about people in the gym, joking and saying things like, 'and who's daughter is she?' about a player who obviously had no game to speak of but for some reason was being permitted to participate in the tryouts. We ragged on everybody in the gym that day. Those we knew and those we didn't know.

There were about six or seven media representatives scattered around the gym. A photographer from NBA Entertainment, had spotted Cynthia and me cutting up and little did I know at the time that he'd decided to mosey on over and eavesdrop. I never saw the camera guy put the furry microphone above our heads, so I kept yammering. Cynthia had abruptly begun to speak in Italian to me. So we proceeded in Italian. Teasing each other about various things. Our age. How much we both liked to shoot. She joked that all I needed to do if we got the chance to play together that night in the scrimmage was to pass her the ball. I rolled my eyes and said okay. She asked me in Italian why I was sitting there cussing her out with the camera listening. I slowly looked over my head and sure 'nuf, there it was.

I took Coop's advice about showing my shooting range and leader-ship on the court. I also wanted to play solid defense because I was smart enough to know that the last thing Houston needed was another scorer. No, if I was gonna make the Comets team, it would be because I played defense. And I knew it. In my many years of playing basketball and trying out for USA national teams, I'd learned a few things. Among them, how to impress at a tryout. So, that was my game plan. Play hard, play defense, and above all, show these coaches that you want this bad-der than anyone on the floor. That was my plan.

Many of the women I played against in college had gone on to coach or had gotten so far out of basketball shape that I'm sure the Comets coaches were just amazed that anyone could take eight years off and still make it up and down the court without fainting.

Around 5:30 that day, after several cuts had been made, Van called me over and asked me a simple question. Would you like to be on this team? I immediately said yes. He said, and I'll never forget this, I think we can win a championship with you here. Needless to say, I smiled wider than the Atlantic Ocean.

I left Houston headed to Ft. Lauderdale to visit my sister, Deb. She had set up several speaking engagements at elementary, junior high and high schools in the area. She wanted me to talk about setting goals and making good choices, two of my favorite topics. At one junior high school, a girl asked me if I knew Sheryl Swoopes and if I could get her autograph when I got back to Houston and mail it to her. The whole class laughed. I thought it was cute. Here I am speaking to her and she wants Swoopes' autograph.

I stayed in Ft. Lauderdale for a week and it was time for me to head back to Texas, I was still riding high from the tryouts. It was a long trip from the bottom of Florida to Texas, so I had to stop several times along the way. When I got to Pensacola, I checked my voicemail and that's when my world crumbled…again. I had a message from Kelly Krauskopf, a big wig in the WNBA front office. She said she needed me to call her back as soon as possible.

I frowned at the phone wondering what Kelly Krauskopf could possibly want with me. I listened to the message again but there was no indication of what she might wanna talk about, so I called her. That's when she lowered the boom. "I just wanted to let you know that the Comets have put you on their list of developmental players," she said. Silence. I didn't say a word. I thought I must've been hearing things. Did Kelly Krauskopf just say that Van had put me on his *developmental* list? The list that was reserved for practice players? I *know* that is *not* what I heard.

Finally I said something. "I'm sorry? What do you mean, Kelly? That's not what Van and I talked about." I was starting to get upset and slightly elevated because I was shocked. And very confused. Not to mention a little over all the games people play with folks' careers. But Kelly was very nice and professional. "Well, that's what the Comets have submitted to the league. But Van is very high on you, Fran. I don't think you're gonna have any problems making the final roster," she said.

I got off the phone with Kelly as quickly as I could because I was about to lose it. And my anger and frustration didn't have anything to do with Kelly Krauskopf. I didn't need to say another word to someone who was just delivering a message. Instead I called Deb and bawled for 30 minutes. Then I called Cynthia and cried for 30 more.

"Where are you?" Coop asked. "Fran, I'm so sorry. I had no idea. They told me that you were on the roster. You had a great trial. You were the best player out there—well, when I wasn't on the floor," she laughed.

"I'm so sick of this, Coop," I said. "You have no idea how over this shit I am. No idea."

CHAPTER 2

We Got Game and Hype and Fans

This is how far women's basketball has come.

Cyndi, a mom who worked in the front office of a professional sports team, had taken her 6-year old son, Jack, to see the Houston Comets play during the inaugural season in 1997. When the game ended, it was around 9:30, over an hour after Jack's bedtime. So, when Cyndi and Jack arrived home, she told Jack that he was to brush his teeth, wash his face and head straight to bed. But while she prepared his clothes for school the next day, she noticed that instead of heading to the bathroom, Jack turned on the television and began staring at the 10:00 newscast in amazement.

"Jack," she said. "C'mon, sweetie, turn off the TV, time to go to bed." Jack didn't move. Whatever was on the screen had him frozen. Five minutes passed and now Cyndi was starting to get frustrated. From the other room, she yelled out. "Jack Peterson, get those teeth brushed right now!" Jack still didn't move.

Cyndi bolted from her son's bedroom into the family room to see what Jack was up to. That's when she noticed the astonished look on his innocent little face. "Honey, are you okay?" Cyndi looked at the television, which was re-playing NBA playoff highlights.

Jack turned to his mom and said, "*Boys* play basketball?"

All of his young life, the only basketball Jack had seen was women's basketball. Stories like his illustrate the amazing impact that the WNBA has had not only on the athletes themselves but also the community. The number of girls participating in basketball has skyrocketed over the last four years, thanks to the WNBA. But the other wonderful thing about being a part of the WNBA is the fan fare. You can look into the stands at any WNBA game, in any arena on either coast, and see girls, boys, men and women of all ages and backgrounds. You see dads with their daughters, daughters with their mothers, and my personal favorite—toddlers wearing jerseys of their favorite WNBA player.

Monday was Memorial Day and we were supposed to be in Houston by that night because training camp was starting on Tuesday. Peggy Gillom had called and told me that they had reserved a room for me at the Holiday Inn Select on Highway 59. I told her that I might come in on Sunday but after I thought about what had happened with the try-outs and the whole developmental list, the less I wanted to be there early. When I arrived at the hotel on Monday afternoon, I saw a tall woman walking toward her room. I didn't know who she was and before I could get within speaking distance she'd vanished behind her door. I assumed she was a Comet.

I'd felt so out of sync heading into Houston that I had literally thrown my things in my car. Nothing was in any order. There was no method to my madness, so I only had a few things to carry up to my room.

The Chicago Bulls had just started playing and I wanted to watch the game. When I came back from the second trip to my car, I noticed a few players sitting in the lobby. Tiffany Woosley, the point guard from Tennessee whom I'd played with at tryouts, was the only one I knew. The others were all new faces. I walked up and introduced myself. The other three were Tina Thompson, our number one draft pick, Racquel Spurlock, a center from Louisiana Tech and Yolanda Moore, who'd played for Van at Ole Miss.

On the way back to the elevator, I saw Catarina Pollina's back. Finally, a friendly and familiar face. I'd met Cat when I played in Italy ten years earlier and then she'd come to the States to play at UT where I'd played my college ball. She and I chatted with the four players in the lobby. That's when I found out that they were waiting on Van to pick them up. He was having a little get-together at his place and we were all invited. Part of me wanted to just go upstairs and catch the rest of the game. But the other part thought that I ought to get through that first interaction with Van since the whole tryout, developmental player incident. After all, I still wanted to be on his team.

On my drive into Houston I had gone back and forth in my mind. Should I say something to him about the developmental thing or just let it go? I'm not the kind of person who just lets these kinds of things go unaddressed but I wasn't sure it was worth it. In the end, either I'd make the team or I wouldn't. Ruffling his feathers certainly would work against me, I reasoned. So, I pasted a smile and didn't say a word. But I knew what time it was. This little incident told me what kind of situation I was going into. It was my wake-up call.

When Van finally got to the hotel we exchanged a cool hello. The initial interaction was over and I was glad. He and Peggy Gillom drove two groups because she was living in the same apartment complex as Van and his wife, Betty. We got to his place and began trying on practice clothes. Van announced that he was the king of Spades and challenged anyone who thought they could stay in the card game with him. And since I've been playing spades since I was eight or nine years old, Van had at least one opponent. I would look forward to beating his butt in cards…especially in light of the developmental list thing. He chose Tina. "Come on, Rookie," he drawled. "Let's take on Harris and who-ever…Harris, who you got?"

Yolanda agreed to play with me and the game began. I love playing Spades and I'm one serious player, skill-wise. Unfortunately, skill can only take you so far. If you don't get any cards—face cards—you can forget about competing. And when the cards aren't coming your way, it's gonna be a long day. It was never a contest. They got the best cards, spanked us and called for their next victims. Betty, however, called for the prayer. Lunch was ready. She had prepared chicken and vegetables, and some delicious deserts. We devoured the food, tried on some more clothes and then headed back to the hotel. The next morning the van was picking us up for physicals around 7:30.

I hadn't been around Coop in 9 years. Hadn't spoken to her since 1991 when we saw each other briefly when we both lived in San Antonio. Cynthia and I are more like family. We go back a long way. Sometimes we manage to be decent friends to each other. but I guess you could call us girls. We have the kind of relationship that's honest and real. We won't talk on the phone every week but when we talk, it's like we've never missed a beat.

I was excited to be playing with her but I knew that I'd also have to deal with her off-court antics. I was actually relieved that she really had-n't changed that much. She walked into the clinic the next morning, singing. Off key and awful. Like she always did. Like she had during the

'86 World Championships. Like she had in '87 during the Pan Am Games. And yes, like she had during the '88 Olympic summer. I knew she wasn't Whitney Houston so I never looked up when she came in totally destroying Erika Baduh's song *Lifetime*. She loves to sing and it's something to watch. How can you fault a person who sings for the joy of it? Even when they don't know the words or sing like a bird.

I noticed the reaction of the rest of the players. They were so tired of hearing her butcher this song that a couple of them decided to help her out with the words. I sat there pretending to read a magazine but I was laughing inside.

A representative from the clinic came out to explain to us what would happen next. We'd be required to give some blood. Go through a body fat analysis. Coop announced that she was first in line. Players rolled their eyes. Me included. I met her eyes and shook my head. Then for the hell of it, I said, 'I'm first'. Just to see what she'd say. "Fran Harris, you're not first…how can you be first when I am…?" Then she proceeded into some verbal aerobics that generally fatigued me too much to stay engaged for any respectable length of time. So, I went back to my magazine.

The physical was supposed to take a few hours. There was an extensive questionnaire bent on finding out if any of us had an eating disorder. It asked things such as do you think about your body constantly? Are you overly concerned with gaining or losing too much weight? Would you say you are too fat, too thin, or about right? I told them my only concern was controlling love handles and consistent ab work was the answer to that little problem.

The next day was Media Day at the NASA Space Center. We loaded two vans and headed to the space center, where a barrage of reporters and camera crews were supposedly waiting to greet us. When we got there we were taken to a secluded area where an NBC crew interviewed a few players while the rest of us ate scrumptious chocolate chip and macadamia nut cookies.

Sarah, from the community relations department in the Rockets office told us it was time to be introduced. We were taken to an area that looked like the back of a rocket and told to stand in a specific order. When our name was called we were to walk through a smoke-filled entrance and stand on a piece of tape. One by one we were introduced to a crowd of about 200. Cameras flashed. Lights from television cameras came on. Women, men, and children of all ages applauded. They had strategically put Coop at the end of the line since she was our marquee player now that Sheryl would miss most of the season. The crowd went nuts when she ran out and stood on the front row.

After the group picture we were guided to a green room where we munched on sandwiches, chips and fruit. There the media clamored over Cynthia, Tina, the two foreign players, Catarina and Janeth Arcain, the Brazilian. The rest of us got our eat on and chatted with each other. The rest of the media wandered around talking to the rest of us.

Our afternoon practice was scheduled from 3:00 to 5:00. There, Kevin Cook, the other assistant coach, announced that we were having some sort of inaugural dinner in which someone from the WNBA was to show up. Practice started out with Van telling us that we were an elite group of athletes and that we had an opportunity to make or break the league. He also said that we had an obligation to be role models for little girls, which we all took to heart. That point really struck a chord with me.

Training camp was a lot of fun, mainly because it was the first one, I think. We had two-a-days for nearly two weeks but when we started losing players to injuries, the coaches wisely tapered off on the training. Van was having a hard time deciding who was going to play with Cynthia, Tina, Janeth and Wanda Guyton. So, we went through about a week of Spin The Lineup. Sometimes I would play on the red team with Coop and Company, sometimes Kim or Tiffany would. He really couldn't settle on a point guard. Kim was faster than a locomotive but sometimes this great asset also made her turnover prone. Tiffany, in my opinion, didn't have a personality that was durable enough to deal with our superstars. And if there was one position where a strong personality was needed, it was point. Even with our point guard drama, one thing was already clear. We were gonna be a lot better than anyone outside of Houston thought we were.

As for me, I let the little developmental thing slide. My job was to lay to rest any doubt that I belonged on the Houston Comets team. And I did just that. I had a fantastic training camp. So good in fact, that I was vying for a starting spot. I didn't have a beef with Van, he's human just like the rest of us. Was he responsible for the developmental list fiasco, maybe, maybe not? But serving up attitude wasn't going to help me in Houston, so I remembered what my mother always told us at home: you reap what you sow. You get what put out. I don't try to punish people for the bad things that do to me because life has a way of working things out. So, I put all the negativity aside and concentrated on doing what I could to help the Comets become a contender.

Training camp was exciting and effortless, mainly because there was such a high level of enthusiasm in the first season. Plus, we had such a unique group of characters on our team that there was never a dull moment. We were very loose, almost all the time. In fact, before each practice, we stretched to music. I'd heard that Van liked, no, make that, loved Jackie Wilson. So, one day I bought a compilation tape that had this song he was so crazy about, on it. "Lonely Teardrops" was the name of it. The next day in practice before the coaches arrived, I had our manager cue up the boom box to the song. When Van, Kevin and Peggy walked in, it started playing. At first, he didn't hear it. He was too busy yukking it up with us. Then, all of a sudden, it hit him. And his face lit up like a Christmas tree. "Turn that up, turn that up!" he said. "Who did that?" Nobody said a word. It really wasn't important to me that he knew that I'd gotten that tape for him. Seeing his expression when he heard it, was reward enough. But after practice, he walked over and said, "Harris, I didn't know you did that. That was very nice, thank you." He looked surprised, which made it even better. "You're welcome," I said. "It's yours." He beamed. "I get to keep it?" I looked at him, smiled and said,"You think *we* wanna hear "Lonely Teardrops"? He laughed and yelled for the DJ to play 'his song' again.

A week later we opened the season at home versus Charlotte in one of two exhibition games and it was then that I got a glimpse of how great our team was going to be. The starters had been Coop, Janeth, Tina, Wanda and Kim but Tammy, Tiffany and I had gotten lots of playing time. Van was so bubbly after the game because I think it had just hit him that he had something special. Very special. "Harris," he said after we beat the Sting. "We gon' be good. I can't hardly stand it." I knew exactly how he felt. Houston was going to make some noise before it was all over. Nobody else in the league knew it, but we sure did.

And Now A Word From Our Sponsors

In 1997, the WNBA made history in a lot of ways. It was the first women's professional league to secure such high profile sponsorships in its inaugural season. The television deals with NBC, Lifetime Television and ESPN solidified the WNBA as a professional sports organization. And what a testament to the female consumer that so many heavy hitters stepped up to the plate early on—Buick, Sears and Lee Jeans, to name only a few. I do have one complaint though. Where was the diversity in the commercials? Not ethnic diversity but more variety. Instead we saw the same commercials over and over and over. I know that advertising is all about repetition, but I don't know what I would have done if I'd had to sit through one more summer of the same tired Buddy Lee commercials. Another one that drove me crazy was the Buick ad, "When you score, I score." My favorite commercial though, over the league's four-year existence was the one where the sassy little girl gave life lessons to the WNBA stars. Especially the one where she told Cooper,'...you had Tina wide open for a three on the wing...you know she's money from down there'.

Where Did Our Love Go?

A few sponsors dropped out in the fourth season and as soon as they did, panic ran rampant in the women's basketball community. "Oh, no," people wrote in their emails, "Isn't this bad for the league's overall stability?" Losing sponsors is never a reason to throw a party but it doesn't have to be a reason to wave the white flag either. We've gotta remember, the WNBA is a business, first and foremost. Sponsors come on board because they're seeking very specific results and rewards. If they don't feel that they're getting a solid return on their investment, of course, they're gonna pull out. It makes sense that they would take their dollars elsewhere. But in my mind, this simply opens the door for a company that may be a better match for the WNBA. It's not personal, it's business. And it doesn't mean that the league is on the brink of folding.

The Original Big Three

Before Sheryl Swoopes, Tina Thompson and Cynthia Cooper could give this title real meaning, the league had decided that another big three would lead the WNBA to the Promised Land. Lisa Leslie, Rebecca Lobo and Sheryl Swoopes' most recent claim to fame at the time was that they'd all been members of the gold medal '96 Olympic team. But they had very little professional playing experience, a fact that left some observers wondering if the WNBA was being run by the cast of Southpark. From a player's perspective I didn't really see how the league could justify shelling out $250,000 to a bunch of twentysomethings who hadn't paid their dues. Dues in the sense of going overseas, toiling on foreign soil and putting up with some of the things veteran players had to endure.

It just didn't seem right. How can you anoint someone who really doesn't know how far the game has come? Anoint people like Lynette Woodard, Andrea Lloyd-Curry, Jennifer Gillom, Cynthia Cooper, and Teresa Weatherspoon. Folks who'd gone to the most heinous corners of the world for the last 15 years to continue playing a sport they'd given their lives to. People who'd left their loved ones and everything that was familiar to them for the sake of continuing to play the game they loved so much. Those are the folks who needed some love in my opinion.

But of course, from a business standpoint, selecting Swoopes, Leslie and Lobo made perfect sense. I wasn't upset that the league had chosen this trio because I knew that it was all about timing. They were the best candidates to sell the WNBA globally. Had the WNBA started the summer after we won the NCAA Championship in '86, nearly ever senior on my team would have been an assigned player, along with Cheryl Miller, Cynthia Cooper, Jennifer Gillom, Clemette Haskins and Lillie Mason. But the timing wasn't right for a league then.

A decade later, Swoopes, Leslie and Lobo were the big names in women's basketball and nobody knew who any of us were. But these three were young and fairly well-known. Lobo and Swoopes had played on NCAA championship teams. Leslie had rewritten the scoring records at USC. They would have long careers in the league, so Val Ackerman could justify making a long-term investment in players who were going to be around to promote the WNBA brand. Plus the partnership between USA Basketball and the WNBA had ensured that everyone in American knew who these three were. Team USA's well-publicized national and international tour coupled with their Olympic triumphs provided the perfect entrée for the WNBA to introduce its new league. I think we all *understood* the method behind the league's madness—but that doesn't mean we agreed with it or liked it.

Training Camp 101

The countdown to the 2000 WNBA season began with the opening of training camp on Wednesday, May 3. And if you've never gone to training camp, you have no idea how grueling these things can be. When people ask me to describe the experience, I say, take your bottom lip and pull it over your head so that it doubles as a ski mask. That's how hard WNBA training camp can be. It's a month-long boot camp designed to weed out those poor souls who are on the cusp of being the 11th person on the team.

You see, the 12th person on the team is easy for a coach to decide on. That player is often what coaches affectionately call a 'project'. A player who the coach sees as an investment towards future championships. The 12th player can also be that player who goes hard, cheers even harder but whose talent pales in comparison to her teammates. This is insurance for the coach. Not so much as actual on-court help but as that one face a coach can look down on the bench upon and see her smiling. This person is happy if she sees two minutes of playing time the entire season. I was never her. If I was on the team, then I wanted to *play*.

Anyway, a lot of people wonder how teams decide who gets invited to their training camps. Well, it goes a little something like this.

In 2000, the Sunday before camp opened, each coach had to provide the league office with this elusive 'list' that consisted of players that they wanted in their camps—players they'd seen in the off-season, in their local tryouts and in tournaments around the country. Of course, this meant that a player could (and probably did) appear on two or more teams' lists. So, in this case the league decided which team got the player, with very special consideration given to the expansion teams.

College and high school preseason training camps are like Sunday School compared to WNBA training camp. Week One is hands down, the most critical week of any team's training camp. If a player can survive—and better yet, thrive—during the first seven days of preseason workouts, the rest of the month will be a piece of cake. Not quite easy street but certainly not hoops purgatory, either. Here's why. Week One is the weeding out week. It's the week that the women separate themselves from the girls. It's the one week that talent means nothing. It's the week that coaches get to read your mail. They find out who's in shape and who's made one to many runs to Taco Bell in the off-season. Week One generally consists of at least four two-a-day practices. You heard me, right. In seven days, it's possible to have eleven practices, each about 2.5 hours. In addition to the team workout, some lucky players can also have an hour position practice with an assistant coach plus a 60—90 minute weight workout with the strength coach. All on the same day as a two-a-day. So, let's calculate that. Five hours of practice, an hour of position work and an hour and a half of weights. That's a grand total of 7.5 hours of training in ONE day. Isn't basketball a 40-minute game?

The Three Basic Food Groups

There are three groups of players in training camp. Every player fell into one of these categories.

The Anointed Ones. The returning superstars, who are usually the highest paid, best-treated athletes on the team. They don't necessarily practice every day and certainly not every practice like the regular players. Somehow they tend to get an usually high number of calls to go their way during the intrasquad scrimmages. And they get away with saying things that other players wouldn't dream of uttering in the presence of the coaches. Things, as one western conference player told me one superstar said to an official during a scrimmage session, "Call a f&*$ing foul or else I'm walking off the court."

The Usual Prospects. The drafted or otherwise highly regarded players who are often disillusioned by the amount of work that is required of them at this level. They sometimes think that being drafted means that they've made the team until they get to camp and find out what V02 max is all about. Hello, rookie. Nobody here gives a rip about your college scoring record. Sometimes these players have even been told by the coach that they're on the team so sometimes they get amnesia when you're trying to run a set play because they know that they're not gonna get cut.

The Bubble Girls. These are the players who are busting their butts every single day because they know they've gotta dot every i and cross every t to even get a for real look by the coaching staff. Sometimes these are fourth round picks or players who made it through local tryouts. So, it's not surprising that an inordinate amount of these players actually make the team because there's absolutely no pressure on them. If you find yourself in this situation, the best thing to do is to carve out a niche. A good example of a specialty player, was Wanda Guyton. Now, Wanda was not a bubble player in Houston but I'm using her to make a point about specializing. Guyton was a rebounding machine. If the ball went up, she had a 50-50 chance of getting it every single time. She was that relentless. The flip side was this: Wanda's hands were not the greatest. She had a strong, sturdy body and she was terrific at posting up but she simply had a hard time catching the ball. You could deliver a pass to her via FedEx and she still couldn't hang on to it.

That's Coach To You

I got into a heated discussion with a good friend during the summer of '98 on the topic of professional players calling their coaches by their first name. I said what's the big deal? She said that if they want to be called 'coach' then that's what you should call them. We went back and forth. I mean, I didn't see why a coach should require players to refer to them as Coach so-and-so versus the name their mama gave them.

When I was 22 and playing on my first pro team in Italy, we called the coach, who was at least 15 years older than most of us, by his first name, Paolo. In fact, every player in Italy called their coach by his or her first name regardless of the age of the coach. It's professional sports and we have a business relationship with our coaches. Sometimes I really think people have a hard time seeing women as equals, so they attempt to create these situations to keep them in subordinate roles. A few years ago I saw one coach get in a player's face and yell at her, telling her to say, 'yes, Sir'. She was a professional player. And I couldn't believe my eyes. I thought I was looking at a military film.

For four years I worked at Procter & Gamble, one of the biggest and oldest companies in the U.S., and I never heard one person, regardless of rank, call another person Mr. anything. One of the company's top executives at the time was a guy named John Pepper. You know what we called him? John. Or Pepper. Never Mr. Pepper. So, I didn't get the whole Coach thing.

In '97, I caught flack in Houston when I called Van Chancellor, Van during a practice. I had a question, so I said, "Van, what do we do in this instance?" Tina Thompson looked over at me like I had grown a third ear. Cynthia Cooper gave me the eye. As far as I'm concerned they were being hypocritical because we all know that every athlete in America calls their coach by their first name behind their backs. Don't lie, you do the same thing with your boss, parents and coaches, too.

Team Meetings

This is how it is when you're the best team in the WNBA but you're not playing like it. Somebody, usually the coach, calls a team meeting. Attendance mandatory. To be clear, team meetings are rarely called because things are going *well*. So, when I heard that we were having a team meeting, I knew it wasn't to pat us on the back. Nuh uh, something was about to go down and it probably wasn't gonna involve champagne and strawberries. We had just lost to Utah, who at the time was widely considered the tank of the league, and our coaches felt that perhaps we were getting a little apathetic in our on court effort. So the whispers started. We're having a meeting in the locker room after practice, I heard someone say on the sidelines as we were conditioning one day.

After workout, we all headed for the locker room. Van, Peggy and Kevin entered solemnly. Van started in by saying that if you had something to say that you should say it. My experience was that when a coach said that, it was the biggest setup in the world. And I didn't bite. I'd already learned to fight the fights worth fighting and to leave that other stuff alone. Coop was already in a funk so I knew she was gonna have plenty to say.

And I was right. "We have too many offenses," she started. "I think we need to stop learning a new offense everyday." I laughed inside and just stared at Cynthia. Our lockers were directly across from one another. "And," she continued. Van interrupted her. "I don't think it's the offenses, I thank we just not playin' hard enough." Coop came back. "Coach, we have too many offenses. We can't learn one before we're given another one." Van looked around the room. "That how ya'll feel? You thank we got too many offenses? 'Cause we can fix that." People nodded. Hell yeah, we had too many offenses. About 20 to be exact. I was watching everyone in the room.

Tammy Jackson was sitting in front of me patting her feet like she was in 11:00 Baptist church service. Rocking like she could've been the star of the movie *Girl Interrupted*. She was stewing over something and I knew what it was. She'd talked about it on a recent road trip. I wondered if she'd have the guts to say in the meeting what she'd said to me in private. Van rambled on about our execution and Coop rambled on about a more effective offensive set. I was tuning them all out. I wanted to hear from Air Jackson. That's the speech I was waiting on. Finally, Coop and Van paused and that's when Tammy burst in like Superman.

"Okay, okay," she said. "I got something to say. You wanna know what your problem is?" Whoa! I almost flew outta my chair. Jackson was about to go off. Van looked at her like 'what the hell?' He'd never seen Tammy this animated either. Neither had I.

"Let's hear it," he said.

Tammy's voice got thunderous. "Your problem is that you've got good players, great players on this team and you don't know how to use 'em. That's your problem." I was praying, Lord, please don't let me get happy in here, cuz Air Jackson is preaching!

Tammy was saying exactly what needed to be said. Here we were, the best team in the league losing to folks like Utah and all because our coaches were only using five players, when he had one of the strongest benches in the league. I agreed with Tammy 100%, but the words were better coming from her for a number of reasons. One, Tammy rarely got upset. Two, Tammy barely had anything to say in team meetings. So, the fact that she'd gotten hot and bothered on a subject was going to carry more weight. I was glad I hadn't needed to open my trap that day. Van had asked for my opinion on numerous things—players, coaching philosophies and so forth. But he and I both knew that he had not exactly been on the up and up with my playing time, so sometimes we walked gingerly around each other. We were cool but we both understood that the air between us was still a little cloudy because of the developmental thing.

I'd learned to pick my battles. Everyone in that room knew that if I opened my mouth, that I was just gonna tell it like it is. Some folks don't like to hear the truth. We had a few of these folks in that room. So, instead of adding anything to Tammy's comments, I simply said a silent prayer of thanks because that was one day that my mouth and opinions didn't get me in trouble. I took Tammy to lunch that day. And this time I treated.

The Best Seats in the House: Tales from the Bench

Toward the end of the season, after Sheryl got back from giving birth to her son, J.J., life for me was a little different. As I mentioned earlier, I'd been playing anywhere from 20-26 minutes a game and was loving being back in basketball. But the league was dropping a quarter of a million on Swoopes and the fans wanted to see their marquee player in action—sooner than later. And even though Swoopes, by her own admission, wasn't in basketball shape, she played just the same. That meant whoever was getting some of her minutes had to sit. That was me. So, overnight I went from playing almost half of a game to a quarter of a *half*. I went from handing Janeth a warm up jacket as I substituted for her in the game, to handing her a cup of water from the end of the bench. Boy, that took some getting used to. I was glad Sheryl hadn't had J.J. in May.

CHAPTER 3

Salt Lake In My Wounds

Knock Knock? Who's There? It's Your Gut Feeling...

I should have known something was up when everyone except the head coach in the Utah Starzz organization telephoned me to welcome me into the fold after the trade with Houston went through two days before the beginning of training camp in 1998. That should've been my first clue. But time was of the essence and the only thing I had time to do was to find someone to baby-sit my car while I was away.

I got on the plane to Salt Lake City anxious about my new situation. I knew a few of the players on the Starzz team but not that well. And I wanted to make a good impression. Sometimes people have preconceived notions about people who come from the best team in the league. But I wasn't about trying to get the Starzz to be like the Comets. Not at all. In fact, it was refreshing to be going somewhere that wasn't like Houston because we'd had our own unique issues.

The first order of business in Utah, was a team meeting. We convened in the locker room at the Delta Center, where all of the games are played. And that's when I knew that my gut had been right on. Denise Taylor, the head coach, barely spoke to me and never said welcome to the Starzz. Nothing. I dismissed it primarily because I didn't have a choice. I had asked for the trade and there was nothing that could be done to reverse it. I'd have to live with it.

That night in my hotel room I played back my conversation with Van Chancellor. He'd said, "Are you sure this is what you want?" I'd hesitantly said yes because I did but I didn't. Houston had been good to me but with Swoopes returning to the team it meant that my minutes were going to be sliced significantly and that wasn't that appealing to me at age 32. Now, had I been five or six years younger I would have gladly played behind Sheryl or I probably would have had more trading options. But that wasn't my reality and I wanted to go to a team where I could possibly start or at least get the minutes I deserved.

Training camp in Utah started with physicals. And wouldn't you know that something showed up on my physical that would keep me out of the first day of practice. That was a shot in the heart because I was already a little unsettled by the coach's lack of enthusiasm about my being there. In all fairness to her she had not orchestrated the trade. She wasn't the general manager. She was *only* the coach and most coaches in the WNBA have absolutely no power if they aren't *also* the general manager, the person who usually spearheads all personnel moves.

The trade, which forced her to give up Karen Booker, a player she really liked, had been initiated by the Comets and approved by the Starzz' top operations man, Scott Layden, who's now with the New York Knicks. I guess I didn't expect Denise to roll out the red carpet but I was disappointed that she wasn't a little more professional. That was very disappointing. But I put my head down and pressed forward. I knew I'd have to work that much harder to achieve my goal of starting or to even make the team with this size obstacle already in my way.

So, as I said, I had to miss the first day of training camp because WNBA rules prohibit players from practicing without being cleared physically by team doctors. So, instead of being on the floor in practice on that first day, I had to sit on the sidelines. Fred Williams, the assistant coach at the time, came over and asked how I was doing, and what the doctors were saying about my release. I appreciated his concern very much because it's scary to think that your career could end because of some physical condition that you have no control over. So, I was grateful to Fred for his kindness.

The next morning I had a series of tests run because some kind of heart abnormality had shown up during my physical. I spent the morning with a cardiologist running on a treadmill. They found out that whatever I had was very common but they had to be sure that it wasn't life threatening before I could be cleared to practice.

I went to the Franklin Covey center where we practiced. All of the players were very welcoming and that made me feel really good. By the end of week one I knew that I was leading the candidates for starting at the three spot. I had to have faith that Denise Taylor would get over the trade and give me a fair shot. I just played ball and eventually the air got better in Utah. I was playing well and getting along with my new teammates, especially my girls Dena Head, Chantel Tremitiere and Olympia Scott. The first round of waivers was upon us but I honestly wasn't worried one bit. I'd made sure that I'd left it all on the court each day of our two-a-day practices. Taylor was becoming much friendlier, which was nice because the last thing you want as a player is unwarranted friction between you and your coach. One day before practice, I was in the restroom and Denise walked in. We exchanged hellos and then I headed for the door. "You're playing well, Fran Harris," she said. I was utterly speechless. She had said all of 20 words to me in two weeks so this was quite refreshing. "Thank you," I said. "I appreciate that, *Coach.*" Denise Taylor was one of those coaches who required you to call her Coach.

If It Ain't Broke, Wassup?

The first time we played Houston in the Delta Center, we took them to three, count 'em, three overtimes. Forty-three minutes it took the champs to beat the Utah Starzz in 1998. How, you may be wondering, in the world did the Utah Starzz take the Houston Comets to triple overtime? It's simple. We were good. I mean rrrreally good. We were talented and we were getting along quite well. So, how, you say again, did a team so supposedly good, end the season so badly? It's hard to make something good out of something that's not quite right from the top. And things just weren't regular in Salt Lake. The management didn't appear to be very enthused about having a WNBA team. And that's a shame because the Starzz had almost all of the ingredients to be a Houston or Phoenix. The fans were enthusiastic, the players were talented and the surrounding communities were excited about us being there, yet the management team appeared to care more about the corn crop in Egypt than they did about our team.

The Starzz owner was (probably still is) one of the wealthiest car dealers in the country, yet we shared vehicles the size of Yugos. The support staff rationed practice gear like it was gold plated. These things may sound trivial to outsiders but when employees are treated well, they're more likely to perform well. That's a fact. It's all connected, if you ask me. In Houston, we were treated very well. First class all the way. The result, Four championships in four years.

So, it didn't surprise me that Utah had already settled into underachievement. There was no real love out there. And you know something's wrong when every player on the team wants out. The first day I got there, Wendy Palmer asked me, "Why would you leave Houston to come to a place like this?" I thought, 'hmmm' and that was from the team's best player. Before the day was over at least three other players had expressed similar sentiments. They all said the same thing basically. *Click your heels, Dorothy, this ain't Kansas.* And they were right. There was no place like Utah.

Nothing but the Tupac in Me

It's a shame that Kim Williams is not still playing in the league, she could be a great pro player. The problem with Kim was that she wasn't all that crazy about practice, see. And that's a problem for some coaches. I played with her in Utah and I didn't log the number of full practices Kim actually participated in but if I had to guess, I'd say it was something like ten…in four weeks or roughly 30 days. When you look at those as straight numbers, it's not that impressive, is it? But she was spectacular in those few practices. She really was.

On most days Kim was as quiet as a cathedral mouse but on this day in practice somebody had apparently ruffled her feathers. I think the coaches had made her mad by asking her to go hard and stuff. She didn't respond too well to those kinds of requests. So what did she do? What any respectable competitor who wants to keep her job would do, she took it out on anyone who got in her way. She was trying to block 7-foot-2, Margo Dydek's shot. She mauled me on a dribble and went down court for a finger roll. She cursed out several people for just looking at her the wrong way. It was actually funny to most of us because no one had ever seen her that riled up.

Cat Eyes, the woman who was easy like a Sunday morning and who didn't usually say a whole lot, was ticked. So, after workout I walked over to her to get the cutters to take the athletic tape off of my ankle. "What's up, girl?" I asked. "Nuttin," she mumbled. "*Something,*" I shot back. "I'm just tired of this shit, man. They gon' mess around and make the Tupac in me come out."

"Is that what they gon' do, dawg?" I asked cracking up. "You laughing but I'm serious, Fran." She fell on the carpet laughing too. She knew that was the best line of training camp. And she meant every single word of it. Believe that.

Spunky

Art Bader had only one request. It seemed like a small enough request. Yet his wife, Sandy, still wasn't ready to give him the green light. Not yet, anyway. It was April 29, 1998 around 4:30 p.m. D-day had come and almost gone and still no word from New York. The Baders sat around talking about nothing in particular, just waiting for 'the call'. Three rounds of the WNBA draft had passed and their spunky point guard and baby girl, Tricia, still had not been taken. And it wasn't looking all that promising. Tricia, who stands not an inch taller than 5'4" was a long shot.

In a league where point guards are anything but half-pints, her chances of making the Big Dance were looking more like none than slim. So when the phone rang and Denise Taylor, the head coach of the Utah Starzz asked for Tricia Bader, the whole house walked around like the floor was a sheet of hot coals. Denise Taylor told Trish that she had been selected as their fourth and final pick of the draft. Welcome to the dance, Trish. Trish beamed. Sandy smiled. And Art went bonkers.

Art marched over to the tall, oak entertainment center and patted the sensible, 19-inch television that rested peacefully on the top shelf. Then he flashed a mischievous grin in Sandy's direction. The week before, Art had polished his sales pitch to a perfect shine. If Tricia got drafted, he'd asked Sandy if he could buy a big screen television to watch her dazzle fans and defenders with her crazy handles and smooth as butter jumper. Secretly, Sandy wanted the 52" inch screen as much as Art did. But of course she didn't tell him that.

Art hadn't missed one of his daughter's games at Boise State in four years and he wasn't about to let a few miles and mountains separate them. When the Starzz played in Salt Lake City, Art would make the four-hour drive to be there. And for away games, he'd have Big Bertha, his big screen, a few cans of brew and a score sheet in breathing distance.

Trish was like any other rookie in training camp. She had good days and those not so fresh days. But her killer crossover deceived her Starzz teammates on a daily basis. Her high arch jumpshot was so fluid that we'd all watched in amazement. And her heart? As big as Texas. But still there were days that Tricia questioned if she truly belonged in the

WNBA. There were days during the summer of '98, when the chiseled athlete with the streaky, strawberry blonde ponytail that swayed gently from side to side when she ran, was just not sure she'd make the cut.

Like the day in practice when she was put on the purple team. The team that as the 15th day of training camp winded down was looking more like the starting five. The day Trish made the purple team she wanted to string herself up on the very goal she couldn't put the ball into no matter how hard she tried. Her jumper had clanked off the side of the rim each time she shot. She had dribbled off her foot more times than the floor. And her defensive player had been like a second sports bra all scrimmage long. Not today, she thought. Of all days, not the day I play on the purple team, she thought.

But Tricia conceded, 'it just had not been her day'. She had left the floor in a funk, a rarity for someone who was so cheerful, she could have easily been a Mouseketeer. Her sweaty, purple mesh #10 jersey drooped off of her gray Starzz Basketball T-shirt. She walked slowly toward the tweed, carpeted bleachers where passers-through often sat to watch the Starzz practice. She talked to herself in a barely audible tone. *Couldn't even hit a stupid jumpshot. Who in their right mind would keep me on their team?* The laces on her shoes were finally undone. The athletic tape that had snuggled and protected her fragile ankles during the two-hour workout, she slung to the floor. Her one chance to strut her stuff and prove that she could play with the big dawgs and she'd blown it. In two hours, she'd been about as exciting as the credits after a good flick. But in two days, she told herself, redemption would be hers. If she got to play.

Phoenix gave heat new meaning. We'd practiced for two hours in Salt Lake and then boarded a 2:50 flight to Steamy Pines. The game would be our first test of the season. And even though it was just an exhibition game, it would still count. Especially in the minds of the five returning players who had endured the pain of a horrendous 7-21 inaugural season. The Starzz had finished the '97 campaign dead last. Eighth out of eight. Anything would have been an improvement. And Trish saw this as her big chance. Maybe God had looked out for her after all. If she could make an impact anywhere, surely Utah was the place.

The Mercury, who boasted hall of fame coach, Cheryl Miller and all players from a playoff team a year ago, seemed to have all of the elements to put us to the test. The pregame introductions had mesmerized the 11,512 fans on hand, including the Starzz. The solar display and fireworks had the crowd bumpin' and the adrenaline pumpin'. All 16 players who'd made the Starzz training camp traveled to the game at America West Arena. Five players from the year before, two trades, four draft picks and five who'd been selected through local tryouts. Sixteen players. Sixteen heartbeats. Eleven available jobs. Trish Bader wanted one of those spots. And every basketball player in the world knows that practice is one thing. Games are another.

Nothing went as planned. We jumped out to an early lead and had the momentum heading into halftime. Trish had started the game on the bench and as the first half wound down, she was still sitting in that seat. Was Coach Taylor going to put her in? Or were the events of the horrible practice haunting her? Trish sat patiently, hoping, praying that someone would call her name other than a teammate trying to get her attention for a cup of Gatorade.

Her name was eventually called, but one minute and forty-two seconds was all the run she'd gotten. It wasn't the way she'd planned it, but at least she'd gotten in the game. The butterflies that had taken residence in her stomach had left. They'd had plenty of time to get acclimated to the air on Mercury. But one minute was hardly enough time to get your rhythm. It was barely enough time to even breathe hard. In basketball time, one minute is a long time. Ask anybody. Games have been won and lost in fewer ticks. But that was no consolation to Trish, who felt that she had at least deserved to sweat.

Later that night at Dan Majerles' restaurant after we'd licked our wounds and soothed our hurts with ice, Flexall and comical conversation, the reality of the situation sunk in. We had just lost the season opener by eight to a team that didn't even have all of its players. Four of the Mercury players who were foreigners had missed the game because they were playing in the Women's World Championships in Berlin, Germany. Trish sat on the barstool and pondered the future. The possibilities. She leaned over and congratulated one of our three teammates seated to her right. "Nice game, T.J.," she said. In between bites of her spicy chicken wings, T.J. returned the compliment. "Phhhh! Yeah, right," Trish said taking a long sip of her beer. "What did I play? One minute? 30 seconds?" Actually it was 1:42, I reminded her as she almost spit up her food laughing.

Salt Lake In My Rear View

It happened so quickly. One of my teammates had just called to ask me if I'd heard about Denise Taylor being fired. I hadn't. I continued to work on a book proposal for a project I wanted to sell. Later that day, our manager called and said that my ride was going to be coming a little earlier to pick me up but I wasn't going to be there, so I asked for a later ride to the gym—it was game day.

When I arrived at the Delta Center, the manager came into the lockerroom and said that Scott Layden wanted to see me. I walked into his office where he and this other Starzz management guy were already sitting. "Fran, we're waiving you," Scott said. I was shocked, though not surprised. "Because…," I replied. "We've decided to go in another direction," he continued. I couldn't believe my ears. "Another direction?" I said, looking for a little more than that as a reason. But then it dawned on me that this was exactly what I'd been warned about when I got to Utah. The players had all agreed. If you have opinions, it's best to keep them to yourselves, because they are not welcome in Salt Lake City.

A few weeks before my untimely dismissal, I'd been yanked from the starting lineup without any warning. So, naturally I was concerned. Not because I wasn't going to start, but because neither Denise nor Fred had pulled me aside to discuss it. After all, it was my job and it was going to affect me. So, I did what professionals do in this situation—I called the coaches and requested a meeting with them. Only I didn't go alone. I asked one of our captains, Tammi Reiss, to sit in on the meeting with me because I wanted someone else to witness the whole thing. I wanted someone else to see that I'd come to them with a positive attitude to inquire about my job. It's sad that I felt that I needed 'a witness' but I didn't trust the Utah organization. It was not one that inspired open communication and trust, two things that I value greatly.

In that meeting, I opened the discussion by saying that I wasn't there to discuss 'starting', I was there to understand how things worked in the Utah system. "It's not that I'm upset about not starting, I'm concerned that no one came to me and said anything." That's when Denise spelled it out. "Well, we don't feel that as coaches, we have to explain why we do anything," she said. It was classic. And I knew what time it was in that very moment. I knew what I'd been up against for two months. But I disagreed with Denise and I told her that. "This is my job," I said. "Playing time is reward for working hard and performing well. Are you telling me that if one day you got your paycheck—your reward—and it was cut 20%, and nobody told you that it was going to be reduced, that you wouldn't be upset?"

For some reason, a light came on with that analogy. "We felt like we needed to make a change, just see different looks," she said. I didn't have one problem with her explanation, but I told them that it would have been nice to hear about it beforehand. Fred interjected, "I see what you're saying, Fran, and we could've taken care of this just by communicating this to you." My point exactly.

After this meeting, things were never the same. My playing time dwindled to seconds. And all of the horror stories the players had told me about in training camp, were coming true. They'd said that the minute you express yourself in Utah, you're done. You may as well bring

Terry McMillan's latest novel with you to the game because you will never set foot on the court again. So, I went from starting and playing 43 minutes in a triple overtime game against the Houston Comets, to rotting on the bench, to being waived. And why? Because I didn't respond too well to slave-like work conditions. I can't work my ass off, be mistreated and just take it in silence. That's not how I was raised. I have too much self-respect.

Dr. Wayne Dyer, in one of his bestselling inspirational audiotapes, talks about the great thinkers and leaders of our time. And he talks about what happens to people who express unpopular opinions, opinions that go against the grain of institutionalized thinking. Instead of celebrating them for what they add to our society, we crucify them because we see them as troublemakers. We get rid of them, we waive them. But without people like Martin Luther King, Jr. or Gandhi, where would our world be?

Later that summer, I asked my friends around the league what they'd heard about the Utah situation and one friend broke it down like this. "You had opinions, a voice," she said. "And that's why they let you go." I breathed a sigh of relief that at least the rumor mill had gotten it right this time. And I was never happier about being waived in my entire life because at least I'd stood firm in my beliefs, treated my coaches with the respect they deserved and done the right thing by going to them, even if it cost me my job.

It was devastating at the time, but what great lessons I learned. I left Salt Lake City with even greater convictions about injustices and speaking your truth. And basketball was again in its proper perspective. I felt good. And I know that my mother was in heaven that summer, smiling her ass off, bragging, "That's *my* baby!"

CHAPTER 4

From the Hardwood to the Headsets: Life as a WNBA Announcer

Lights, Camera, Action

You'd think that with my broadcasting and basketball credentials, that I would have been able to parlay my various skills and talents into a multi-million dollar empire by now. That there'd be at least one street named after me. That I'd be mobbed in airports and restaurants worldwide. That I'd be invited to play in that famous celebrity golf tournament in Vegas that Michael Jordan and Charles Barkley play in each year. That there would be a Millionaire question with my name on it. Or that my wall of fame would have at least one ESPY mounted on it. Instead, I'm constantly asked if I'm Sheryl Swoopes and if I'm not, do I know her? And if I do, can I get her autograph for someone's 11-year old daughter? Even as an athlete who's reached the pinnacle in my sport, my life since my retirement has been quite the opposite of my male counterparts.

As a broadcaster, not only do I have to compete with other women who are in pursuit of the next best microphone gig but I've also gotta get my hustle on against guys who know the guys, who know the guys whose Daddy owns the company. You see, there's no Title IX in sports-casting. There's no legislation that says that women should at least be given a shot at covering a sporting event. And I'm not saying that there should be. I am saying that I'd like to see more networks nurture female talent because there's a lot of it out there.

I can't complain too much because my initial transition from the hardwood to the broadcasting booth was actually smooth primarily because I went from playing basketball to covering women's basketball. Don't get me wrong, there are obstacles still facing women in pursuit of sports careers. The opportunities available for men, say, in broadcasting, double mine. A male broadcaster can cover both men's and women's sports, while a woman is often relegated to women's sports or the sidelines of men's sports.

After our team won the national championship in '86 and my stint in the Italian pro league in '87, I felt fairly confident that I'd be able to find a job in the sports broadcasting industry after I got home. After all we've come a long way, right, baby? Sorta. In 1991, when I inquired about becoming a basketball analyst for a major sports channel at that time, I learned that there were very few women currently in analyst or play-by-play roles. And moreover, I was told that they had no plans of changing that fact in the foreseeable future. This was the late '80s before the proliferation of cable television, when there was only one women's basketball game televised each year. It was CBS' national championship telecast and Hall of Famer Ann Meyers Drysdale had that gig sewn up.

Still, I kept pounding the pavement, calling producers and attending every networking event in the country. Trying to convince them that even though men were playing the game, that basketball was basketball and that if I could cover a women's game, surely I could handle a men's event. The game didn't change because the reproductive equipment did. Finally in January 1992, ESPN gave me my first analyst job—an SEC women's basketball game between LSU and Auburn. Other assignments soon followed over the course of the next few years but the trend I started to see concerned me.

While women were being given more analysts jobs (on women's events), men still outnumbered us on these events and more importantly, many were filling the perceived important job of play-by-play announcer. Fine for a guy who knows the sport or who's at least seen the sport in the last oh, 20 years. But the guys who were (and sometimes today) my broadcasting partners were often former baseball or football players who were not very basketball savvy and even less enthusiastic about covering the women's game. I worked with guys who were so uninformed on women's basketball that they were startled to learn that the half-court game died around the same time John Wayne had. They'd say, 'It's been that long? Hmmm, where've I been?' These same guys were being paid, in some cases, three times what I made as the expert on the game.

Then when I saw that Charles Barkley had decided to hang up his sneakers and the one-size-larger-than-he-used-to-wear-before-his-injury shorts, I had to laugh. And I wondered where the next Sir Charles sighting would be. Would he be reunited with his close friend and golfing buddy, Michael Jordan in the Washington Wizards' organization? Would he begin jawing in the broadcasting booth with Hannah Storm, Isaiah Thomas and Peter Vescey on NBC's Showtime? Or would he follow through on his threat to run for governor of Alabama? I'd heard that the World Wrestling Federation was looking for a few big butts. Point is, Chuck's options were endless. He recently signed a sweet deal with TNT to be a studio analyst alongside Kenny Smith and Ernie Johnson. No surprise to anyone because Charles likes to talk. And he's not afraid to say how he feels—about any given subject at any given time. So, not only are we about to be graced with the opinions of the guy who became known as the Round Mound of Rebound, but some poor soul's about to be out of a television job. Oh, no, wait. Guys just move over when another guy retires. Psst, E.J. and Kenny, slide one.

Sometimes it seems so unfair. If I were a guy I'd be making a killing as a broadcaster right now. My agent and I wouldn't be hounding folks to get me a TV gig. But the retirement situation is not the only discrepancy between men's and women's sports. When I made the Houston Comets squad in 1997, my 1-year salary for the compact 90-day season was less than my speaker's fee at the time and tip money for my boy, Shaq. And had I not retired in 1998, I still would not have earned a million dollars from my entire professional basketball career.

Here I was staring at my contract letter from the WNBA wondering how I would possibly continue with my Hollywood lifestyle on the cheese the league wanted to pay me. Meanwhile, my counterparts were moaning in labor talks about the virtues of making $11 million a season instead of $7 million. Guys, do me a fave. Don't talk to me about hard times. Try being a veteran female sports announcer trying to persuade a network exec to pony up a measly $200 raise and seeing him look you dead in the face saying, "Fran, I'd love to give you more money, I really would, because you deserve it…it's just not in the budget." And then two weeks later, learning that the new kid on the block—the recently retired Rogaine-using quarterback from the team that never won anything—is getting a whopping six-figure deal to sit in the studio in his Armani suit to state the obvious. That my friends, is strife.

The Darkest Hour

Beverly Williams remembers where she was when the ABL folded. So does Edna Campbell, Natalie Williams, Jennifer Azzi and about 90 other players who'd played in the league for 2 and a half years. Was I sad that the ABL folded? Of course. We all were. December 22nd was a dark day for women's basketball. It was on that Tuesday, three days before Christmas, that the ABL suspended operations and announced that they'd be filing for bankruptcy.

The players—the 100 or so who filled the nine-team league rosters—were stunned. Many of them going about business at home as usual when they heard the news. Some of them admitted that they knew something was up but they didn't know what. "I knew something was wrong when I couldn't get anyone to return my phone calls," said Beverly Williams, who played for the Long Beach Stingrays along with Yolanda Griffith and Clarissa Davis-Wrightsil. "It was wild because they didn't tell us anything. Nothing. We had to find out from the people in the community who were asking us what we were gonna do next." That's how the news was broken to Beverly.

Someone called Clarissa on her cell phone. Others turned on the television and heard it on the news. The ironic thing about the way the ABL ended is that it had touted itself, almost in a self-righteous manner, as the league that cared about its players. Several players and members of the league's management team had gone on the record and crucified the WNBA, saying that the NBA didn't care about women's basketball and that the women who chose to play in the league would be treated like second class citizens.

But here the ABL players were, in the dark and out of the loop on a decision that would have tremendous impact on their lives. The same organization that had included the league's marquee players in the business planning process was now not returning phone calls to some of those same players? Who was being treated like second class citizens now?

I've talked to dozens of former ABL players since the league folded and every single one of them had nothing but praise for that league. Words like family, community, a sense of ownership and loyalty are among the things that always came up when they reflected on the experience. They even spoke fondly about those early morning flights and back-to-back-to-back games, because I think for them, they felt like they had truly been a part of building a league of their own.

Edna Campbell was an All-Star guard who played for the Colorado Explosion, who says that it was very common for ABL players to call

ABL senior management to simply shoot the breeze or to talk about serious issues affecting the league. That was the kind of atmosphere the founders had nurtured. So, she knew something was awry when Steve Hamms had not returned her many phone calls. She then called the Explosion front office and was told that the league had folded. Edna said that she was so shocked that she sat in her car for almost an hour. "I couldn't believe it," she said. "I was just numb and I couldn't cry until maybe two days later."

What's even stranger is what former ABL players say when you ask them how they felt about the league not telling them that it was in trouble. "If I were dying," Edna said. "I'm not sure I'd tell people either." An interesting way to look at it, I guess. But wouldn't you rather hear it from them and not some stranger walking down the street? "Yeah, I would. I guess I just loved playing in that league so much. It was so united," she said in almost a sad tone.

In many ways the league did hint to the players that the organization was struggling, though not in those terms. In the summer of '98, Gary Cavalli asked all players to consider a 10% pay cut to help with the league's operating expenses. A plea that fell on deaf ears leaguewide. "People were like, nuh uh, you ain't getting none of my money," Edna laughed. "But I think had Gary put it to us by saying, 'Hey, if we reduce your salaries by 10% we can finish the entire third season', I'm sure we would have responded a little differently."

No ABL Players Allowed

It was going to be my first full season as a WNBA broadcaster with Lifetime Television and the biggest story heading into the 1999 season was the availability of the ABL players. There were rumors that ABL players were being blacklisted from the WNBA and their staunch fans wondered if this were true. Not only was it not true, it was ludicrous.

How stupid would it have been for the WNBA to keep some of the best players in the world out of the WNBA? Very. And although I don't know Val Ackerman that well, I do know that she wants the WNBA to be around longer than a New York minute. You don't get a big job like President of the WNBA if your IQ borders on single digits. I mean, can you imagine the WNBA without Yolanda Griffith, Adrienne Goodson, Shannon Johnson, Katie Smith, DeLisha Milton, or Natalie Williams? We saw a good product in 1997 without these players but we see a great product on the floor *with* them in the mix.

The WNBA has one objective: long-term stability. Blacklisting elite players for any reason would not have served them or their objective well. So, no, ABL players were not being kept out of the WNBA. Now, in 1999 with the first Collective Bargaining Agreement, there were rules that limited the number of ABL players a team could sign—but only in 1999. The following season, in 2000, it was fair game and all ABL players were.

And I believe that any player who should be in the league will eventually find her way there if that's her goal. Having watched a number of ABL players in pre-draft camp this past spring, I know that while some of them will eventually land in the league, many will not. Like the WNBA, the ABL had its cream and most of them have risen to the top ranks of the WNBA already. Yolanda Griffith wasted no time making her mark. But Yo's a special player. She was going to show up regardless. Occasionally I'll hear players (former ABL and former WNBA) moaning about being blacklisted for reasons that range from a coach not liking them to their affiliation with the ABL. I don't think this kind of thinking is very productive, so I usually tell them (and their fans) to focus on making the right contacts in the league because the best deterrent against injustice is always excellence. Take it from someone who's been there, got the DVD.

Fans

You wanna talk about folks with issues? Fans. Some fans got plenty of
stuff. Stuff that makes you laugh. Stuff that makes you go 'huh?' Don't
believe me? Okay, let's go back to 1998. The playoffs were approaching
and the dirt on the street and the Internet was that Coop and Swoopes
were fighting like a couple of alley cats over a can of Meow Mix. Brian
Donlon, the President of Lifetime Sports had this brilliant idea to do a
Meet the Press, debate-like halftime show called Jump Ball. In this segment, Mary Murphy and I would toss around issues that were affecting
the league as a whole or specific teams within the league. Over the
course of the week approaching the playoffs, the executive producers
and I had gone back and forth over what the three or four topics should
be in this segment. He told us that we'd have about four minutes tops
and we needed to come up with what we felt the issues of the day
should be. Both Mary and I agreed that Houston defending their title
was paramount. We had to talk about them repeating. Next was expansion, as well as men coaching in the WNBA. We'd mapped out a plan
and figured some folks would get their feathers ruffled but what the
hell, it'll be fun. We were gonna really have a ball.

As we rehearsed the night before, I could tell that we were gonna
deliver a great halftime show. With Maura moderating, things wouldn't
go too long or get too far out of hand, since neither Mary nor I are ever
short on opinions. So, it's game day and we go on the air. The segment
runs without a hitch. Our producers loved it. Tons of fans emailed saying how great it was to see me and Mary make good arguments. But as
is the case about anything, a few fans got their undies in a big wad. And
not just Houston fans either. A lot of non-Cometheads got in on the
action. *Can you believe Fran Harris? How could she go on television and
say those things about Swoopes and Coop? Of all people, I would think that*

she would have shown more loyalty…She's just bitter that the Comets traded her…"

And as the Faberge shampoo commercial goes, and so on and so on and so on…

I was amazed by these comments. Completely dumbfounded. First, let's point out a couple of things. Number one. All was not well in the Comets' paradise heading into the '98 playoffs. Anyone with eyes could see that there was some mad tension between Sheryl and Cynthia. Number two. Sheryl and Cynthia had already both acknowledged this tension publicly in their respective interviews in the newspaper and on television. Number three. I was not a Houston Comets player who happened to be announcing on Lifetime Television. I was a journalist with a job to do. The fact that I'd played at Houston was totally and completely irrelevant to the issue. My mother used to say, if you don't want your business in the streets, then don't put it out there. And I was with Mama on this one. My exact on-air comments were, *if Sheryl and Cynthia don't put their personal issues behind them then some team's gonna sneak up on them and then we're gonna be saying WHO-ston?* That was it. I wasn't saying anything that everyone else looking on didn't already know. But the fact that I had played in Houston seemed to cast a different light on the issue. It's not as if I said something stupid like, "Coop told me that she hated Sheryl and Sheryl told me that she hated Cynthia and both superstars say that they're not going to pass the other one the ball this game." This ain't the National Enquirer, it's entertainment on a well-respected national television network. If I ever say something that's unprofessional, believe you me, the powers that be will let me know.

The bottom line is that fans don't wanna hear the sometimes unflattering truth about their favorite teams and players because they watch sports with rose-colored glasses on. That's fine. It's not real, but that's fine if that's how you wanna flow. But don't expect me to flow in that fantasy world with you. I live in the real world. And in my world, hit shappens.

But it's not just the fans who close their ears to the truth. Families can be worse than fans. When I was in college, my sister, Debra, wrote a book that revealed some pretty unflattering things about a few members of my extended family. They were things that were true based on her experiences. But this book threw the family into an uproar because some people disagreed with her depictions of certain respected members of our family. She'd outed bad behavior and some folks just didn't appreciate it. And they let her know that they didn't like it. They didn't speak to her. They were mean to her when she visited our hometown, Dallas.

I respected her for having the guts to say what we all knew anyway. That favoritism had run rampant in our family for generations. That some kids were treated better than others. All of it was true and we all knew it. But the angry ones just didn't want anyone to give the ugliness a voice. Isn't that the way our society works? We let things like child abuse and domestic violence grow and fester in our homes and communities because we don't want anyone to know that these horrible things are happening. Often we let perpetrators go unpunished and on about the business of hurting folks because we're too afraid to call out the bad behavior. Or we're too afraid of what people will think of us for blowing the whistle.

Same thing with the Houston comment. I had put it out there for millions of viewers to hear and the family didn't like it. And like my sister, they let me know it. And it wasn't just in Houston. I heard from fans from coast to coast who were die-hard Comets fans. But at home, I'd walk into the Compaq Center in Houston and some fans would roll their eyes at me or whisper to the person sitting next to them. Like the person who told a friend of mine that I never seemed to have anything good to say about the Comets. That's such bull!

I'm grateful for the few souls who actually had the nerve to actually say something directly to me. One person told me that they agreed with the sibling rivalry comment I'd made on Lifetime but that they hated that it (the saga) had drawn so much national attention. And you know what? I respect people who can admit that even their favorite players behave badly sometimes. I respect them much more than I'll ever respect those folks who sent me anonymous emails whining about how unjustly the networks had been to Sheryl and Coop. My mother used to say, 'If you don't want your business in the streets, then don't put it out there'.

I'm also thankful for those fans who got bent out of shape by my comments, because that's the real world. You're never gonna please everyone, so why bother? I tell young women who want to be in broadcasting a few things. If you're a people pleaser, this ain't the job for you. If you're the type who'll lose sleep over a few bad reviews, then maybe you should look into being a professional baby-sitter. Above all, though, to be the best in this business, you've gotta have some scruples, values and principles by which you live.

Walk The Talk

And another thing, fans can be very hypocritical. Why do I say this? C'mon, keep it real for a minute. As long as the Houston Comets won, the fans didn't really give a damn whether Sheryl and Cynthia got along. The crowd at Madison Square Garden could care less if Teresa Weatherspoon and Vickie Johnson go out for ice cream sundaes after their Sunday afternoon games. You know why? Because fans care about one thing. At the end of the day, did you drop 30 points? Good. Did we win another championship? Terrific. That's all that matters. The average fan could care less about team harmony and accord. Sure, there are some of you out there who know that chemistry is critical to long term success. And you folks really do want players to get along and like each other. I will give you that.

But do you think the average fan cares that the star player cursed her point guard out for not passing her the ball? Please. Does the average person sitting in the stands with a bag of peanuts and a foaming brew care that another player just walked by the coach and yelled an expletive that couldn't even air on Howard Stern's dirty little show? Nope. When the final buzzer sounds, fans wanna know one thing and one thing only. Did the home team score more points than the visiting team? Period. And anyone who tries to sell you something different is blowing some serious smoke up you know where.

I'm Glad I'm Sitting Over Here

There are days that I wish I was a WNBA coach but draft day is not one of those days.

The biggest dilemma facing every WNBA coach as we headed into the WNBA draft on April 25th was whether to take Georgia grad and 5-time Olympian Teresa Edwards if she announced her plans to play in the league. Many felt that even at 35 years old, that Edwards was still the best guard in the pool and many remarked, "If Teresa decides to play in the WNBA, how can I not take her—she's a legend?"

Since the teams that finish last usually get the earliest picks in the draft, those first round selections often come with a lot of speculation and nervous anticipation. The right pick could catapult a cellar team from the bottom straight to the top of the league. And the wrong pick could cost a coach his job. But is there any way to truly know how a player will perform once training camp begins? Do all top picks live up to their hyped billings?

These are the questions that coaches are paid the big bucks to answer correctly. And there's no formula to calculate whether the player a coach is drooling over will actually turn out to be all that a franchise bargained for. It's a pray now pay later system.

Is There A Draft In Here?

It's 8 a.m. on April 24th, the morning of the 4th WNBA draft. The first bus for the players and the first limousine for the talent (that's me) leave hotel en route to the NBA.com TV studio in Secaucus, New Jersey. When we arrive, makeup and hair commence immediately.

The players are sufficiently nervous although part of most athletes' makeup includes the Cool Factor. The yeah-I'm-in-awe-of-what-I'm-about-to-go-through-but-I-ain't-gonna-show-it facade. They all had it. Except for Maylana Martin, who'd been wearing a smile a mile long when she blurted out at dinner the night before, 'Yeah, I'm excited, I'm not gonna lie.' I decided to take her at her word since she's at least 6'3 and a huge hockey fan. Even if she weren't excited, I wasn't going to push the matter.

Around 9:30, the director of our show finds me primping in my dressing room and informs me that 'I'm needed on the set immediately for rehearsal'. I jaw a few more minutes with the players about the movie Love & Basketball, and everything inconsequential and unrelated to the draft and then I head to the studio. Which by the way, is fabulous. Imagine, a basketball floor to work on! The big, glass globe ball with patches of orange leather that hangs on the wall behind the draft podium, was now swirling about. And the production crew had started to test the Teleprompters and cameras for a run through.

Emotions and expectations were high for this first-ever-televised event. And our producers and directors were sure to remind us what we were and were not to say on the air, no matter how tempted we got. In other words, even though we got the word very late that Teresa Edwards was not going to be in the draft and even though everybody and their dog already knew it, we were not to dilly dally on this particular subject. We must move on. Let the healing begin.

It's now around 10:00 and the players are starting to get a little uncomfortable in all the makeup so they start getting silly, calling each other names and clowning each other's eyes, hair and lip color. Ah, the good old days. I sure miss all of that. But it's 60 until ShowTime and I'm starting to get fairly pumped. I'm walking around in my heels high-fiving all the crew, pretending to be stoned when I say Summer Erb's name. And basically just being the way I am when I'm at home watching a game with my friends.

I stumbled upon Naomi Mulitauaopele and told her that her hair weave was off the hook. And then I told her that since I'm phonetically impaired that beginning June 1 that I'm nicknaming her Rapunsel. It's better than messing up her last name all summer. She was courteous while she repeated the proper pronunciation and handed me a Hooked On Phonics gift certificate. That's Moo-lee-tau-woh-pay-lay, in case you're wondering.

It's 10:30ish and the players are tripping on how giddy sideline reporter Vera Jones and I are. And I'm sure they're tired of us asking them questions like "Where do you wanna play this summer?" When all they care about is hearing their name called—preferably earlier than later. We're talking about climates and jersey numbers and the only sentence they wanna hear within the next hour on this fine morning is, 'For the __ pick of the 2000 draft, the ___ select 'insert their name'.

They wear nervous and forced smiles as they file inside to be seated in their designated area of the court. Dressed to the nines. Tamicha Jackson in a long, taupe jacketed pants suit, Einstein-like spectacles and a black briefcase in tow. The woman is making a statement before anybody even thinks about mistaking her for just another jock. She's got the air of someone who knows she's going in the top ten.

Earlier Tausha Mills, who is just the coolest, had barged into my dressing room with her do rag on, asking the obvious. Yo, Fran, 'sup? You got a comb? To which I said yes. Got a brush? Yes, again. And can I use yo' iron (curling)? Mills is 6'3 both ways, what do you think happened next? I plugged that puppy right into the nearest outlet and offered to style her tresses, that's what.

Ten 'til air and I go around distributing dap to all the talent, Matt Devlin, Ann Meyers Drysdale, Doris Burke, and Sweet V (Vera Jones). From a distance we hear, 'Seven 'til air' and everyone's in place. Parents with their cameras. Media with their steno pads. I don't know why, but I'm as nervous as a cat near a rocking chair. My hands are shaking like a leaf and you'd swear I'd never been on television before. I guess for a second I thought *I* was getting drafted.

To sit in that room as players tried to be unattached to their names being called was something to watch. We all pretty much knew who'd go 1, 2, 3. But the next 13 in the first round were toss-ups in terms of order. We soon discovered that the players we thought might go higher had dropped for one reason or another. Coaches are fickle that way. For one solid week, for instance, Nancy Darsch had talked about Grace Daley, and then she takes Tausha Mills. Which incidentally was exactly what she should have done. The Mystics needed a post player like The Artist formerly known as Prince needs purple.

I had my opinion about all of the draft choices. Let's take a closer look.

Best overall draft by an expansion team. Portland got Lynn Pride, Stacy Thomas, Maxann Reese and Rhonda L. Smith. Lynn Pride, was one of the most versatile players drafted, who when surrounded by equal or superior talent will thrive in this league at the three spot. Stacy Thomas is a sleeper. If Linda Hargrove's staff can nurture her talent and athletic ability, Stacy will be an All-Star off guard by her third pro season. She's gotta work on her outside jumper but the other elements are already in place.

Worst overall draft by an expansion team. Miami Sol. They got Jameka Jones and Milena Flores, two guards. They gave up their picks for trades in the off season and now with Elena Baranova's torn ACL, they're hurting in sunny south Florida. Add to that point guard Debbie Black's back injury and a very good team just went south.

Best overall draft by an existing team. Minnesota will be fast but they're not very big. Brian Agler drafted for the future, which I hope includes moving the Lynx to the eastern conference or they may never make it to the playoffs with Houston, Los Angeles, Sacramento, Phoenix and Utah to deal with. Grace Daley, Betty Lennox, Maylana Martin, Marla Brumfield and Keitha Dickerson will all be terrific pros one day. Lennox already proved she belonged.

Worse overall draft by an existing team. New York Liberty needed a solid back up point guard for Teresa Weatherspoon. They took Olga Firsova who didn't get to help because of injuries. Not a great draft for the Liberty but an early trade to get Tari Phillips kept their title hopes alive.

Biggest surprise pick of the draft. Ann Wauters over Tausha Mills as first pick. I felt like Cleveland was either gonna be really good this year or really bad. Dan Hughes stocked up for the future by choosing Wauters and it almost got him into the 2000 eastern conference finals.

Biggest surprise diss of the draft. Anita Kaplan out of Stanford was a solid 6'5 post player that could have helped a team like Seattle. She had a good camp, plus, she's American, which means a lot in a league that's had several foreign players decide for whatever reason that they weren't spending the summer stateside.

Best trade by a coach. Detroit Shock sent Azzi to Utah Starzz for two early first round picks. Nancy Lieberman-Cline got Edwina Brown (Texas) and Tamicha Jackson (Louisiana Tech), two guards who could easily be All Stars by their third season in the league.

Cinnamon Rolls & Loaf Management

The absolute worst thing about retiring is that you've gotta find time to workout. If you don't, you get out of shape. And then when you go to try to get into a pick up game, you suck. See, when you're playing on a team, your workout time is already scheduled for you. If you're involved in a structured activity that gets your heart rate up, keep it up, I'm proud of you. I wish I were still on a team for that very reason. Oh, sure, I have a membership to the gym and I go five times a week. But I don't get the same kind of workout I'd get if I were playing basketball for two hours straight.

That's how I first developed cinnamon rolls. You know, love handles. I never had handles when I played ball. You have to work real hard to get pudgy during the WNBA season. After I retired I vowed that I'd keep working out and keep my lean machine in shape. And it worked...for about two months and then something happened. December happened. And we don't even have real harsh winters where I live. It just gets cold enough for me to have an excuse not to go running.

All of a sudden I start to feel the beginnings of a cinnamon roll and that's when I miss the WNBA the most. Clarissa also called that area around your mid-section, a loaf. We'd see each other in the gym in the off-season and say, how are your cinnamon rolls? Or, 'girl, you look good. I see you're keeping your cinnamon roll on the down low'. Or, 'I can't wait for the season to start because my loaf is getting out of control'.

Most athletes I know are very vain when it comes to their bodies. And sometimes, so are broadcasters whose playing days on the professional level are over. So, these days I'm really taking stock of my loaf because television is not kind to weight gain. And the last thing I need is a producer coming up to me saying that they love my halftime interviews but they're thinking about putting me on a loaf management program.

Legends & Stars

One of the greatest things about my job is that I get to work with and rub elbows with some great people. When Ann Meyers Drysdale, who announces for the Los Angeles Sparks' local television package on KCAL, had a couple of conflicts with other WNBA games on NBC, she recommended me as her replacement. I got to work with the legendary Chick Hearn, who has been the voice of the Lakers broadcasts for more than 60 years.

Also in '97 I got to meet Penny Marshall and have since had the opportunity to send her a few of my screenplays. I'm optimistic that one day she'll read one of them and want to make a movie out it. I'm not sure if I would have been this close to so many different kinds of people—politicians, actors, directors, rappers, and other flavors of millionaires had I not played in the WNBA. I think the women are just now starting to get a taste of what the guys get to experience and how the exposure can often propel them into successful careers away from the basketball court.

Are you disappointed?

Some journalists are a rare species. So rare that sometimes I'm just looking for any signs of intelligent life when they open their mouths. And I gotta admit that there are days I have trouble finding it in myself. But where certain reporters are concerned, it's often very hard to know if they're trying to be funny or if they're just a little on the stupid side. Being a reporter, I try to understand them, I really do. But when they ask really stupid questions, I don't have a lot of patience.

When my college team lost to Western Kentucky in the Mideast Regional in 1985, the year we were hosting the Final Four in Austin, I had a reporter ask me, "Are ya disappointed you won't be playing in the Erwin Center for a national championship this year?" No, Gomer Pyle, I'm *happy* that we won't get to play in our own backyard this year! I mean, what kind of question is that? Of course, I was disappointed.

Since I'm a broadcaster I know that there's no school for us to attend to learn how to ask intelligent questions. I have an advantage because I've been an athlete for most of my life. I've had the benefit of being asked some all-time dufus questions. And I vowed a long time ago to never ask ridiculous questions. I wanted to ask the tough questions, but not the stupid ones. And asking good questions can really help you in this business. Players and coaches will willfully talk to you. But if you get into the habit of asking bad questions, players will avoid you like a pair of smelly socks.

Another thing that used to bug me as a player were unethical journalists. Folks who'd print things that they'd gotten off the record. People who disclose the names of sources who want to remain anonymous. There are few things worse than talking off the record to a reporter only to see what you've shared in confidence, smack dab in the middle of the Sunday Sports section. And then they wonder why some players won't give them interviews.

In this business, you're nothing if no one wants to talk to you. You got no story. No feature. No scoop. Nothing. So, sometimes I don't blame players for refusing interviews with some reporters. The same guy who's misquoted her three times in one season wants ten minutes. Forget it. The same woman who wrote a lot of negative and untrue things about her wants fifteen seconds right after shoot-around. Are ya crazy? That's the way it goes and with good reason. For while most people I know in this business are very ethical, there are lots of reporters who are not. These are the characters players avoid and ignore on a regular basis.

Who's That Girl?

Madonna's popular song "Who's That Girl?" could be the national anthem for some WNBA players who transform themselves into other people when a television camera comes around. I understand that it can be a little nerve racking to have that big camera and bright light beaming down on your face. But some players go overboard.

After the All-Star game in Phoenix, I tuned into NBA.com TV in the hotel and caught an interview with one of the West players. An interview that started out great but quickly went south because this player kept repeating herself. And each time she'd speak, she'd insert a bigger word into her sentence. A word that didn't make sense. A word that was longer than my legs. A word that was totally out of context. It got so bad that I forgot what the question had been. That's how far off she went. Three minutes later, she's still going and the words are getting funnier and funnier. So funny that I thought maybe this player was *trying* to be funny. But she wasn't. She was just caught up, I guess. Fortunately, a reporter interrupted her and the torture and the 20-letter word marathon ended.

It's My Body & I'll Exploit It If I Want To

When tennis media darling Anna Kournikova made the cover of Sports Illustrated this year, I knew that we'd taken three steps backwards to the Stone Ages. Here we go again. Another woman letting the establishment use her body to sell magazines. Well, I ain't Anna's mama or nothing but I do have three words for her: win something, girlfriend. And SI, you just can't help yourselves, can ya? Does the phrase 'dirty old men' mean anything to you? Apparently not.

Although the furor has subsided surrounding Kournikova's, well, spread, in SI, the question still circling in the minds of women who want women's sports to be celebrated without the sex, is, when will the exploitation stop? Kournikova's thing beats the annual swimsuit issue, though. The pre-teen pictures of her are despicable. Baby Anna better be thanking her lucky stars that I'm not her mama.

I almost climbed through the television during the Wimbledon coverage when Chris Evert-Lloyd said something that I know had to have come from The Flintstones Guide to Tennis Commentary. On Kournikova's SI fame, she said, "She's not the most popular girl in the locker room these days but I think it's because the other players are jealous." Oh, yeah, Chris, I'm sure Serena Williams is real jealous of Anna. I'm sure Lindsey Davenport is too. I mean, after all, all they do is play phenomenal tennis and win a lot of money. All they do is show millions of little girls that hard work, dedication and commitment pays off. What earthly reason could Anna's peers have for being jealous of her? It can't be the money. It can't be the media hype. It must be the raunchy pictures in SI. Yep, that's exactly why women are so mad at Anna Kournikova these days.

No, wait. Maybe it's because they want to be featured on a life-size billboard that says, "Your balls are the only things that should bounce" or whatever the bra ad says. It can't possibly be that we're sick of seeing women prostitute themselves in the name of ad sales and moving a few magazines. Why, the pictures of a pubescent Kournikova in Sports Illustrated have some folks calling her Pornikova. No, we're just mad because we're not blonde and Russian with a driver named Serg, right? Please.

Gimme a bloody break. Couldn't Evert-Lloyd have used her six seconds of airtime to say something other than that women never focus on the bigger picture? Couldn't she have denounced the notion that there's always a feline brawl in women's locker rooms when one of us excels? Couldn't Chrissy Evert-Lloyd have gotten her tush off the fence and told the media that focusing on a woman's beauty and body instead of her talent and skills as an athlete, is unacceptable and deplorable? Obviously not. I mean what's next? Hooters as the official sponsor of the Olympic swim team?

We Gotcha Covered (Yeah, right)

When will we see more televised games? It's a question I'm asked each week during the WNBA season. And it's also one that I often ask myself. Soon. I'd like to think that we're heading in the right direction. The entire playoffs were televised in 2000, as well as a number of preseason match-ups. But remember, ratings help to drive supply in the television business. Ratings are to television execs what blood is to vampires—a lifeline. So, I tell folks, if you want more games, you have to *watch* them when they are televised. Even if you don't like the announcing team that night, watch anyway. Just turn the volume down. I do it all the time. Besides, it's a lot easier to make a case and evangelize for more television coverage of the WNBA when the ratings are healthy.

You may have heard that the WNBA ratings were down this season. Let me tell you that ratings are always lower in the summer because this is prime vacation time. It's beautiful outside and not many people are glued to television when they could be on the beach. Ratings for sports in general slipped this year—across the board—but overall, the WNBA's television audience continues to grow.

When I say we need more coverage, I'm not just talking about *more* games on national television, I'm talking about quality here. Maybe a pre-game show and decent post-game interviews or press conferences. The league wants our game to grow at home and abroad but sometimes I feel like our games are treated like the redheaded, buck toothed stepchild. We get on the air quickly and we get off the air even quicker because the networks wanna get to their precious programming.

I mean, if you've seen one Lindsey Wagner "Don't leave me, not now," movie, you've seen a million, right? And who cares about the National Bowler's Association Championships anyway (don't email me, bowlers, I ain't mad actcha)? And does that red clay in the French Open hurt anybody else's eyes? My point is this. Sports are emotional. Part of the ride is hearing what teams say before and after the contest. Our fans miss the chance to connect with the game in this way because we get on and off the air so fast.

What we really need is a women's sports channel so that we can stop surfing in search of those 5-second WNBA highlights on CNNSI or Sportscenter. I'm talking 24-7-365 women's sports. Similar to what NBA.com TV did during the playoffs this season. Another option is a women's sports show that provides features, in-depth reporting and highlights. ESPN does an around-the-WNBA highlight show during the summer that's nice. It's a good start. But I always say, nobody knows what you want unless you ask for it. And there's a lot that we can do to improve women's sports coverage on a local and national level. Here are some suggestions.

- Call your television, radio or newspaper sports directors/editors to have a little chat with her/him about what you'd like to see as it relates to not only the WNBA but women's sports in general.
- Commit to sending a weekly email/letter to your station's sports department reminding them that they're coverage is pathetic.
- Applaud your local media (with a letter/email) when they do well. This will go far in getting what you want the next time!
- Offer to HELP them cover your sports better. Feed them story or feature ideas on a regular basis.
- Be unrelenting in all of your efforts to elevate women's sports in your community. It's a 24-7-365 commitment made easier by email and the Internet.

Lord Have Mercy, If I Hear One More Player Thank Jesus For Helping Them Make That 30-foot Desperation Shot

I grew up going to church nearly every day of the week, and twice on Sunday. So, hear me when I say that I don't have anything against religion. Why, religion has stopped me from cussing a few folks out in the last three months alone. So, I got no beef per se with religion, spirituality or anything else people get into to help them become better human beings. But I do have a problem when players thank Jesus a hundred times in a 30-second interview. Hey, we only have so long on the air, remember?

And I can't stand it when they say things like God was on their side and that's why they beat a team by 52 points. Jesus ain't got nothing to do with you slaughtering a team by 50 points. In fact, beating a team like that is not very neighborly at all. So, I have a problem with thanking Jesus for stuff like that.

And maybe you can help me with this one. Why is it that players only get on national television to thank God only for the *good* things happening to them? Huh? You never hear anybody saying, "I'm so thankful to God that I shot 1 of 15 tonight. Praise the Lord for those 13 turnovers I committed!" Ever heard someone say anything like that? Nope. And you won't.

I Swear If I Didn't Have to Pay My Mortgage, I'd Give You A Piece of My Mind

Have you ever just wanted to tell someone exactly what you thought of them and their behavior but you didn't because you might not be able to pay your bills that month if you did? I have. And I continue to be amazed at how crazy our world is getting and how unaware people seem to be when it comes to simple, old-fashioned manners. I'm also amazed that some of the rudest people I've come across in a while work in the front offices of WNBA franchises. People who hold very important positions but have the personality of a paper clip. I guess I can't fault people for being boring but can't I at least rag on them for being jerks? And poor examples of professionalism? One executive is known for walking past every single person on the Lifetime Television crew enroute to say hello to Reggie Miller. I love Reggie too but if I were the owner or general manager of a team, I'd at least know enough about public relations to acknowledge the other members of his broadcast team instead of acting like they're invisible. Geez, am I missing something here?

The ABC's of Broadcasting

Just about every WNBA athlete out there thinks that when she's done playing ball that she'll become a broadcaster. And I think that's great. More power to the sisters. We need more of us in the business. But before they take over the airwaves, a few folks—and I ain't calling no names today—gotta learn their ABC's. I'm talking the basics of being on the air. And let's face it, no one knows the rules until they join the broadcasting ranks but some folks, I can already tell, are gonna have a hell of a time making the transition if they don't get a better grip on the fundies (fundamentals) of being on TV.

First, the A. A is for accuracy. You don't go on the air and say something that you don't know to be actual factual unless it's your opinion, that's different. It's difficult to keep a job in this industry if you come from the he-said, she-said school of broadcasting. You never hear Diane Sawyer say, "Well, I heard that Fidel Castro was planning to leave his post as Cuba's big dawg." It just won't happen. You never hear Oprah

Winfrey saying, "I think Julia Roberts was married to Lyle Lovett for a year and a half. I think."

On this note, one of my personal peeves is hearing announcers speculate on an injury that occurs during a game. We're broadcasters, not doctors, so until we get an official report from someone who actually knows what's taken place, I think we should shut up or talk about the effect the injury could potentially have on the team. I don't think we should say, 'Well, it looks like an ankle but it could've been her knee'. I think it's better to say, 'We'll have an official word on the injury before the game's over'. But you won't believe how much pressure some announcers feel when they put that headset on. They think they should have an answer to every question.

Next is the B, and this is a biggie. B is for brevity. Be brief. Television and radio are both about getting in and getting out. You get on the air, do your thang and get off. No easy task for a person who loves the sound of her own voice. And believe me, there are some long-winded women in the WNBA. You've seen those little snippets during the telecast where the game will be going on and all of a sudden the network you're watching inserts comments from a player or a coach, right? Well, that's called a soundbite. Because you *hear* it, it's called sound. And because it's supposed to be brief, it's called a bite. But some players haven't caught on to this concept yet. Some of them don't know when to shut up. You ask them a question that should take them about ten seconds to answer and instead they go on until New Year's Eve. It's very funny. Sometimes. And other times, it's a little annoying because producers want soundbites, not sound *encyclopedias*. We have only so much time. A basketball game is only two hours long!

One time we were getting bites from a veteran player and one of her answers took two minutes and six seconds. I'm not joking. I thought she was giving a keynote address to a second grade class. It was incredible. She used one period in her entire sentence and it was at the end. Then there was this other player who we asked about four questions and she said 'you know' 64 times in less than three minutes. I know, because I counted. Is that amazing? These are no-no's in this business.

The last one is C. C only comes into play if you violate B. If you go off on a tangent, you're not being brief. So, we have to cut you off. C is for cutting you off. Even if you're accurate. If you're not brief, we *will* cut you off. Ever see someone's lips moving after you no longer hear the soundbite? Those are violators of the B rule. Lots of those in the league.

You Down With MOP?

I'm starting a campaign to rename the WNBA's top individual award from Most Valuable Player to the Most Outstanding Player. I know, I know, who wants to be called a MOP? But let's think about this one for a second. The word 'value' sounds like a team would be in deep doo doo if they didn't have you, right? Which could actually be the case for lots of players on lots of different teams. In other words, a player can be valuable, almost indispensable and not be outstanding, which is the premise of the MVP award anyway.

Take New York for instance. If the Liberty's individual players could be traded on the NYSE, then Teresa Weatherspoon—in terms of *value* to her team—would be traded like the latest, greatest Internet stock. She's *that* hot. Let's keep it gold—as Spoon goes (emotionally) so does the Liberty 99.9% of the time, right? Her value will never be measured in points, rebounds or steals even though she won the Defensive Player of the Year in '97 & '98. She's valuable because her emotion makes the players around her take their games to another plateau. At best, the New York Liberty is a good team that's playing great and Spoon deserves part of the credit for their turnaround. Will she ever win an MVP award? Nope. Why? We'll get to that in a second.

Next, let's take Cynthia Cooper. We saw in Game 2 of the Los Angeles—Houston face off at the Great Western Forum, just how valuable her break-you-down-off-the-dribble services were. She'd sustained an ankle injury against Sacramento the week before and she just couldn't play. Houston has two other great players in Sheryl Swoopes and Tina Thompson, but break you down off the dribble players, they are not. Create a way out of no way ballers, they are not. When the Comets needed someone to put the ball on the floor and exploit the Sparks perimeter defense with penetration, Houston had no answer. That one aspect of her game makes Cooper undeniably valuable to Houston. But will she win the MVP award in her supposed farewell season? Nope.

The two players considered the forerunners for my Millenium MOP award were Sheryl Swoopes and Lisa Leslie. Both valuable and outstanding this year. And here's why it came down to these two players for the coveted award. Both players are gunners, they score lots of points. You'll never see an MVP or an MOP who doesn't score, it just won't happen. And while scoring's not everything, the point of the game is to put the ball in the hole more times than your opponent.

Second, they played on good teams, this year's best. You wouldn't have seen an MVP or MOP from the Seattle Storm in 2000 because they didn't have a sterling season. The players on really bad teams are rarely recognized. Next, both of these players are multidimensional. They can do a lot of damage all over the court. Sheryl was the league's top perimeter defender and led the league in steals at various times during the season. Lisa was the league's most formidable inside defender, swatting about 3 shots a game.

There were never really any other contenders for this year's MVP or MOP. And now that you've seen why these two players were the favorites, maybe you can pick the 2001 MOP.

Chit'lins & Hog Maws

It was our first Orlando game of the 2000 season and we were learning all kinds of interesting things about the players. Nykesha Sales liked to cook quiche. Taj McWilliams apparently thought that she might make a cameo appearance in the movie *X-men*. Why else would she get those gray-looking contact lenses? And even though I hadn't been there to hear the interview, I knew exactly what Shannon Johnson had cited as one of her favorite meals.

We were in the middle of a production meeting when Michele Tafoya said that she'd gotten some great stuff in the Shannon Johnson interview. Apparently, Pee Wee is a good cook and she'd shared some of her culinary secrets with Michele, who pulled out her pad and said, "Oh, here it is! She said she liked to cook…," she rummaged through her notes. "Chit'lings and *Hog Maw*?" I fell out laughing. Just the sound of my girl, MT, saying it cracked me up. So I asked her to repeat it like five more times. Finally she caught on. Most people know what chit'lins (chitterlings for you city folk) and hog maws are—pig intestines. They are the foulest smelling things I've ever come in contact with. They're so funky that they've inspired me to coin another catch phrase for my on air analysis. Instead of saying that a player is stinking up the gym, I could say, "She smells like a pot of chit'lins and hog maws."

Mo Money

In mid-September 1997, a week after my Houston Comets teammates and I had won the inaugural WNBA championship, I hopped on a plane and headed back to Baden, Switzerland, where I'd played the spring before to prepare for the WNBA season. During that first summer, the WNBA exceeded everyone's expectations, particularly regarding attendance—we averaged nearly 10,000 fans. And although I wasn't surprised at how well our game had been received stateside, what I saw upon my arrival in Baden, told me just how global our game had gone in three short months.

Our team was stretching, about to begin our first practice, when one of my Swiss teammates told me that she had a surprise for me—that it had been hard but that she had found the jersey of her favorite WNBA player and she was going to be wearing it in practice that night. Given the fact that she had told me all spring that I was her favorite player, had cried when I left and told me to hurry back to the team in September, I was prepared for her to pull out a #20 jersey, the number I'd worn with the Houston Comets. She ran over to her bag and grabbed a red jersey. "Look," she exclaimed, "You think you can get Sheryl Swoopes to sign it for me?"

After I comforted my bruised ego and snapped back into reality, I realized once again how powerful television really is. Because of television, the WNBA had reached far beyond American borders and was now building an incredible fan base in other countries.

Say My Name, Say My Name

Do me a favor. If you don't want me getting on the air and botching up your daughter's name, please name her something like Jane Smith or Lisa Brown. Anything else and we broadcasters are bound to screw it up. I'm conscientious but I mess up on occasion too. Like during the 2000 draft when I called Usha Gilmore, oo-sha instead of YOU-sha. The draftees laughed and shook their disapproving young heads. Thankfully I got to redeem myself later when the Indiana Fever drafted her. At least I didn't spend an entire day mispronouncing it. I hate that. But can you blame us? Names have gotten to be so complicated.

Gone are the days of Ann White and Kim Jones. Kids today have names like Briannica and Rhodeshia, which actually sounds like it should be a suburb of Rhode Island or something. Don't get me wrong, there's no excuse for mispronouncing a name on the air. All announcers have to do is ask the player or the team's media relations director for the proper pronunciation. They even give us pronunciation guides with the names broken down phonetically and attached to game notes to help us out. Which brings up a good question. Did Cleveland Rocker Mery Andrade change her name or has it always been pronounced AHN-drahd and nobody knew? Not even her sports information director at Old Dominion University, where she played her college ball. We've been calling her An-drah-dee all this time. Finally in the 2000 playoffs we get a memo saying that it's AHN-drahd? Huh?

Parents hate it when broadcasters mispronounce their kids' names and I don't blame them. So, on behalf of all announcers who've butchered an athlete's name, we're sorry. But you know, you can help us out. If you're thinking about having a kid that you think will eventually play sports, do us a favor. Don't name her Zephrynetta Monifa Aquarenesha Magillicuddy. You're just asking for trouble.

Oh-ho Say Can You...Get The Words Right?

It's gonna happen. I know it is. One day, someone's gonna sing the correct words to the Star Spangled Banner. One of these days, we're gonna all sing the same words during the nation's greatest sing-along. And what a glorious day that will be.

This song has been around about as long as the Bible. And almost as long as women's sports have been ignored in sports pages across the country. Okay, maybe not that long but you get my point.

Do we need an MTV video to this song to get it right? It's not even that long! And the author, Francis Scott Key, is probably shaking his head faster than a windmill in a rainstorm at how much we've messed up his lyrical masterpiece. And the rockets red *blare*? Whatup with that?

I'm an old spelling bee geek, and blare does not go with red in any language. Oh, and they really lose it on the stars and stripes part. Work with me, ya'll. Someone sang "whose *bright* stripes and *white* stars." Another well-known singer thought it was "whose broad stripes and *white* stars." And what about the ramparts? Were they so gallantly gleaming or streaming?

I used to know the words to this song like the grooves on a basketball, but now even I'm confused! So, I just don't sing. I hum.

Bobby Caldwell is one of my favorites, but during the inaugural WNBA season, I noticed that the Bobster apparently hadn't gotten the memo either. He botched it up beyond bandaging. And I was so carried away by gospel diva Yolanda Adams' soulful rendition three WNBA seasons ago, that I went to church the following Sunday thinking maybe she'd actually gotten the words right. She hadn't, so I prayed for her too...for good measure.

I think what we need is the mother of all karoke machines, complete with that little bouncing ball that pounces on the words. Maybe then some of the singers wouldn't feel compelled to make up their own words.

Okay, maybe I'm a little cynical. But it's not as though these people have never heard this song. It's probably the most sung song on the planet. And it's certainly a bigger group song than "We Are The World." Perhaps the singers get nervous with all of the hype and excitement in the arena. Or maybe it's similar to when ball players miss wide-open lay-ups or free throws. We know the drill, we've shot it a million times. Yet on that one night, that fine day when Aunt Fordie Mae is sitting in the stands watching her first basketball game, that night that everybody and their dog has decided to come see you play — that's the night you couldn't buy a bucket if it were marked down 75 percent and put on the Blue Light Special rack.

You're probably thinking that you've got better things to do than to learn the words to the Star Spangled Banner, but think about it. If you'd written a song and it was one that people all over the country had to sing at every important event, wouldn't you want them to at least sing the words it took you three years to come up with? Of course you would.

For those of you who, like me, sometimes find themselves humming along, here are the correct words to "The Star Spangled Banner:"

Oh, say can you see, by the dawn's early light, What so proudly we hailed at the twilight's last gleaming? Whose broad stripes and bright stars, through the perilous fight, O'er the ramparts we watched, were so gallantly streaming? And the rockets' red glare, the bombs bursting in air, gave proof through the night that our flag was still there. Oh say, does that Star-Spangled Banner yet wave O'er the land of the free and the home of the brave?

An Interview With A Vampire

The following interview was titled, "Ask Fran" and ran on June 14, 2000 at **thehoopslink.com**, a website committed to women's basketball. The writer who interviewed me (Sharon Bibb) wasn't the vampire but I sometimes felt like the questions coming from the fans were so fierce that they sucked the blood right out of me. So, I'm happy to share this interview with you because I think it gives you some insight into what people like to talk about sometimes. Of course, it's been reprinted with the permission of the owner, Kat Fox.

theHOOPSlink.com: There has been talk on online bulletin boards about remarks you've made in the past, and we'd like you to address some of them here for everyone.

Let's start with complaints by some readers that you can't be impartial about the Houston Comets, that you rarely have anything good to say about that team and perhaps it's because you're bitter about Houston trading you to Utah in 1998. Can you respond to that?

Harris:
Well, let's just start the hoopla surgery with no anesthesia!

This may be hard to believe, but I also get lots of, "What is this love jones Fran has with the Houston Comets, sometimes she acts like they are the only team in the league?" So, there's no winning here. My affiliation with the Houston Comets as a player seems to be all people remember. The pro-Houston folks feel that I should have this blind allegiance to the Comets (even though I only played there one year) and the anti-Houston fans think I should rag them and never say anything good about them even though they're obviously great. I think if you truly listen to me on the air, you'll find that I'm very fair with every team and I don't give teams special treatment because I played for them.

Fans are great and I love ya'll to death. I mean, one fan got bent out of shape about something written in one of my columns that could only be interpreted as Comets-ragging if you're Ebenezer Scrooge and are looking to bash me (which apparently has become quite a popular pastime of the galactically bored). At least read all of my archived WNBA-related columns before you cast stones—especially the one where I hailed the Comets as the bloody Second (Fourth) Coming! It's titled, CAN THE COMETS BE STOPPED? And it's located at www.sportsfor-women.com/Just_hoops.html

And while I'm ranting, let me address another comment on the Board. There's nothing filthy or deviant about the Comets trading me, it's business, baby. I averaged nearly 20 minutes of time and even started a game or two at Houston so obviously I wasn't garbage. You don't play 20 minutes in Houston if your game sucks, you stand on the sidelines and wave a white towel. So, do your research before you go running your mouth. Or better yet, my advice to folks is to not comment on things that you have no knowledge of.

And finally, if why I was traded is so important to the 'board' people, ask Van Chancellor about it the next time you see him or have a chance to chat online with him. Put plainly, my services were no longer needed when Sheryl returned, so Van and I had a heart to heart and made something happen. I don't need to be bitter, I carved out a small slice of history in Houston and I got the ring to prove it! By the way, Tina Thompson may not have added the off-the-dribble dimension to her game 'because' I pointed it out on Lifetime Television as one of her development areas, but she sure as hell didn't do it BEFORE I said anything either! And incidentally, Tina Thompson is writing the foreword for my book SUMMER MADNESS as well as the jacket endorsement for my WNBA novel, HOUSTON BY MORNING, due out next spring. She must be soooo mad about my comments that she's taken an interest in my literary career.

Yes, I played in Houston and it will always be special to me. And there are a few Comets players who I'd have in the delivery room with me when I have my first child, but as an analyst I can't get on the air and talk about what a great time we had lounging by their pools or on our last vacation together! That's professional suicide. The bottom line is that I have friends on every single team in this league but when the headset goes on, I'm an analyst and they're a player—no more, no less. And the players understand that. They give me a hard time about clowning them but they respect my work because I don't chum with them and then dog them. When I interview them I tell them, 'Now you know if you play bad, I've gotta talk about you, right?' And they say, 'And you know if you clown me on national television, I'm gonna let you hear about it, right?'

It's the fans who seem to be gnashing teeth these days. Sometimes fans are so attached to their teams that they can't digest anything said about them that won't go in a Good Housekeeping article or worse, they can't stand for an announcer to say something positive about a team OTHER than their fave team. I'd be lying if I said this kind of stuff hasn't bothered me on occasion. I mean, I'm human, I wanna be understood and not misrepresented just like the next sister. But as a broadcaster, my comments and performance are on stage for millions to see and I know that this kind of criticism is inevitable and all a part of the game, so I don't lose much sleep over it.

You know what? Fences across America are overcrowded. I have opinions that I'm willing to express and sometimes that's hard for people to accept. They want a fence sitter (especially if you're a woman) and that's simply not me. I don't respect people who sit on the fence. Have a spine, speak your mind. This is one of my values and my friends always know exactly where they stand with me. I've got plenty of friends, I don't go on the air to make friends. And I don't go on the air to be controversial but I have a job to do and that's to analyze (not criticize) what goes on between those 94 feet of hardwood. It's not always going to be popular or fashionable but at least people know where you stand.

The Internet boards are often a place for people with vents to convene…hardly anything on those things are positive, so I don't frequent them. I think it was Diane Keaton who said, who wants to read something negative about themselves? I've never been a big reader of my own press, that's my publicist's job. My goal is to be the most prepared person on the air. When I sit down at that table, I ask myself, "Does anyone in this business know more about the players, coaches, or game than you?" If the answer's yes, then I say get your butt in gear and start studying!

theHOOPSlink.com: That said, do you think Houston can or will win a fourth championship?

Harris:
Absolutely! Are ya nuts? Yes, there's parity in the league but the longer we go without someone coming close to beating them (when it counts), the more the mystique grows and the tougher it'll be to beat them. I wrote a recent column that said that although Houston may be simply more superior talent-wise to other teams, what makes them particularly

lethal is their mental fortitude…they don't fold in the clutch and that's a quality that other teams don't seem to possess yet. **And Sheryl Swoopes is *%&$ing amazing!**

theHOOPSlink.com: You've also been taken to task for being too critical of players, as if you don't remember what it was like to be a player yourself. Further, some have wondered, if you're such an expert analyst, why aren't you on a coaching staff in the WNBA?

Harris:
Well, people CHOOSE their professions and I'm no different. But I've certainly had at least two opportunities to coach in the league but that's not where I'm going right now. That will always be an option for me. In terms of being critical of the players, I think that's not altogether fair to say. Fans watch the games with rose colored glasses, therefore, anything said that's not filled with sunshine is perceived as critical. I've played a lot of basketball. Some nights I was awesome, some nights I sucked the big one. Is an analyst suppose to say of me, "Oh, Fran's such a wonderful person and normally a wonderful player…too bad her shot's off tonight?" Huh? Is that what an announcer should say? Of course, not! They'd get a pink slip first thing Monday morning. Instead they'd probably say something like, "Fran told me she was building a new house this summer, but she didn't tell me she was starting tonight!" Do you get how bad I'm shooting from that statement? Of course you do. Is it critical? Only if you think the truth is critical.

You also have to understand that I'm the only announcer in the league who's been on both sides—I've played and coached. So I'm sure you hear the coach in me when I talk, but that gives me a unique perspective. You'll also probably never find a more compassionate announcer when someone's struggling. For example, in Friday's game between New York and Sacramento. I felt soooo bad for Spoon because I know how much she wants to win and perform well. So, I couldn't trash her, I just couldn't. It wasn't necessary and even if it were, the player in me wouldn't have allowed the announcer in me to pour salt into the wounds.

theHOOPSlink.com: One of your fans thinks you're one of the top analysts in the game, but finds that Lifetime's coverage (at least in the 1999 season) has been too chatty sometimes. Can you shed some light on Lifetime's broadcasting style?

Harris:
Thank you for the compliment regarding my work.

I actually agree that sometimes last year it got a bit chatty. I think that's probably because we had a 3-person booth and conversation unrelated to the game is a bit more probable with that kind of set up. But also, from a corporate standpoint, we try to tell more stories than NBC or ESPN because that's what our producers feel makes the game more compelling and interesting. We want our viewers to get to know the players.

theHOOPSlink.com: One reader wants to know what you think about Cheryl Miller saying she'll coach one day in the NBA. We'd like to know, more generally, whom you see as top candidates to break that barrier first. Cynthia Cooper, for example, has said coaching an NBA team is one of her goals.

Harris:
I loved reading Cheryl's comments in USA Today and she'll probably be the one to break the barrier because she has major connections in the league and because she's had relatively good success in Phoenix. She knows the players (NBA) and coaches. Top candidates? Hmmm...Pat Summit, C. Vivian Stringer, Tara VanDerveer. That's news to me with Coop, I thought she wanted to OWN a team. But with

Coop or anyone, experience is the key and if she gets that coaching experience either in college or as a pro assistant, then I think coaching an NBA team is quite realistic.

theHOOPSlink.com: Now for a few questions of our own. First, we've already seen contentious play this season—just Saturday, between Bridget Pettis of Phoenix and Lisa Leslie of Los Angeles. What should the league do, or what can it reasonably be expected to do, to hold these players in check and maintain some decorum in the women's game?

Harris:
Can you say fine? The league can. And it will not hesitate to impose strict penalties when unsportswomanlike behavior is displayed. And I think the WNBA has to make a statement because I certainly don't want the league's image to be tarnished or the play diminished over a few knuckleheads. But I also think officials have to talk to the players during the games. Go to them and let them know that you're (refs) watching. Warn them and speak to them like their professionals. Sometimes I see the officials in the women's game ignoring the players and I don't like that. It's totally okay for a player to question an official's call, there's nothing wrong with that. And there's also nothing wrong with an official walking over to a player and telling her that he'd hate to have to toss her, so clean up her act. That's professionalism.

theHOOPSlink.com: Game officiating doesn't seem to have changed for the better over last season, yet there are officials at the games observing the refs. Why haven't we seen any improvement and what hope can we have that the situation will improve if players and coaches have a gag order against publicly criticizing the referees?

Harris:
Well, no one wants to be fined and the league is firm on lashing out at officials. My main concern with the officiating is that it's inconsistent, horribly so. The officials are under tight scrutiny, believe it or not, and they're committed to getting better. But I think part of the problem is that many of them officiate college and don't make the transition to the pros come June. So, you've got them calling games as if it's the NCAAs. They've gotta make a mental mind shift and many of them overblow their whistles. Or worse, they're so determined to NOT call it like college ball that they let a player maim another before they blow. We need to pay them more so that they can live off of their WNBA game salaries. Or they need to review their work and just get better on their own.

theHOOPSlink.com: Back to Houston for a moment. WNBA President Val Ackerman has said it's ridiculous to suggest she's concerned that a fourth Comets title would adversely affect the league—that fan support for other franchises will suffer if Houston continues its dominance. What's your take?

Harris:
Actually I think Houston's dynasty is good for the league. As with the Bulls, the Comets give the league instant credibility and recognizability. Even non-WNBA supporters know that Houston has won at least two championships. Why? Because we remember what's repeated. If we'd had three different champions for the first three years, there'd be mass confusion out there! People file into arenas on both coasts when the Comets come to town and that's factual. They may miss Phoenix versus Indiana but they're not gonna miss the Mercury game when Earth, Wind and Fire roll into America West Arena.

theHOOPSlink.com: Hours before the deadline to re-sign their WNBA contracts, more than 50 players still were holding out over money. The overwhelming fan reaction was that players weren't being paid what they were worth, while the league was insisting the salaries were fair and within the constraints of its budget. From your vantagepoint, what can you tell fans so they better understand the realities of this issue?

Harris:
I don't think the players are paid enough but they're locked in for at least two more years under the CBA (collective bargaining agreement). A minimum of six figures or pretty damn close is what every player in the league should be making. Our days of 'having' to go overseas should be over. But the WNBA is a completely different business model than the NBA, so it's not really fair to even compare the salaries at this point for a variety of reasons. WNBA teams are not owned by the individual franchises, they're owned by the league, which eliminates (unfortunately) any room for individual financial negotiations at the team level. Players are slotted at a level and basically, there's little to be done about it until the next CBA session.

theHOOPSlink.com: In assessing the early rosters of the expansion teams, you had described Indiana's players as "Gerber graduates" and Seattle as a team that might surprise. Would you like to adjust your assessment, and do you see the tide turning for teams such as Sacramento, Detroit and Charlotte—teams that were expected to do well but are struggling at the onset?

Harris:
It's a long, short season and anything can happen. And no, I don't adjust my assessment one bit—I'll just be wrong! Seriously, we've seen teams come on strong early and fizzle out at the end (hello Charlotte). And we've seen teams struggle at the beginning and hit a stride when it counted (think Detroit in '98), so you just never really know. What I do know is that Anne Donovan is my leading candidate for coach of the

year at this point in the season because of how she's helped to transform Kara Wolters.

theHOOPSlink.com: You'd said last time around that none of the college seniors were truly ready for the pro game, but players such as Grace Daley, Betty Lennox, Tamicha Jackson and Stacy Frese are playing with confidence. Are you surprised at their performances?

Harris:
C'mon, be fair to me. I said no underclasswomen were totally ready for the next level. I've always thought Lennox, Jackson and even Edwina Brown would immediately help a team but like every rookie, Holdsclaw included, they have an adjustment period. Lennox was in a terrible shooting slump recently but is finally working herself right out of it. Tamicha Jackson only played 8 minutes in the Shock's 80-78 win over Indiana, so not every top rookie is flourishing at this point in the season.

theHOOPSlink.com: Are you surprised that so many promising college players taken in the draft were either traded or waived?

Harris:
No, didn't I say that they weren't ready??? LOL. It's a tough business, the WNBA is. And coaches are under pressure to put a good product on the floor. It's not personal but many college players have no idea how to make it at the next level. Shawnetta Stewart is a terrific player but if you bring 30 extra pounds to training camp, you'd better still be as quick as Sheryl Swoopes or as tall as Margo Dydek.

theHOOPSlink.com: Finally, Fran, what's happening in the WNBA that's so right this year, and what about the league needs to be fixed but quick?

Harris:
I'd like to see the league help more players with endorsement and off-season career opportunities. Yolanda Griffith needs her own shoe, her own signature cause (like Lisa Leslie's Breast Cancer spokesperson gig) and maybe a Tampax or Lexus commercial. The league could actually spread the love better in this area. Our players will only become household names when we aggressively market them in every nook and cranny of the world. We'll get there within the next 5 years. And putting Sacramento on national television every other day was a good start. We also need a WNBA small business or professional development initiative to help players cultivate their passions into business enterprises.

What's good about the WNBA right now? I love how this season started. Teams that weren't supposed to be good, are. Teams that we thought would steamroll right past everyone else, struggled. It's bubba-licious. That's what's going to keep folks watching the games and coming to the arenas. Sure, there'll always be dominant teams in any team sport but it's those teams who are waiting in the wings and getting better each year that make watching the WNBA particularly enjoyable for me. I did not leave my sofa during the L.A./SAC game on June 11 and I have a feeling it's gonna be that kind of season. At least, I hope so.

Dear Abby,

I thought it might be cool to share some of the questions I was asked during the 2000 season.

Why in the world should the top team have to go away to play their first playoff game?

Like most new businesses, the WNBA has financial considerations on the brain. But your query is a good one and one that is a point of contention for players and coaches throughout the league. Here's why the playoffs are set up the way they are. Since the WNBA playoffs are based on a best of 2 out of 3 series and not a best of five like the NBA, the league felt that sending the home team away first would lower operating costs. If the WNBA had set up its best of 3 series as the NBA formats its best of 5 semifinals series, then the higher seeded team would get Game 1 at home, then travel away for Game 2 and if necessary, travel back home for the third and final game of the series. Not gonna happen. Too much moolah for the league to shell out for airfare, lodging and per diem.

The argument beyond the finances is that in theory, the higher seeded team would win Game 1 anyway regardless of where the game's played. Then they would play the second/championship game in their own house. But wait a minute. Doesn't that give the lower seeded team the advantage from the start? Yep. It's one of the few times that it actually pays to be second. It doesn't seem right and I think the league needs to revisit this policy and instead reward the team that's gotten it done all season long. These higher seeds have earned the right to play that first game in the comfort of their own backyard.

Do you think the WNBA expanded too quickly?

No, I don't. I think it expanded in good quantity. People have complained that the quality of play has been poor and sometimes I agree. But sloppy, uninspired performances are as much a reality as great basketball. It comes with the territory. But it doesn't mean that the talent pool has been drastically diluted or that the league made a mistake by adding four teams this summer. I think some fans became so fixated on the lack of success with Seattle and Portland, that they forgot that the Miami Sol almost made the playoffs. Yes, it would have been difficult for them to advance to the WNBA Finals, but heading into the week before the last regular season game, it was still mathematically possible for the

Sol to finish fourth in the eastern conference and advance to the Eastern Conference playoffs.

Think about the WNBA in terms of the bell curve—10% of the teams fall to the left of the hump—these are the league's elite teams—Los Angeles, Houston, Cleveland, maybe New York and Sacramento. The largest portion of the bell, the 80%, is where most of the teams fall, which is why this year's run to the finish became so exciting. The right 10% of the bell represents the cellar teams, Seattle, Portland, and Charlotte. So, you see, overall the league was quite vibrant and competitive. There will be no expansion in 2001 but there may be a team coming to your city in either 2002 or 2003. The team pushing the hardest to acquire a team? San Antonio for the 2003 season.

Do you think there's a conspiracy against the Houston Comets? It's obvious the league doesn't want them to win a fourth title—that's why the officials are so anti-Comets.

Fans. You gotta love that loyalty thing. I've also gotten similar questions from Sparks, Monarchs, Liberty and Starzz fans who think the league doesn't want their respective teams to win either. I'm not an employee of the WNBA, so nobody's paying me to say what I'm about to say. I don't think the league cares *who* wins the 2000 crown. Val Ackerman and Company just want the journey to the championship game to be exciting. An exciting championship run makes fans, media, sponsors and advertisers happy. Has the Comets dominance been good for the league? Absolutely. Whether you're a hater or lover of the Houston Comets, you've gotta admit that you want to watch them play, whether you're cheering or booing. The Comets are part of the reason the WNBA has thrived because the team became a household name not only in the states but also abroad where everyone knows the Comets' Big Three by name and number. The buzz in the media all summer long was about the Los Angeles Sparks and how magical it would have been had they been able to bring a WNBA championship trophy home to place alongside the Lakers' hardware. Maybe next year.

Charity Begins At Home

One of the things that the WNBA has done is to help broaden economic and exposure opportunities for the players. Many are spokespersons for various causes. Coop is tied to breast cancer, as is Lisa Leslie. Sheryl Swoopes is connected to the March of Dimes. For the most part, the partnerships are win-wins for the player and the charity. But I've heard some horror stories where charitable organizations are asking WNBA players to give them everything including their first born.

I'm all for giving back to the community and I'm involved in several causes where I completely donate my time and expertise in a variety of ways. Or I help on a pro bono basis. But you can't always give it away each and every time someone calls with a sad story or a worthy cause. Sometimes you have to talk business or say no.

After my second season in the WNBA several foundations approached me, one in particular wanted me to be the spokeswoman for a national initiative that focused on empowering girls. It sounded interesting to me, so I called the coordinator back and we talked for a good 30 minutes. I liked what they were trying to do and wanted to continue conversations with them. Everything was going smoothly until we got to the compensation part of the conversation and I heard, 'Well, we were hoping that you would donate your time to this project'. This coordinator had just told me that they'd secured one major sponsor who was donating a buttload of money to the program. But now she was telling me that they were just a little not-for-profit operation who didn't have any money? It didn't compute. I've worked with non-profits enough to know that some of them stretch the truth when it comes to how much money they have.

After explaining to the representative that they were asking me for a significant commitment, I recommended a figure that I thought they might be able to stomach. The amount I suggested was so small that it would have covered per diem when I had to travel, and maybe minor business-related expenses. In return, they'd get me as their ambassador for one full year. I'd speak at events and attend important functions nationwide. It was an incredible deal. One she knew she couldn't resist. So we agreed verbally with the understanding that she'd have to get final approval from someone in the organization's executive office.

A week later I get a call from this coordinator saying that while she agreed that I'd presented her with a fantastic bargain, that her supervisor had essentially vetoed her decision, saying that they don't pay their spokespeople. Keep in mind that they'd never even *had* a spokesperson before they approached me. So, how was it that they had this iron clad policy in place? Again, it wasn't adding up. And I was starting to feel like I was in the Twilight Zone with all of the back and forth phone conversations. Shortly afterwards, I gracefully bowed out and wished them well.

Hot Air

Shouldn't the broadcasting booth on WNBA games belong to women announcers? I'm so sick of hearing the men refer to the players as girls. Plus, I don't see us calling NBA games. These are actual comments and questions from viewers who are concerned that women broadcasters will become extinct on WNBA broadcasts, much like female coaches in the league. For me, it's all about opportunity—whether we're talking about broadcasting or coaching. It's all the same. There are obviously more available qualified men in sportscasting than there are women simply because they've had access to the jobs longer than we have. But I feel the greater issue is that people in power at the networks, on some level, feel that we need men to validate us. Or else there appears to be this prevailing notion that a male presence is needed to draw in the male viewer to watch the WNBA. I disagree. I believe that true fans will watch a good game, no matter who's on headsets.

True, in the WNBA, half of the on-air positions are filled by men. And I'm not so sure that many announcers, with the exception of Reggie Miller, have a real interest in women's basketball at the college or pro level. That's just my experience. That's from listening to them talk about it amongst themselves. And that disturbs me. Would you want an attorney representing you who has no passion for your case? Of course not. So, why do we stick guys who look down on our sport in key broadcasting roles? I don't get it.

Would I like to see women play-by-play announcers teamed with women analysts and sideline reporters? Absolutely. But I also have to give all three WNBA broadcasting partners—Lifetime, NBC and ESPN—credit. They've all at one time had all women teams, but the format, for whatever reason, didn't stick. NBC tried it in 1997 with Hannah Storm and Ann Meyers Drysdale. ESPN did it with Robin Roberts, Pat Summit and Tiffany Wright in 1999. Lifetime's other on-air team in 1999 featured Suzyn Waldman, Mary Murphy and Christine Brennan. And before Reggie finished his 2000 NBA playing season, Michele Tafoya, Percefone Contos and I were the only all female broadcast in the league. So, it's been done. Will it happen again? I'm optimistic that it will. What bothers me most is that I don't feel the partners have ample patience for women announcers. They almost appear to be operating under the 'We tried it once and it didn't work' rule. They're so quick to bail and that bothers me. Do they ever stop to consider that maybe they didn't have the right combination to begin with? No. Of course not because that would mean that they did something wrong. And my experience tells me that most TV executives would rather have a root canal than admit that they made a mistake.

There are no easy answers on this subject. I'm *inside* and I still don't get satisfactory answers. I did hear one executive at a major network say that 'there just aren't enough qualified women play-by-play announcers out there'. To that I say, that's fair. There aren't a whole lot of us in those positions yet. But then my response to this executive is, then do something about it. You make stars out of men all the time. How about some love for the women.

Give The Media Lemons And They'll Make Lemon Meringue Pie

Okay, now that I'm on the other side, I can tell you for a fact that the media will milk a story like it's a 3-ton cow. I'll give you an example. It's a scenario that I hate to bring up, but it illustrates the point I want to make here. The '98 Swoopes-Coop saga was worked until it looked like a pair of faded Levi 501 jeans. Every time I turned around, someone was talking about it. This story got old quick for me. Even when it resurfaced in the '99 season and again in the 2000 campaign, it was still old.. You know what else I'm over? The Ruthie Bolton-Holifield mega family story. Over it. Not that it's not amazing for 20 children to be in one family, it is. But there are so many other things about Ruthie that were interesting and needed to be told. Her clothing line, Ru-ware. Her musical talents and interests. The Ruthie Bolton-Holifield Foundation and possibly things that we don't even know about because we're (journalists) too busy focusing on the Twenty Is Enough angle.

And what about Chantel Tremitiere? She's very talented musically, which is not to be confused with vocally. Not at all. But Chan can play the ivory off of the keys of a piano. And she also has dreams of starring in the movies. LaTonya Johnson, the Utah Starzz' underused small forward, has a beautiful voice and by far, the best bark in the league. Olympia Scott-Richardson is producing her first CD on a record label that she and her husband, Al, started last year. Monica Lamb is self-publishing her first book on fitness and spirituality. Dawn Staley became the head coach at Temple University this year. Wouldn't you like to have known how she feels heading into such a new situation without any prior coaching experience? I know I would. These are the stories, that as a fan of the game, I'm interested in. I wanna know what makes these women tick. What they do away from the court in the community. What business aspirations do they have?

One of the reasons I was very proud to be a part of the Lifetime team this summer was because I think our producers made a commitment to show the fans and viewers the many faces of the WNBA players away from basketball.

I nicknamed Cynthia Cooper the Drive By Diva in 1999. I also called her Pebbles because of the ponytail.

My sister, Debra and I in South Beach, Florida. She tried out for the Sol...I was so proud!

Look at the facial expressions on these two rookies, Helen Darling and Tamicha Jackson.

Sheryl Swoopes enjoying yet another win in the Compaq Center and looking just like J.J.

I was Kedra Holland-Corn's coach and camp counselor when she was a 7th grader. See the similarities in our shooting forms?

Brandi Reed is a straight up baller who emerged as one of the league's deadliest scorers. Remember that interview I mentioned in chapter 4? Hmmmm...

Eva Nemcova is one of my favorite players but I bet she doesn't remember that I shut her down in the inaugural season at Gund Arena.

Rookie of the Year Betty Lennox checks her conscience, not her ego, at the door.

Edwina "Winky" Brown about to break another Texas alum down off the dribble. It was not pretty.

After being traded to the Portland Fire, Sophia Witherspoon broke out to have a great year.

Teresa Weatherspoon is so over being a bridesmaid. Maybe she'll get her crown in 2001.

Chantel Tremitiere eats a candy bar before every game. One day she's gonna have a serious dental bill.

Ticha Penicheiro is a Globetrotter who likes mustard on her hotdog and a splash of relish.

The shot heard round the world belongs to Tina Thompson, the WNBA's top pick in the inaugural season in 1997.

Edna Campbell tellin' folks how to play Seattle ball. She plays in Poland in the off-season and says it's possible to live off of $100 a week for food there.

MVP to MVP. Yolanda Griffith soars above the league's top defensive player. Then gives Swoopes an oops upside the head.

I still got skillz, baby. It was great to play in front of the league's best fans. Go Cometheads!

Lifetime's Triple Threat. Reggie Miller and Michele Tafoya are two of the greatest people to work with.

Robyn Simmons, a committed '98 Los Angeles fantasy camper. How's that jumper?

(Above) A Comets sandwich with Lisa Leslie filling. What a great 1999 Western Conference Finals in 1999. (RT) Swoopes, the human shot swatter.

Me, my Chaka Kahn hair and the incomparable Olympia Scott-Richardson and her mom, Dr. Jacqueline Scott.

Working for Lifetime gave me the opportunity to interview players and fans alike. Pebbles and I talk about her injury and place on the Comets bench during a crucial game in Los Angeles in 2000.

A send-off befitting a queen. The Cometheads know a good thing when they see it and Coop gave them lots to cheer about for four seasons. They will miss her and so will the WNBA. Stay tuned for Coop TV.

Kim Perrot represented the warrior in all of us. On July 29, 2000 the dedication ceremony had us all choked up. We love you, Kim.

CHAPTER 5

Pick-Up Hell and Why Sports Talk Guys Can't Stop Dissing the WNBA

Boy Meets Girl

It's a familiar scene. Girl walks into gym. Boy stares. Girl asks who has next. Boy stares at her like she's not talking to him. Looks around at other boys. Girl asks again. "Who's got next?" Boy mumbles and points to other boys standing on the sidelines. Girl says out loud, "Who's got next?" All boys imitate mutes. Girl shakes her head. Walks by boys and says, "I got next, then."

Behold! It's a miracle. Boys can talk. "I got next," the first boy says.

Girl says, "You got yo' team?"

Boy lies. "Yeah." Girl smiles, knowing he's lying, especially since there are only two other boys sitting on the sidelines. "Where are they? Your team? Where is it?" she asks. Boy wasn't expecting that response from girl. "Oh, they're coming." Girl smiles a knowing grin. "OK," she says, "I got after you."

Boy walks off dribbling, sizing up girl, hoping his imaginary boys will walk through the door so he doesn't have to pick girl by default. Game in progress ends. Boy's team arrives. Boy is relieved. Winning team loses a player. Baller on the winners knows girl. Asks girl, "Wanna run?" Girl spills a sinister smile in the direction of the lying boy. Damn skippy, she thinks. Let the games begin.

Game gets ready to start and boy thinks he's hot stuff now that he's surrounded by his boys. None of whom, girl thinks, were worthy of passing over her for. But oh well. Since girl is now on the winning team she gets the ball first. Boys on other team all walk around looking lost, trying to check other boys on girl's team so that they don't have to check girl. Boys hate checking girls. Girl rolls ball out to no one in particular and yells, "Check." Boy from other team has to get the ball and thus, check the girl. He concedes, looking around at his boys, "I'll take her."

By now, new boys have walked into gym. One yells, "Man, you 'bout to get schooled." Boy who's checking girl gives an arrogant, 'yeah, right' look and then throws ball back to girl, who gives him a reassuring eye. Reassuring in the sense that his ass is grass. Game starts and girl passes it around. She doesn't have to prove anything, after all, her team just won and with good reason—they're good.

Boy on girl's team passes back to her and admonishes, "*Do* him." Girl passes to another boy and sets a screen away from the ball. Boy passes back to girl and says, "*Do* him. Whatcha waiting on? Initiate dat fool." Girl looks into the nervous eyes of the boy guarding her and thinks for a second. Drive or stroke? She's about 25 feet away from the nylon, well within her range. But boy doesn't know that. So, boy steps back. Almost challenging her to give him a facial. He's thinking, 'Yeah, right. Girls can't shoot from that far out.' Girl hears what boy's thinking and decides that boy needs some strong medicine. So, she lets it fly. And before the ball ever reaches the basket, she yells out, 3-0 and winks at boy defender, as she backpedals to the other end.

You'd think that after more than a decade on this campus I could just walk into the Rec center at the University of Texas and get some respect. But I often forget that the Osh Kosh B'gosh tots in there now were still in their Huggies Pull-Ups when I was dropping dimes back in the day. To them, I'm just another girl trying to get a nut.

You see, this little scene is just a microcosm of the larger backdrop looming over women's hoops these days. Somehow boys have it in their minds that women's basketball is out to get them. They think that we're plotting like mad scientists to steal their money, fame and notoriety. As if anybody could ever be as naughty as little boys with balls.But at least this explains the angst I hear in the voices of male callers each day on sports talk radio. "Why don't the girls just give it up, yo? They'll never be as good as the guys. The WNBA will never outshine the NBA. They can't even dunk, man." And the beat goes on. This is all laugh out loud material, you realize. And sometimes I call in just to tick 'em off even more.

Nevertheless, it boggles my mind. Why is it that guys are so threatened by women playing ball? And when will *we* stop measuring our successes by what the men do? Face it, if women had invented basketball, the ball would never have been as big as it is anyway. Deciding to go with a smaller ball wasn't a slap in the face of women's sports — it was an attempt to customize a game that was made without any thought whatsoever to our gender. A game that certainly didn't consider something as insignificant (to them) as our hands size. Maybe these callers didn't get the memo. We're not imitating high flying, Barnum & Bailey stunts because that's not necessarily our game, period. Believe it or not, we don't all wanna be like Mike.

A lot of women could teach flight school, though. I saw Lynette Woodard dunk to get warmed up back in 1979 in Plainview, Texas, at Wayland Baptist's Flying Queens Tournament. She just jumped up and grabbed the rim. So what? I was more impressed with how still her 'fro stayed as she dazzled the crowd with her ball-handling and scoring prowess. As a high school sophomore desperate for role models, I was sold on our game because it stressed fundamentals and team play.

Fast forward a decade and a half and we're still saying, "Hey, look! Over here, we're as good as the guys." We made such a big bloody deal about Sylvia Crawley dunking at the ABL All-Star Game in 1998. Big whoop. Women have been dunking forever, right? We just don't feel the need to pound our chests and slit our throats when we do.

Let's call it like it is. Men, in general, are built differently than us. Anatomically they will generally be bigger and faster. Big whoop again. It's a physical thing. But somehow the word "superior" got thrown in there and the verbal wars have been in full force ever since. I don't think any human is superior to another, so the thought of the men's game being better than ours is a thought that flees at Mach 10 speed.

But let's be real. Most of us have been influenced by the people who taught us to play or by those we played with growing up. On many occasions those influences included a brother, dad or cousin or two. And although the guys will never admit it, they learn a lot about the way the game was meant to be played when they see women do it. But give us props? Fugitaboutit. Everything's always about *them*. My brother tells me it's just a 'man thang'. Sounds more like a moron thang to me.

Can You Dunk?

It's a question that every WNBA player has been asked. And it makes me wonder what's wrong with Reggie Miller. Take Game One of the 2000 Eastern Conference Semifinals, the Indiana Pacers versus the Philadelphia 76ers. The guy scored a measly 40 points. Shot a pitiful 11-18 from the field, including a rather dismal 7-10 from French Lick and a pathetic 11-12 from the charity stripe. And to top it all off, he only dunked once. One dunk in 48 minutes!

What gives with this guy? Hasn't he been listening to sports talk radio lately? Has he even bothered to pick up an English speaking newspaper in the last, oh, decade? Doesn't he know that dunking is where it's at? Maybe he didn't check the NASDAQ on Friday at the close of market. So, he didn't know that DUNK stock had skyrocketed in the last week.

That must be why he shot a lay-up on a breakaway situation when there wasn't a Sixer in sniffing distance. Yeah, that's gotta be it.

If Reggie weren't busy trying to get through training camp with new coach Isaiah Thomas, I'm sure he'd answer my emails and confirm that he doesn't give a rip about dunking. He'd tell me that red, white and blue pigs singing "I'm Going Back To Indiana" and playing electric guitars could fly through Conseco Fieldhouse and he'd care more about that than the last time he stuffed leather. Truth is, Reggie has one serious stroke and he doesn't have to prove his manhood by dunking a basketball.

And I'd bet you cash money that Shaquille O'Neal would have happily traded in a couple of those tomahawks for about 20 free throw percentage points heading into Game 2 versus Portland. No doubt about it. Pardon the sarcasm but I've just about had it with certain hosts and callers on certain sports talk radio shows. Those Jethro Clampitt-types who excelled in 1977 Pop Warner league and who headed the All Intramural team in college, are the ones I'm talking about. The Ralph Kramden look-a-likes who call in spouting off about how the women's game will never be on the level with the men until they dunk on a regular basis.

Let me let you in on a couple of hints, ladies and gents. One, if I were 6'8, with calves like cantaloupes and had a 41-inch vertical leap, I'd dunk the hell out of that ball, too. No question. But that's not how I'm built. I'm a woman and we don't normally come in industrial size. It's not about skill, it's about biology. It's also about socialization. Guys are about dominance. That is why you dunk. That is why you like to *see* guys dunk. It's an exclamatory athletic move, a dunk is. But don't go crazy, it's not bigger than the game.

The women's game doesn't need the sexiness of a monster jam to validate it. That's insane. Of course, there are women who can dunk. Lisa Leslie, Sylvia Crawley, Charlotte Smith, Margo Dydek and Michelle Van Gorp to name only a handful. But who cares? It's only two points.

If dunking meant that basketball had arrived, the Boston Celtics wouldn't be considered one of the greatest teams in hoop history. Magic Johnson wasn't a dunk meister, he was a passing wizard and without his sorcery, Showtime would not have being coined. Besides, I'd like to see anyone of you tell John Wooden or Pat Summit that what they teach is not basketball. Or that their ten and six NCAA championships respectively mean bupkus because their teams failed to produce the desired number of dunks required by the Hoop Gods.

You wanna know why I was glued to this year's Knicks-Heat series? Because of the competition, the hustle, and the slicing and dicing. I wanted to see Spreewell elevate and then drop, drop, drop it like it's hot. I wanted to see Tim Hardaway come down, lull Charlie Ward into comatosia and then pull up from Ft. Lauderdale.

I ordered in because I didn't want to miss those crafty passes that left defenders scratching their heads and catching flies. I didn't leave church early on Sunday to catch Game 7 and then wait for an event (dunk) that might make the 11:00 highlight package on Sportscenter but doesn't even show up on the freakin' stat sheet.

I don't defend the women's game. It needs no defense. It is what it is. I respect the sport of basketball when it's played in one euphonious tone. I don't care if the person playing it sports a jock strap or a bra strap. On nights when five players have managed to perform like the percussion section of an orchestra, basketball is a beautiful thing. And if the game ever gets to the point where stingy defense and razor sharp shooting lose their luster, then this game will lose lots of fans ergo, money. And then where will the coveted dunk be?

Enough Is Enough

And another thing. I've had it with tired, homophobic male sports talk radio hosts dissing the WNBA. One Phoenix male radio host said, "I wouldn't take my mother to a WNBA game, have you seen that crowd? The stands are full of lesbians!" His caller chimed right in to support his idiotic brother. I'm driving along thinking, 'What does sexual orientation have to do with a basketball game? Can someone tell me that?'

Some guys are so insecure that the only way they know how to feel secure in their manhood is by bashing the WNBA. Here's a quick story. When I was a sophomore in college there was this guy living in the same apartment complex as my teammates. He was a neighbor and he told one of them that he'd like to go out with me. He seemed like a nice guy so I said, why not. We went to dinner and it was while we were breaking bread that I discovered that he had the personality of a stamp. So, when I got back to the apartment, I said thanks and goodnight. He asked if we could go out again and I said no. I told him that he was nice, the meal was great but that I didn't want to see him anymore. "I didn't feel like we had any chemistry," I said.

He seemed to accept that after he kept saying how great he thought the date was. About a month or so passed and he'd called a couple of times. Then I saw him one night after one of my games. He came over with this sheepish look on his face. I spoke and kept walking.

"Fran?" he said.

"Yeah."

"I think I figured out why you don't wanna go out with me anymore," he said.

"Oh, really. And why is that?"

"Well, I hear all of the basketball girls are gay, you know. I didn't think you were like that but apparently this is sort of common knowledge and I just didn't know it," he said.

What I wanted to say to him was, 'No, the reason I don't want to go out with you is because you're boring and you have no soul.' That's what I wanted to say but I didn't. He wasn't even worth my time. So, I said, "Well, Lenny, whatever. I don't owe you anything. If that's what you wanna believe, then believe it." And I left him standing right there catching flies.

Everyone's entitled to his or her own opinion. I've got no beef with that. I had no problem with Lenny thinking that I was gay. I guess for him that was easier than accepting rejection. Some folks have a hard time with that. But what Lenny did is exactly what I see and hear men doing all over the country to women in sports. It's a control mechanism in my opinion. And women have told me that they didn't play high school sports because they didn't want anyone thinking that they were gay. Or that they over-feminized themselves to keep guys from accusing them of being lesbian. Women have actually given up sports because some guy said that women who play sports are lesbians. Fear can be a powerful tool and many women have succumbed to society's ignorance. I personally know women who've prostituted themselves just so no one would think that they were gay. For them, the worst thing in the world is to be accused of being gay. What a sad commentary on our society.

Sports talk radio has produced some of the most bigoted voices in our society today. Guys who never hesitate to bash women athletes. Guys who hide behind their own fears of being homosexual. Guys who can't stand that the WNBA is here to stay. I don't have one problem with these guys not liking the league. But don't stoop to insulting the fans.

This summer I appeared on an Internet sports talk show in which the host asked me if I thought the league was taking care of its 'core' fan base: lesbians. I started laughing. "Is there some instrument out there that runs from the seats in WNBA arenas into a special device connected to sports talk radio equipment that tells you guys who's gay and who's not?" I asked. "How do you know the core fan base is lesbian?" He had to laugh himself at that one. "Well, c'mon , Fran, you can just tell by looking at them?"

What? I told him you're making a big assumption based on what you see. There are folks that I think look like stereotypical Mafioso but I don't go around saying that all the folks at the New York Knicks games are involved in organized crime. C'mon, that's stupid.

The other camp of sports talk guys who hate the WNBA say that they've seen better basketball at their 5-year-old's little league games. One host on One-on-One sports, a national radio show with a 90% goober fan base, said and I quote, "I tried to watch the WNBA but it was just ugly…missed layups, bad passing and a lot of turnovers. I couldn't stand it, I turned it off."

Let me tell you, I've watched *thousands* of basketball games and I've yet to see a game without missed lay-ups and turnovers. Not in the NCAA, not on the playground and nope, not even in the NBA. What's funny is that these same guys rarely bag on the women's World Cup Soccer team, maybe because soccer isn't considered a 'man's' sport. It's more of a socially acceptable sport for women, it's supposedly gender appropriate. I wonder if that's because there's not the kind of contact there is in hoops or football?

I've also never heard sports talk guys compare the men's and women's soccer leagues. Yet that's all I hear when people express their dislike for the WNBA. *They can't play like the men. If you put them in a game against the NBA guys, they'd get creamed.*

Okay, so you'd rather watch the guys. Fine. But why must you hate so hard on your little talk show, that's what I wanna know? That same Phoenix host said that he hates being force fed the WNBA by his station managers and feels that he shouldn't be forced to talk about the WNBA when he doesn't think it's a good product. Can you believe it? So much anger over 20 whole seconds of airtime? All this angst over a few box scores? I couldn't believe it, so here's what I wrote to one host.

The WNBA showcases women who are both strong and graceful. Women who effectively combine power with finesse. And women whose muscular physiques reveal their commitment to being in supreme condition and top physical shape. Aren't those the qualities of champions, regardless of gender? So, what's all the fuss about, guys? Scared there won't be enough airtime to

talk about the escapades of your many upstanding professional male ath-
letes who are beating their wives, evading arrest, ordering hits on their preg-
nant girlfriends, stealing VCRs, making racist and bigoted comments, or
running in and out of court to deal with palimony suits?

Postcards From The Edge

I get emails from folks all the time. Emails about everything from how to shoot a jump shot properly to setting some poor fool up on a date with Nikki McCray. And I'm pretty good about answering my emails personally. If you have something somewhat intelligent to say—even if I disagree, I will answer. Sometimes people just send me emails to vent and that's okay. I don't mind hearing that someone's sick of seeing the same WNBA players get all the glory, that's a valid point. And I don't mind that some folks think that Lifetime's coverage of the WNBA is sometimes sexist. So, I thought it might be fun to share some of the more famous emails that I've responded to over the last year. Or I should say, infamous.

Dear Fran, what is up with the WNBA players not combing their hair. If they want this league to last, they should pay more attention to the way they look on the court.

FH: A sore subject for someone who tells little girls all over the country to focus on how hard they play the game, not whether their hair is out of place *while* they're playing it. Needless to say, this email got a speedy response. I said, who cares what her hair looks like. As a fan of the game I'm not sitting in the stands saying, "Gee, I wish she'd worn her hair in two ponytails instead of three tonight. Well, that's it, I'm never coming back to watch this team again!" On the point of the league lasting, I said that the league's success is not dependent on how the women look as much as it is on how well they play the game. If the WNBA puts a poor product on the floor, grooming will be the least of the league's worries. The players can all look like goddesses but if they can't play, the WNBA will last about as long as the movie Blue Streak did at the box office.

Dear Fran, the phrase is player-to-player, not man-to-man. These are womyn out there and I'm sick of the patriarchal terms being used during the game by all announcers.

FH: First, have a chill pill on me, why don't you. I'm a women's advocate and I understand the basis for this gripe but in practice it just doesn't work. Person-to-person sounds like it's a collect phone call. Player-to-player just won't roll off the tongue as well. But I'm open to trying 'woman-to-woman', even if it reminds me of that R&B song by Shirley Brown, "Woman To Woman", about a woman who was sleeping with a married man.

Cover Girls

A few years ago I went to the Rec center on the UT campus to play in a pickup game with my little brother, Chris. I'd just come from an appointment and was probably wearing a little makeup and a pair of earrings. I ran to the restroom to swiftly change my clothes because I wanted to be upstairs before the guys started shooting for the teams. Shooting for teams, in case you've never played pickup, is a process by which every person shoots a three pointer to see who gets to be one of the ten players in the first full court game of the day. So, I didn't wanna miss my turn to shoot. When I walked through the door, Chris beamed. He was always glad to see me, so he said. I walked over to him, we kissed and did our usual bantering. That's when he let me in on a little secret. "You look cute," he said. "Did you have a meeting or something?"

"Yeah," I answered.

"Where's your scrunchie?" I'd never known Chris to take that much interest in my hair but I pointed to my Nike bag just the same.

"Why?"

"Cuz, these fools gon' think you can't hoop, you know, with you rollin' in here looking like *that.*"

I smirked. "Oh, now I gotta *look* a certain way to get picked up?"

"Naw, naw...well, yeah," he laughed. "If you wanna play."

I knew my brother was right. At least about the perceptions of men when it comes to what a good female basketball player should look like. Come to the gym looking frilly and guys don't take you seriously. Talk about not wanting to break your nails and you won't get the ball on the wing when you're wide open. Squeal in delight when you nail a jumper and you'll never touch the rock again, trust me. I'd heard it all during college. Let a shorthaired, hard-bodied woman walk in and the guys would start. *Man, she looks like a dude. I bet she can ball.* Looking like a guy was supposed to be a compliment to the girl, of course.

I can't remember a time in my recent past that I've cared what people thought about what I look like, especially when I'm playing basketball. I would never intentionally wear makeup to play ball—pickup or for real. It doesn't make sense to me. Cosmetics are not functional in sport in my opinion. And the only time I actually wear makeup is when I'm on air. Then, I'm an entertainer. But mascara on ball players? During a game? Just don't get it.

CHAPTER 6

And The Franny Goes To...

Swoopes There It Is...Finally

I bet last year Sheryl Swoopes knew how All My Children soap star Susan Lucci felt those first 12 years she didn't win an Emmy for her portrayal of Erica Kane. In 1999, Sacramento's Yolanda Griffith had a monster season and she deserved to be recognized for her efforts but I still think Swoopes was robbed of at least co-honors for both MVP and Defensive Player of the Year. So, to make sure that props go to the players most deserving of post-season honors, I'm announcing The FRANNYS, awards given to the players and coaches who I feel gave us the most memorable on and off court antics during the Millenium WNBA season. Remember, these were given in July so some of the numbers and statistics may have changed by the end of the season.

Most Valuable Player Award:

Sheryl Swoopes led the WNBA in scoring with 20 ppg but more importantly, she's got the goods in every single category. She's a scoring machine who also thrives on defense—a rarity for great scorers.

Best Defensive Player:

Swoopes there it is. I call her The Great Anticipator of errant passes and she'll blow by you so fast you'll suffer whiplash. She's the league's top pickpocket with two steals a game and when it comes to defense, she's smart, intuitive and tenacious.

Rookie of the Year:

Betty Lennox, Minnesota Lynx. The most electrifying newcomer in the WNBA averaged 16 points per game. She backs down to no one and loves to stop and pop it from the great beyond on the fast break. What I love about Lennox is that like all great offensive players, she checks her conscience at the locker room door and has yet to meet a shot she didn't launch.

Most Improved Player:

Tangela Smith of the Sacramento Monarchs may have been Griffith's backup last season but she is the main reason Sacramento had a real shot at the western conference title this season. She's quick, nimble and slight for the power forward position, but no one is quicker to the basket on a rebound, except for maybe last year's MVP.

All Defensive Team:

Three of the league's most lethal offensive weapons are also defensive stoppers. Mess with them and you'll be eating a double-decker leather sandwich for lunch. Sheryl Swoopes, Yolanda Griffith, and Lisa Leslie join Orlando's Shannon Johnson, Cleveland Rocker Mery Andrade and the New York Liberty's Teresa Weatherspoon on my All-D team.

Most Likely to throw a Bow:

Lisa Leslie, Los Angeles Sparks and Margo Dydek, Utah Starzz have elbows that should be registered as deadly weapons. They're pointy and they hurt—just ask my throat. At 6'5 and 7'2 respectively, they get their share of 'little people' poking them in the stomach so they make sure that they send their opponents home with lovely black and blue parting gifts.

Most Likely To Whine About a Call by the Official

'Hey, ref! Watch the hacking!' This quartet will approach an official during timeouts and re-enact the scene of the crime, complete with sound effects. Cynthia Cooper (Houston), Mery Andrade, (Cleveland), Jennifer Gillom (Phoenix), and Natalie Williams (Utah Starzz).

All Six Pack Team:

That area below your breasts and above your waist is supposed to feel like steel trap doors according to these ab divas. Kelly Gibson, (Houston), Ruthie Bolton-Holifield, (Sacramento), Adrienne Goodson, (Utah) and Sylvia Crawley (Portland). I've got two words for all of ya'll: not fair!

The Staremaster Award:

Don't make these players mad because if looks could kill, you wouldn't last ten seconds in a room with this trio. Sheryl Swoopes, Tina Thompson and Yolanda Griffith. None of them are very vocal, but if they were to star in a movie, it would be called Lethal Eyes.

Coaches Most Likely To Get Teed Up (Technical Fouls):

Los Angeles Sparks coach Michael Cooper said that he was not going to let poor officiating deprive his Los Angeles Sparks of a championship. So his assistant coaches purchased harnesses for the playoffs because Coop had a tendency to leave the bench in pursuit of a few bad zebras. Phoenix Mercury coach Cheryl Miller has had more coaching-related injuries than any other WNBA coach. Last year she got so upset with a call that she kicked the scorer's table. Maybe she and Coop can star in Rocky 6.

Players Most Likely To Get Teed Up and Thrown Out:

DeLisha Milton did not earn the nickname D-Nasty because she has horrible table manners. This woman gets in the trenches and fights for her team even if that means giving the officials a piece of her mind. A big piece. Although she smiles when she disses them, the striped shirts don't always find her sentiments DeLishous.

Off the court, Edna Campbell of the Seattle Storm is one of the wittiest people I know. On the court, she can be maniacal if she thinks the officiating stinks. Two weeks ago, she was ejected and sentenced to the locker room for the duration of the game. Apparently, she didn't have closure because ten seconds later she returned to finish what she'd started with the official who threw her out!

Most Likely To Grab Your Jersey When The Official Isn't Looking

I love old school players because they know how and when to pull one over on their opponents. You'll never see anything overt from this tricky trio because their antics mostly happen away from the ball. Sue Wicks-New York Liberty, pulls big girls' jerseys so that they can't jump and grab rebounds. In one game during the inaugural season, Teresa Weatherspoon was guarding me and as I got ready to screen across the lane, she grabbed my shorts. After I dug my undies out of my butt, the play was foiled. Rhonda Mapp of the Charlotte Sting is 6'3 and about 200 pounds, and she's got lots of tricks and treats for big women. But when she has to go against smaller, quicker post players, what does she do stop them from beating her to the ball? She grabs their arms, plain and simple.

The Hair(do) Club:

They never have the same hair color or style for two weeks straight and sometimes even we broadcasters have a difficult time identifying them in the lineup. Another reason we screw up their names, right? Here are my favorite looks for each player.

Andrea Stinson, strawberry blonde woven into her brown tresses. Sheryl Swoopes, twists that roll into a Rapunsel—like ponytail. Merlakia Jones, the Shirley Temple look. And Chamique Holdsclaw can go from Pocahontas to Annie all in one week.

The Player Most Likely To Get Evicted If She'd Had To Depend on her WNBA Salary

There may be a thin line between love and hate but the gulf between the lowest and top paid player in the league in '97 (and even now) was pathetic. When I tried out and made the Houston Comets' roster in the 1997 inaugural season, my $10,000, three-month salary was less than my one-time speaking fee. In fact, the salary range on our team that year went from $5,000 for our developmental/practice players to $250,000 for our marquee talent and the team's first assigned player, Sheryl Swoopes. That's the equivalent of the Atlantic Ocean in terms of money between players on the same team, in the same league. And it didn't seem quite right.

Unlike the now defunct American Basketball League, which paid its players $40,000 to over $200,000 for a conventional 7-month season, the WNBA, from the outset, reasoned that its salaries were, well, reasonable. Was there *that* much difference between Swoopes and the practice players? Not necessarily in terms of talent but more in terms of marketing value to the league. Between Swoopes, Rebecca Lobo and Lisa Leslie, there was about a week's worth of professional basketball experience. How in the world were they supposed to be able to compete at the professional level without any tenure? According to the league, the Big Three had just played integral (except for Lobo) roles in helping the '96 USA Olympic Team bring home the gold—*this* was their experience.

More importantly, the six-figure salary that the league was about to pay Swoopes, Leslie and Lobo in 1997 was not only for their on-court efforts, but also for their face time in commercials. It was also covering compensation for marketing and helping to make the WNBA a household brand. In short, Swoopes, Lobo and Leslie were the shoulders on which this league would rest, so we were told. And that was why they were being given Filet Mignon and the rest of us were blessed with only Happy Meals.

Since 1997 things have changed some in this area, but not nearly enough. In 1999, the average WNBA salary was $55,000 with a great proportion of that being carried by the salaries of players like Swoopes, Leslie, and rookie All-Star, Chamique Holdsclaw. Even after winning the league's first MVP award in 1997, Cynthia Cooper was still not close to being the highest paid player in the league because she wasn't in the WNBA's long range marketing plans. Said another way, why should we (WNBA) spend millions to market players who won't be around for more than five years? I can answer that one. Because she's brought tremendous exposure to the league. She carried it for two years. So, she wasn't 25 years old. She was still the best thing going in the WNBA and she deserved to be paid like she was the best.

The ultimate sign of salary shame came in the spring of 2000 when the league was unable to come to terms with 5-time Olympic basketball legend Teresa Edwards. Before the April 25th draft, Edwards telephoned me to say that she would not be playing in the WNBA in the 2000 season because they couldn't agree on the terms of her contract. Translation: they weren't willing to pay her for her extraordinary talent or for what she had done to elevate women's basketball over the last 15 years. Edwards had earned (and deserved) a six-figure salary for hoops since 1988, mostly in European or Japanese leagues. She was a founding member of the ABL, where again her hard work and elite talent had commanded one of the league's highest salaries.

Can the WNBA afford to lose players like Edwards on a regular basis because they're not a twentysomething who'll be around to carry the league? Absolutely not. Will prospective WNBA players then opt for greener pastures overseas where they can be paid what they're worth? Yes and no. In 2000, players like Cindy Brown (Utah) and Andrea Congreaves (Orlando) chose to sit out or go overseas because they felt that the WNBA was asking them to play for such paltry salaries.

Chapter 7

On The Road Again

I rarely drink and I have a good reason. A very good reason. Besides the fact that I've seen what alcohol abuse has done to people I love and respect, it's just not good for your insides. And it makes you do really stupid stuff. Gets you into awkward situations, too. I was a sophomore in college and you couldn't tell me anything. Over spring break, 1984, one of my close friends, Cara, had been invited to New Orleans to visit a man who wanted to date her. He'd told her that she could bring a friend along so she asked me to go. He picked us up at the airport and dropped us off at this ritzy hotel in the French Quarters and told us he'd pick us up later that evening for dinner.

We walked into the room with eyes the size of egg yokes because this room was bigger than any hotel room either of us had ever seen. It had a dining area, living room and a huge television in the center of it. We slowly took it all in. Then we noticed a door. She walked over and opened it and it was another room almost identical to the one we were standing in. "Oh my God," she said. "It has a twin." For two days we toured New Orleans and had a good time.

On our last night we were having dinner with this guy and he asked if we wanted drinks. Neither of us were drinkers so we declined. "Oh, c'mon," he persuaded. "You don't drink? At all? Then you've gotta be pretty thirsty." He thought he was so funny. So we said okay. We'll have one drink. "One drink? You can't come to New Orleans and have one drink," he said. "Tell ya what. We'll have a little bit of a lot of drinks, that way you'll end up having one drink." We looked at each other and although we'd both made the dean's list the previous fall, we said the first dumb thing we could think of. "Okay."

The night went on and we'd lost track of time. All I remember is laughing at every thing anybody said that night. We did a lot of laughing. Finally it was time to go back to the hotel. We had an early flight because we had an early evening practice waiting on us back in Austin. I felt fine all the way home. We talked about how much fun the Quarters had been and how we couldn't wait to go back. You have to understand that NO DRINKING was one of our team rules, so we were already feeling guilty about having violated something that had been so sacred just a year before, when we were lowly freshwomen.

We vowed not to tell anyone about our little taste test. Not a soul. Practice began and as we stretched, everyone asked how our trip was. We said fabulous and that we were already planning a sequel. About 30 minutes into the workout I asked Cara how she felt. "Not good," she said.

"Me either. I feel like crap," I said. "You think it's the drinks?" Cara asked.

"Way to go, Sherlock. I'm *sure* it's the drinks, are you crazy?"

"I think I'm gonna throw up," she said.

"Don't do that…people will know that we've been drinking."

"You're right," she said. "But I don't think I can hold it."

"You've got to. If you don't, we might get in trouble." There was nothing like getting into trouble in college. It meant public ridicule even if no one knew but you and your coach. We were sure that everyone else on the team was abiding by all the team rules (yeah, right) so we felt like we had let our teammates down by being these little heathens with apparent alcoholic tendencies. Above all, we wanted to keep the details of our trip on the down low. We lasted through practice but they knew. Everyone knew. We were two of the team's best shooters and all practice long neither one of us could hit a bull's eye with a soccer ball. But no one ever said anything. We used to say that our coach could have easily been one of those airport dogs because she could sniff trouble and drugs a mile away. Somehow she always knew who'd been up to mischief. Yep, she could have made a nice little side salary if she'd wanted to.

Low Rollers

Just like I don't drink, the same goes for gambling. When I was a junior in college, our team played in the 7-Up Desert Classic in the City of Sin, Las Vegas. After we won the tournament I took the rest of my per diem and went down to the black jack table on the lower level of our hotel. My goal was to triple my money before I headed up to my room at midnight. I got a few of my teammates to go with me to the casino but they only wanted to play the slots. I hate the slots. Too boring. Not enough strategy for me.

So there I am all by myself at the black jack table with a bunch of feisty but very cool senior citizens who were spending their social security checks. I started off on a roll and won three straight hands. Then I lost one. I'm not too panicky, so I kept playing. Around 10:30 some of my teammates came in from a movie and started messing with me, calling me Black Jack Fran. I had almost doubled my money and I was just where I wanted to be. Almost at my goal and on my way up to my hotel room for some serious room service. My girls kept egging me on, telling me to quit while I was ahead. But I didn't listen. I kept ordering cranberry juices and eating potato chips.

By then I was up to almost $300, a fortune when you were in college back then. My roommate, Yulanda, grabbed me after I won a hand and said, "Stop it. Right now. Get your stuff and let's go. You gon' lose it. That's the way it works," she said all nervous like somebody's grandmother. I said, "Nah, see that's how it works when *you* play. But this is me, baby. And I know what I'm doing." She shook her head and looked at me pitifully. "Okay," she said walking away. "You gon' be crying on the plane tomorrow, watch." Buh bye, I said and then I swiveled around and told the dealer to hit me.

By 11:30, I had gotten back down to $100, exactly what I started with but I was determined to change my luck. That was my first mistake. This is how people lose their homes and the shirts on their backs. Thinking they're gonna change their luck. So, me being the stubborn and competitive person I am, I stayed there. Determined to win it all back and then some. Around 12:30 a.m. I had $25 left. I could've just walked away with at least enough money to buy some lunch the next day. You would have thought I'd have sense enough to just get my happy butt up and go to bed since we did have an early flight. But I didn't. I played one more hand. And lost. I dragged myself up to my room and got right into bed. The next morning when I woke up I was ticked off. And I marched around the room throwing clothes in my suitcase, mumbling like crazy. Yulanda knew not to say anything to me but she just couldn't help herself. She just couldn't pass up the opportunity to tell me 'I told you so'. "Fran, how did it...?" she said. That's when I cut her off. "Don't you say a word," I said. So she kept her mouth shut. But I know she kept laughing because I could see her shoulders moving up and down.

When Gas Calls

Why is it that gas shows up when you least want it to? It doesn't happen when you're the only one at home or driving to the post office. No, it won't show up then. It waits until you're in the dentist chair. Or in an important meeting that could change your life. That's when it shows up. And you know where else it likes to make an appearance? The airplane. 30,000 feet above the ground. 1,000 miles from your Pepto Bismol.

Because Tammy Jackson and I have traveled most of our adult lives to foreign countries playing ball, we've racked up quite a few frequent flier miles. Sometimes on a road trip, we'd get free upgrades with our miles and get to sit in first class. This one day, I don't know what was going on with my insides but I had incredible gas. The kind that rumbles around in your intestines takes a couple of violent U-turns at the intersection of your colon and bladder and then heads south. That's the kind of gas I had. I know how much I hate it when someone lets one go in a confined area like an elevator or car, so in all honesty, I wanted to hold it in until we got to our destination. And the thought of bouncing up like a jack-in-the-box every ten seconds to go to the restroom just didn't sound that appealing to me.

Tammy and I were seated in seats 3E & 3F. And after holding it in for about 15 minutes, I just had to let one go. Remember, Tammy doesn't say a whole lot. She kept turning the pages of her Essence magazine. And I kept reading my book, hoping that because *I* didn't smell anything, that maybe this was one of those odorless farts that we hear so much about these days. Another five minutes passed and I had to let another one out. This one I smelled. And it was foul. Boy, was it rank. I kept my eyes on the same spot in my book, but out of the corner of my eyes I could see Tammy looking at me. Her eyes about to water. I turned to her slowly.

"Is that you?" she asked.

"Huh?"

"Is that you?" she asked again, knowing the answer.

I nodded yes. She just shook her head slowly, disapprovingly. "Don't make no sense," she said, continuing to flip through her magazine. "Can't you get up and go to the lavatory?"

"I could but I'm just gonna have to do it again as soon as I get back," I said trying not to laugh and breathe at the same time.

"Uh, uh, uh," she said again. "Don't make no sense. Something don' died in there, girl."

"I know, I think it's something I ate."

She frowned again. "Well, whatever it was…you might not wanna eat that again, okay?"

I laughed hysterically. "Yeah, yeah, you're probably right."

"Cuz, that don't make no sense. Uh, uh, uh. Don't make no kinda sense for somebody to sit up in here and do something that smells that bad."

Smiling Faces

If you're ever walking down the street in a WNBA city and you see your favorite player smiling, it's probably because it's a per diem day. No matter how crappy practice was or how bad a player is performing, they smile on per diem day. If you're a player and you played your cards right you could have a nice little stash, especially when your team was heading on an 11-day road trip. Those kinds of trips were good for at least a grand. But Tammy and I were always happy on these days because we'd hit up a lot of the homeless people in Houston or the people who sold the Houston Chronicle at the intersections we passed by on our way to one of our favorite post practice restaurants. We'd give them $20 on most days, $50 if we we'd had a good practice or were getting a day off.

Teammates would ask us why we gave our per diem away when these people could be buying alcohol and drugs with our money. I guess that's one way to look at it. But we always believed that our intent was more important than what these individuals might have done with the money. We always said something encouraging to them and for us, that was our little way of giving something positive back to the community.

Single Black Female Looking To Dump Mandatory Roomie

My biggest complaint heading into the 1997 WNBA season had to do with the league's lodging arrangements. In a word: mandatory roommates. I did not want a roommate. I like my space. I like to have the television and radio on at the same time sometimes. I like the air conditioner at sub zero temperatures when I go to bed. I did not want to have to look at another person every night before I went to bed and every morning when I got up. Her hair products would have to share space with mine. If she didn't like Oprah we'd have to compromise. I didn't wanna compromise. And I'm just not a Jerry Springer kinda woman.

Besides, I had to compromise all day in practice when I wanted to shoot and somebody else was open. I didn't wanna have to do it when I got home too. I mean, think about it. You spend three, four hours a day with the same teammates, the last thing you wanna do is go home with them. At least I didn't. But the WNBA was trying to save money and these were the realities in 1997. Even though I feel like I could probably live with anyone, except maybe Coop because she's a bigger chatterbox than I am. Actually, that's not true. In private, Cynthia's extremely calm and laid back.

But anyway, I didn't want a roommate. And even though I had close friends on the team, I did not look forward to rooming with anyone, I didn't care how close we were. Fortunately, at Houston, Van didn't get too involved in these minor matters, so we at least got to choose our own roommates. And I really appreciated that about him. On most of the teams I've been on, it always sorta happens that people hang out in twos, so the rooming situation was fairly easy in Houston. Tammy Jackson and I roomed together and it was perfect. At least at first.

Well, Tammy and I are girls but we have different extracurricular activities. She likes music, books and going to bed at a decent hour. And I like music, books and staying up writing on my laptop until I collapse on the keyboard. In other words, she spent many nights listening to me clack on my keyboard and I know it drove her crazy…because she told me it did. If I weren't writing, I was on the Internet, having instant conversations. That drove her nutty too, I'm told. This is why roommates are bad. Very bad. People should be able to nurture their own bad or unusual habits without offending someone else and with the way the league had it set up, this just wasn't possible.

Tammy's a very quiet person. So, when she started to lash out vocally, I knew I needed to make some concessions. "Okay," I told her. "I'll write until 10:00 or so and then I'm done for the night."

She liked the idea.

But when the urge to create hits a writer, he or she has to fill that urge. Needless to say, that little agreement didn't last that long. I came up with another solution. Sleep with your headset on, I told her.

She liked that idea.

But then I kept the light on because I was straining too much to look at my computer screen in the dark. Bad for the eyes. That didn't last too long either.

"Okay," I promised, "I won't get on the Internet after 10:30 no matter which coast we're on."

And I stuck with that. I didn't get on the Internet late at night anymore. I got on the phone instead. And as Tammy likes to tell it even today, I giggled under the covers like a little 12-year old. Tammy and I are good friends. And boy, did that first year put our friendship to the test.

CHAPTER 8

Teammates, Coaches and Zebras

It was during training camp 1997. We were practicing at this cozy little sweatbox, Houston Baptist University. Coop had been getting hacked all day in practice by every player in the gym. That's what happens when you're the shit. And sometimes when you're not, but especially when you are. She had been cussing us all out all day for fouling her. She had screamed at the coaches to start calling fouls or else there would be serious consequences. I was on the white team at the time and I egged them on, "Good D, ya'll…keep it game-like."

That's when it happened. Coop received the ball at the top of the key with me almost in her shorts with her. She caught the ball over her head, growled like a tiger and got ready to throw one ferocious elbow that had she followed through, might have knocked out my front tooth and made me look dangerously like Leon Spinks. "Girl!" she squealed looking me dead in my eyes. I rolled my eyes as if to say, "You ain't that crazy and you sho' ain't *that* mad." I had my elbow in her gut so she settled for slapping it off. I got no problem with an offensive player protecting her body as long as she doesn't lose her mind and start throwing punches. And Coop and I went too far back for that kinda nonsense. So, I didn't retaliate when she vigorously slapped my elbow down. But instead I did something that really gets most frustrated players' goats. I winked at her. And smiled. So what does she do? What a drive-by diva does, she ducked her shoulder and took my butt to the hole. *And* one.

Volcano Tammy

Like I said, Tammy's not too vocal so I wasn't really expecting her to tell me what all was going on with her when she was upset. But I sure didn't expect her to be a complete punk in practice either. This one day, we were both on the white team and she had gotten to a spot late on defense and this mistake had resulted in the other team scoring. So, I went over to her and said, "Say, man if you need me to stay a little longer until you get there…" She cut me off. "Back off, Fran. Just not now." I was shocked. Tammy seemed angry and had for at least a few days. "Cool," I said. I'm not gonna push the issue with a woman as big and strong as Tammy is. I like having teeth. So, I said, "*Excuse me*, I was just trying to help us not get the snot beaten out of us in this scrimmage."

I was trying to joke with her, trying to make her laugh. I can usually make Tammy crack up no matter how mad she is. But she was not in a comedic mood. That's when I knew something was really wrong. So, I let it go. When we got to Phoenix my plan was to just let Tammy have her space. I wasn't going to press the issue but it was really uncomfortable being her roommate with her acting so strange. She was still walking around with her lips dragging the ground. "You gon' tell me what's wrong or do you want me to just leave you alone?" I asked. "Just, just thangs," she said. "I'm not in the mood to get into it with you right now."

"Well, when you do get around to it, I want you to know that I didn't appreciate you going off on me in practice yesterday."

"I just wasn't in a good mood yesterday," she said. "Whatever," I said with a serious attitude.

She offered to bring me some food back but I declined. I didn't know how mad she was but I didn't want her dropping anything in my food that might cause me any digestive problems later on. When she returned she was still in a funk so I put my headset on and got on the Internet. A few hours passed and finally she blurted out, "Fran!" I heard her but I ignored her. Pretended my music was turned all the way up.

"Fran," she repeated it. "You know you hear me, girl." I kept pecking away at the computer. So, she walked over to the desk where I sat and pulled my right earphone out. "Fran Harris!"

"Oh, so you talking to me now? What do you want?"

She gave me those puppy dog eyes. "I'm sorry."

"Sorry? You think that's gon' fix it? As you would say, you went slll-ap off on me in practice yesterday."

"I know, that's why I'm saying I'm sorry."

I just stared at her like she was crazy because she was. "What is yo' problem?" I asked.

" I was just mad at how I've been playing?"

"So you take it out on me? I'm yo' friend. You know what? You got issues. Some serious issues, girl." We started to laugh.

"I was wrong, I know. But I really am sorry. Look, I brought you something."

I smirked at her as she tried to hug me. "If it's food, I ain't eating it…ain't no telling what you laced it with." She laughed as she took out a piece of pie she'd brought me. Dessert's my favorite course. "This helps," I said. "But next time you go off like that, I'm gon' beatcha like you stole something."

Where my girls at?

I think that a woman has a better chance of becoming President of the United States than being hired as a head coach in the National Basketball Association. How pathetic is that? A woman can run the country but she can't coach a men's professional basketball team?

I shouldn't have to tell you that I think that if a qualified woman *wanted* an NBA job that she should have it, period. But the Boys Club is a tough nut to crack. And I'm not so sure women even *want* to join. It all depends on how you perceive the role of coaching women versus men. It's like broadcasting. The first thing people wanna know when they find out that I'm a broadcaster is whether I cover men's or women's basketball. Somehow, I'm supposedly perceived to be a more legitimate announcer because I also do men's basketball. And quite frankly, I don't consider my work on men's NCAA basketball a promotion or validation of me as a broadcaster, although some women do. And men certainly do. No one can deny that from a business perspective, that men's basketball is bigger than women's basketball. And yes, a sportscaster is more likely to double, even triple her income by covering a men's event. But the battle I'm more interested in fighting is the one that is waging to pay women what they're worth, regardless of the event.

I used to be very critical of the league for not having more women as head coaches and I'm still quite concerned that the number of women WNBA coaches is on the decline. In 1997, there were seven women head coaches in the league and one man. Heading into the 2001 season, there are eleven (11) male head coaches to five females. And recently, one of the league's biggest draws, Cheryl Miller, left her post in Phoenix and rumor has it that she'll be replaced by, you guessed it, un hombre. No wonder most of the female college coaches I talk to aren't willing to make the leap from college to the WNBA. A lot of them aren't prepared for the harsh realities that coaching in the WNBA may bring. The travel is grueling. The media is relentless and often unmerciful. It's difficult for some coaches to adjust to waiving players during the tryout and training camp process. And without question, the uncertainty and instability that comes with high expectations is a lot for most people, of either gender, to withstand.

WNBA owners appear to be less patient than university presidents are when it comes to win-loss records. A coach who finishes .500 in Division I basketball may have little trouble having a contract renewed. But we've seen what happens to WNBA coaches like Linda Hill-McDonald of the Cleveland Rockers. After leading Cleveland to a strong finish in the inaugural season and then to the Eastern Conference Finals in 1998, she was bounced like a troublemaker in a night club after her 1999 Rockers underachieved and finished a miserable 7-25.

Women coaches had been like revolving doors in the Los Angeles Sparks organization, where the search for the right team-coach chemistry to lead them to their first WNBA championship seems to have ended with former Laker and NBA champion Michael Cooper. Penny Toler, former Sparks point guard turned General Manager told me that the entire management team is high on Coop and believe that the Sparks can win a title under his tutelage. I'd still like to see more women entering the WNBA coaching ranks but I also recognize the advantages of having NBA coaches in the league—they know what the pros are all about in every regard. They know that coaching at this level is like having one foot in the unemployment cemetery and the other on a banana peel. Therefore, they're more likely to leave assistant jobs and take a stab at the WNBA.

Many female college coaches have told me that they just aren't ready to give up the security of the college game for the uncertainty of the next level. Plus, with so many women vying for college basketball jobs, if a coach tries and fails in the WNBA, the competition to get *back* into the college game is much stiffer.

On the NBA front, I'm not as eager to see a woman coach in the NBA as I am to at least have her be given a real *opportunity* to do so if she so chooses. And to be clear, the bar is so high for women coaches that only someone like Pat Summit, with six national championships in her pocket, would have a genuine shot at leading an NBA team. And that's one reality that we've gotta change.

Sign of the Times?

I mentioned the WNBA coaching realities a few paragraphs ago, but can the same thing be said at the college level? What's *really* going on? Well, to understand what's going on in the WNBA we have to understand the landscape of women's hoops period, not just today but yesterday. According to a recent study, in 1992, 28% of Division I schools had no women in sports administration. In 1996, out of 305 athletic directors at DI schools, 17 were women.

The league now has a policy that says that at least one member of each franchise's staff must have women's basketball experience. Does that mean if you've been a manager for women's hoops, you qualify? Nope. Must be women's basketball *coaching* experience.

Now, I don't sit on the fence about anything but I'm wondering where this issue's going. I mean, I want women to hold these positions. And if one more person says the job should go to the best person for the job, I'm gonna barf. That has to be the most overused cliché in women's sports. People who say this apparently have no clue about the impact that the WNBA can have on women economically and professionally. No, we shouldn't put buster coaches in the WNBA but we shouldn't hire buster coaches in high school either. Overall, I think the individual franchises have done just fine with their hiring (coaches) decisions. I don't think it was the smartest move to give a high school coach the challenge of coaching professional athletes but that was nepotism at work in Los Angeles. And I don't think you go out and give every opening to a recycled NBA coach or every retired NBA player who thinks he wants to give coaching a stab. There's growing debate about whether having professional basketball coaching experience gives a candidate an edge and I say not necessarily. And just because somebody's coached a pro team doesn't mean that they were good at it and it certainly doesn't mean that they'll be successful in the WNBA.

I think there are a few key components to being a top coach in the league. One, talent. There's no substitute for good players who understand the game. Two, understanding of professional athletes, their motivations and how to get them to bring their best game in a season where there's a game every other night. A lot of the problems players share that revolve around coaches in the league, seem to center around three things.

First, they (coaches) treat players like they're teenagers. Second, some coaches act like teenagers themselves. And third, some coaches don't know how to relate to professional athletes. Some think that threatening players is the way to motivate them. Coaches don't realize that players often reflect their coaches. If the coach is professional and hard working, the players will be. If a coach plays mind games, that behavior invites mind games from the players. If a coach nurtures honesty and integrity, players will know that those two things are a part of the team's culture.

Don't Make Me Stop This Car and Other Silly Things Coaches Say

For the record, players hate to be lied to. It is the single worst thing a coach can do to a player. Sit 'em on the bench. Tell 'em not to take that 35-footer. Make 'em share a room with the player who has the funkiest feet on the team. But do not lie to them. I've played for coaches who were so afraid of hurting a player's feelings that they would make up stuff just to avoid telling them the truth. I once had a coach tell me that he wanted to alternate the starting job between me and one of my teammates because he thought that she would lose her confidence for the rest of the season if she didn't start. I stared at this coach wondering, do I have stupid stamped across my forehead? You wanna start her 'cause she's yo' girl, is what I thought. But what I said was, "You know coach, starting don't matter to me. I just wanna play."

I Just Wanna Play and Other Silly Stuff Players Say To Coaches When They Don't Wanna Ride the Pine

When you're in college, you're just a few steps away from being an out of control, totally messed up teenager. You think you got it all together because you don't live with your parents and no one tells you when to turn off the television. You think you've got it all under control but you don't. You try to be cool but you're not. And when it comes to ballin, you're just like a five-year old. You want a coach to tell you how wonderful you are and to pat you on the back when you come over to the bench. In the old days, when a player was recruited and a coach asked if starting was important to them, they'd say, "Coach, I just wanna play." That was between 1970-85. I don't know what happened but toward the end of the '80s, stuff started to change. Fifteen-year-olds were telling coaches that they'd better be a starter or else they're heading across country to the rival institution.

Another thing we do as players is answer questions that don't have answers. If a coach is mad in practice and she starts ranting, saying things like, 'Did she just grab another rebound after I told you that she'd better not touch the ball again?' Don't answer. This is one of those questions that don't have an answer that's gonna satisfy your coach. If he says, "What did I just tell you? Huh? Didn't I tell you not to let them get the ball inside to the post player from the baseline?" Don't answer. This is another unanswerable question. He *knows* he just told you that. He's not interested in your answer. He just wants you not to let them get the ball into the post player again.

See, the mistake that a lot of players make is opening their mouths when coaches are mad. Thinking that they're gonna outsmart the coach or prove to the coach that he doesn't know sugar from shineola. Even if you are smarter than your coach, the worst thing you can do is prove it in front of everyone in practice. So, it's best to just nod and silently disagree. And remember, most coaches think they know more than anyone else in the gym. It's not your job to give them a reality check. If you do, just go ahead and find a nice, cozy little spot on the end of the bench, 'cause your playing days are numbered.

Me & Phil Jackson

I hear that there are NBA coaches who hate Phil Jackson because he doesn't rave like a bloody maniac on the bench and up and down the sidelines like some folks you and I know. I don't buy it. I think they hate him because he's won seven championships without foaming at the mouth every time an official makes a bad call. Last season on a national sports report, a member of the management team of an NBA franchise was quoted as saying, "I'd just like to see Jackson sweat a little bit…arrogant son of…" He wanted his team to beat the Lakers so Phil would get upset. Please. Phil understands the spiritual side of peak performance.

Does he get mad at his players? Of course. He got after Michael Jordan and Scotty Pippen all the time. But does he disrespect his players? No. And therein lies the magic of Jackson. He gets good players to play great basketball. And he gets great players to play together. And that spells championship more times than it doesn't. But if you ask me, people are jealous of winners, period. And the fact that Phil can be poised and cool on the bench and still get results, just ticks off a lot of coaches. Coaches who feel that you need to yell and degrade players to get them to perform. I'm with Phil on this one. He's my mentor. And if I ever decide to coach again, Phil Jackson will be the second person I call after I hang up with my shrink.

You Better Start Hustling Or We Gon' Run Until *I'm* Tired

Every coach in America has used this tired ass line. Not me. My tired ass line as a coach was to call the team into a huddle and say, "I think it's so stupid when coaches stop practice when a team's not hustling and makes them run sprints, don't you? Don'tchu guys agree with me? Is that just insane or what?" For some strange reason, they always agreed. And for an even stranger reason, practice always seemed to pick up 200% after I asked this question. It's not psychology, it's logic, it's common sense. And it's honest. I do think it's stupid to punish players by making them run. Losing is punishment enough for players who truly have a champion's mentality. No amount of running in the world is gonna make them truly value the ball instead of turning it over. Sure, suicides (line drills) and other forms of torture may render a coach short-term results, but over the long haul, the only thing it does is tear down bodies and promote injury.

No, I don't blame coaches for getting a little chapped when their team misses five consecutive lay-ups or fails to get all the way through an offensive set without turning the ball over. But scaring them by threatening to make them run sprints is not the solution. And anyway, running as punishment is all about control. But like I said, a lot of coaches are about control. In fact, on the Coaching Aptitude Test, it asks a point blank question, "Are you a control freak?" If you answer no, the monitors snatch your test from you and send you right down the hall to the Careers in Fast Food window.

Jack of all trades, master of none

If I were running a WNBA franchise, I'd make sure that we had experts on our staff. In addition to our coaches we'd have an exercise physiologist, a sports psychologist, a strength coach and a nutritionist. And if we couldn't afford to have these folks on salary, they'd be our regular consultants. Here's why. Coaches are just that, coaches. Well, some of them. And that's fine. But some coaches haven't the foggiest idea about how to condition basketball players. So, who ends up getting hurt in the end? The athlete. Some coaches think that if they run you until your tongue is mopping the floor that they're doing their job, when in reality they're doing more harm than good. You wouldn't hire a cardiologist to work on your car, would you? No, of course not. So why do we let basketball coaches determine how much conditioning a team needs? This is the job of an exercise physiologist. The problem for some coaches—not all—is that they wanna control every single aspect of their teams. If a player looks tired, the first thing a coach thinks is 'she's out of shape'. And what follows this thought? The coach might suggest that the player get in some extra running or push herself more in practice. There's a difference between a player who works hard but for some reason just doesn't have the stamina that other players have. I've seen coaches humiliate players in practice, saying things like, "When I said hall ass, I didn't expect it to take you two trips."

Coaches rarely think that they overtrain their teams. But a lot of them do. A sluggish team doesn't necessarily mean that your players are out of shape. They could be tired. And you might need to back off of the four-hour practice the day before the game. What a lot of coaches fail to realize is that physiologically we're all built differently. And while we're on the subject of how we're built. I've seen many a strength coach do more to promote injury than prevent it by encouraging players to lift more than they are ready to lift.

What about the psychologist? Face it, some folks got issues. I ain't talking about the small issues we all have. I'm talking about *issues.* Issues they haven't dealt with before they got to the WNBA. Issues that will rip a team to shreds if they go unaddressed. Issues *they* can't even explain. So, a sports psychologist is a must. I'd want my players to be able to work through some of their stuff so the rest of us don't have to suffer. I've played on teams that desperately needed a therapist on staff. I've played with kleptomaniacs, compulsive liars, potheads, religious fanatics, sex addicts, alcoholics, and last but not least, Starbucks fiends.

Is Anybody Home, Coach?

Some coaches have brilliant basketball minds. But there are a few coaches out there who, when it comes to creating exceptional team unity, aren't always the sharpest knives in the drawer. Why is this important in the WNBA? Because in professional sports you're as much a manager as you are a coach and some coaches still haven't gotten with that. As a manager it's your job to create a positive working environment where the organization's values are nurtured. Some teams have never had conversations with their manager/coach about team values. And this is, in my professional opinion, why some teams will never be good. This is why some teams will never make it to the playoffs. Values are simple. What do you believe in or stand for? That's it. On a basic level, it means treating every player on your team with respect, if respect is one of your team's core values. Sometimes coaches want to receive respect but they don't know how to give it. They think that they don't have to respect players. That they're God. The ultimate authority figure. They think they should be able to say whatever they want, however they want, without consequence. That's what's so bugged out about sports sometimes. Some coaches take their leadership roles for granted. And a lot of them abuse their positions.

You wouldn't hear my ex-manager at Procter & Gamble screaming at me for not meeting my sales numbers one quarter. She might express her concern but she wouldn't pitch a fit the way some coaches do when players miss lay-ups. And another thing. As a coach, why would you kiss one player's butt and totally ignore another one? This is very bad. It creates classes within teams and that is always poisonous. Why would you, as the coach, allow one player to curse you out without some recourse? It just doesn't make sense. But this is the kind of stuff that goes on in sports, and yes, the WNBA, these days.

Every team I've ever coached has discussed team values. Things that we as a team and staff believed we had to uphold in order to be successful on the court. The first things I want to know about a player I'm coaching are her values. That's important to me. On a team, these are not things that you, the coach, decides you won't tolerate but rather things that your team agrees are best for the team. It's amazing what teams can accomplish when they are all on the same page. Most teams don't have the talent of the Houston Comets. Most teams are made up of good players who will perform at a much higher level in a system that fosters certain ethics and value systems.

Why Charlie Brown Would Be A Great WNBA Coach

Face it, Charlie Brown was a people person. He was gullible as hell but he was good people. He never beat Lucy down for moving that football every time he ran up to kick it and she pulled it away; and I love him for that. As a WNBA coach, half the battle is won by being a good person. Being a WNBA coach ain't hard. You've got the best players in the world on your team. The best facilities and the best fans. You make at least $200,000 a year. So, what's the problem?

The problem is that sometimes coaches complicate the hell out of their jobs. They over coach and under manage when what they need to do is chill out in the coaching department and learn to deal with their players better. I'm not saying that strategy isn't important because it is. Knowing what to do in a pressure situation will win you a lot of ballgames. Having your team prepared might even get you into the playoffs, but the key to success on the professional level (besides talent) is rapport between the coach and players. Think about it. Most WNBA players have been playing basketball since they could walk; they know how to play the game. But can you get those 12 superstars to gel and play together? That's where the magic lies.

The truth is, a lot of coaches are one person in front of the media and somebody else in private or in practice. That's why I always pay attention to body language. I rarely ask a player about her relationship with her coach because I already know what her relationship is just by observing. Plus, I'm a journalist, no player (except my friends) is gonna tell me exactly what she thinks about her coach. They're too afraid it'll end up on the air or in the newspaper. They're not that crazy. So, I never go there. I just watch and learn.

You can also learn a lot about coaches by watching how their player's react when they talk to them. Some players never make eye contact. That leads me to believe there's some fear and low self-esteem in the equation. Some players look their coaches dead in the eyes when they talk. That's respect and self-confidence. Some players never and I mean, never, interact with their coaches during a game. That player doesn't like that coach period. And when it comes down to it, most players will tell you that they'd prefer to like *and* respect their coach. But if given a choice, they'd take respect.

A player can't respect a coach who treats her like a piece of navel lent. It just doesn't work that way. But if you talk to your players like they're professionals, try to enhance their games, they'll listen to you. If you treat them like people—from the superstar on down to the watergirl—they'll run through asphalt for you. Charlie Brown would never mistreat his players because he knows that people are your most valuable assets. Chuck knows that if you took a billion-dollar empire away from someone, that they would be able to rebuild it in fewer than ten years because *people* build greatness.

Why Michael Cooper Was Coach of the Year

Los Angeles Sparks coach Michael Cooper is a good person. And his players genuinely like him. You can tell by the way they respond to his coaching. The next time you see the Sparks play, check out the way they look and listen when he's in the huddle. They're cued and they pay attention. Coop is also a good coach, he knows his stuff and he's played on three championship teams with the Lakers. So, he knows what he's talking about when he says defense wins championships. He doesn't play mind games with his players and most importantly, he's fair. Players like fair. They can deal with fair.

So, what do you get when you cross a coach that the players like and respect with a coach who knows the game? A team that will buy into your system, run through brick walls for you in pursuit of the team's goals. Players who'll get your back when other players (or the media) around the league try to clown you. When I was in Hawaii covering Team USA for ESPN, I heard one veteran player laugh about how shiny Cooper's forehead is when he gets all dressed up for his games. I gotta admit, he does have one of the more polished heads in the league. And Lisa Leslie laughed (because it wuz funny) but she quickly added, "Don't talk about my coach." Then she laughed some more because Lisa knows Michael's head *is* shiny. But I respect Lisa for that. She didn't have to speak up, but she made a statement. A lot of players wouldn't have done that. But then a lot of players around the league aren't that crazy about their coaches either.

A Word on the League's Zebras

There are some good refs and then there are some Zebras who just bite. During a late season game between the Los Angeles Sparks and the Minnesota Lynx I saw something that was just ridiculous. The officiating had hit an all time low, with the referees calling everything from sneezing on another player to running funny down the court. It was pathetic. I've seen some zebras let elbows fly and folks run over players like dump trucks. But in this particular game you couldn't hold your ground against an out of control offensive player because you would get the foul called on *you!*

On this one play, DeLisha Milton had just committed a foul and it was a bad one, so she was stewing. On the very next play, she actually did foul and the official called it again. But this time when she ran down to play defense she looked at the official who'd blown the whistle, leaned in his direction and clapped her hands as if to say 'good call' but definitely in a sarcastic way. Well, I thought it was pretty funny but this bozo didn't appreciate it and he got very triggered and gave D a technical. The technical was her sixth foul, which meant she was done. Sometimes crime doesn't pay in life and basketball. And officials tend to be very sensitive people, so you have to watch what you say to them. They make bad calls but they don't wanna hear about it from the players or the coaches. Especially the players. This is something that I think needs to change. I don't think players should headbutt or physically assault referees. I think that's inappropriate. But I do feel that players have every right to question a call if they think it's a bad call

Here's a sample of what officials were zeroing in on during the 2000 season.

1. **Unnecessary bumping of the cutter.** Last year a player making a cut across the lane from one box to the other could not do so without Gladiator gear. Officials are now saying that a defender cannot impede an offensive player's path with neither their forearm nor backside (butt) but instead must proceed in a denial position (one hand and foot in passing lane).

2. **Hands off, please.** The issue of hand checking is giving sly defenders like Teresa Weatherspoon and Shannon Johnson fits. Under the new rule, a defensive player (in the backcourt) may not so much as

fingerprint the dribbler. And once the ball is advanced into the front court, then any contact with the hand must be intermittent only. Contact with the forearm is the preferred method of 'hand checking'.

3. **Keep your elbows to yourself.** You probably have noticed a growing trend where rebounders do what we call 'clearing out', once they retain possession of the ball. When a player clears out, they grab the ball and then swing their elbows sometimes in a zig zag motion—no harm unless those elbows accidentally or intentionally connect with a member of the opposing team—and the official thinks it was mal-intended.

4. **Bodying up.** This technique has been around as long as Johnson's Baby Powder yet it's becoming less tolerable in the league. I like to call it 'tired D' because you see it used when players are too tired to get down and move their feet laterally. When an offensive player dribbles toward the basket and the defender decreases the amount of space between their body and the dribbler by standing almost upright and sorta riding along in the same space, this is bodying up and it's a no-no.

Lucy, Warrior of the Airwaves

If opinions ruled, Lucy would reign supreme. Here's a woman who believes that the world deserves to know how she feels about everything on the planet. She runs the Peanuts gang and nobody messes with her. And this is one reason she'd be a great sportscaster. In fact, she'd be the best analyst in the world. This role is all about knowing your Xs and Os and stating your opinion on a myriad of topics. You cannot sit on the fence and be a great color commentator. It just doesn't work that way. And we all know that Lucy is not short of personal commentary. In the business of being an analyst, if you don't have an opinion, you don't have a job. I don't care how cute you are, who your daddy is or how many producers you've slept with. Well, actually I hear that that last one works for some people. I wouldn't know. Lucy and I don't plan on sleeping our way to the top.

Master C

Not everyone can dress like an Untouchable and get away with it, but Cheryl Miller does it well. During the playoffs of the '98 season I had to do a double take because I thought we were filming the sequel to Goodfellas and Miller was making a cameo. Her long pinstriped suits were the talk of that season. I'm constantly amazed by what people talk about in post-game chats on WNBA.com or any other forums. Did you see what Miller had on? She dresses like a man, I think it's bad for the league's image. Have you seen the way she sits on the bench? Yada, yada, yada.

One day I got into a discussion with a broadcasting colleague about this very thing. Cheryl Miller and her impact on the WNBA. This broadcaster's position was that Miller should dress differently. Softer. My response was why do you care how Cheryl dresses. Why are you so insecure about who you are that you need Cheryl Miller to dress a certain way? I just think it makes people talk, that's all, she said. "People are always gonna talk," I said. "If Miller wore a solar orange, red and purple (the Mercury's colors) habit and a crucifix the size of a license plate around her neck, folks would still talk. What she was implying was that Cheryl's style brings out the homophobia in most folks. So, what? She wears ties and pants. Jesus wore a dress but I'm pretty sure he wasn't a cross-dresser.

C'mon, let's be honest for a second. It's not just Cheryl's dress that makes people uncomfortable. It's her persona that they're afraid of. A woman who gets emotional and goes head to head with anybody, male or female? Something's gotta be wrong, huh? This kind of scrutiny is nothing new for Cheryl. She's always been a little outrageous. I've known her for 16 years, played against and with her and I know that Cheryl's just being Cheryl. It's not an act. It's not for attention. It's who she is.

She's passionate about winning. Always has been. As a player she was high energy and flamboyant. She played to the crowd and even sometimes to coaches. About ten years ago, someone told the story of one game when USC was playing Tennessee. Cheryl was apparently getting off, *getting off*. She wasn't just having a good game, the girl was going off. And as the story goes, after one amazing offensive move to the basket in which she embarrassed somebody, Cheryl made the basket and then ran by the Tennessee bench, her arms spread eagle like an airplane and said in the direction of the Tennessee coaches, 'Get somebody in here to guard me'. Aircraft sound effects and all.

Don't let me get started on the things she says to WNBA officials. They are not Rated G comments, so I couldn't put 'em in this book. But this fact might explain why she leads the league in technical fouls, ejections and fines given to coaches. Here's the thing. You can't punk Cheryl. If you make a bad call, she's gonna call you out on it, which is so funny for me to watch personally because in private, Cheryl's very quiet. On the court she's boisterous and showy because that's her stage, it's where she's most comfortable.

Off the court, she's quiet, reserved and almost reclusive. Back in the day, she was one of the team's biggest pranksters. During one USA national team trip to Moscow in '86, Cheryl played practical jokes on everyone on the team. Shorting their sheets. Putting water balloons in their shoes. You always had to check your room, lockers and belongings if Miller were around because you never knew what ingenious ways she had set you up to be tricked.

Where's My Consultant's Fee?

Lin Dunn is one crazy woman. But she still owes me some money. First, let me tell you that my first experience with Dunn as a player was 13 years ago. She was one of our assistant coaches on the 1987 Pan American team that won the gold in Indianapolis. Cynthia Cooper, Teresa Edwards, Jennifer Gillom, Andrea Lloyd-Curry, Clarissa Davis, Sue Wicks and Anne Donovan were all on that team. And Lin kept us in stitches all summer long. She has an excellent basketball mind but it was her snappy one liners that we'd wait for every day in practice.

Lin's a good person too, which was why I was glad to hear that she'd gotten the head coaching job for the Seattle franchise. So, happy that I helped her out even before she was named the coach. That's why she owes me a few dollars.

You see, in the summer of '99, Reggie Miller and I had a little contest in which we gave the new expansion teams names, some of which were pretty clever. Only the cities had been named but no mascots or anything. So, we went to work to come up with some ideas to help these franchises out. Reggie came up with the Indiana Racers and among my outstanding selections were the Indiana Speed and the Seattle Storm.

A few months after the contest I worked a college tournament at Texas Tech for Lifetime Television and Lin's there. The night before the game a few of us go out to eat at this world famous steakhouse. Well, it's famous in west Texas. Anyway, Lin Dunn is cracking jokes and making us all laugh while she tries to get us to tell her who we'd take in the 2000 draft the following spring. Only I don't say a word, see. I'm keeping my cards close to my chest because I'm thinking about the fact that she still owes me for naming her team. I'm not about to give her any more of my brilliant ideas. She's on her own with her draftees. So, I keep eating.

The server brings the check to the table and we all reach for our cash but Lin snatches it from him. She wants to pay for our dinner and nobody there is dumb enough to insult her. So, we all keep mowing.

And that little name thing just sorta fades to the back of my mind while I'm ordering the blonde, caramel, chocolate coconut brownie dessert that the woman sitting next to us is mowin' on. "You know, Lin," I said. "I'd take that Vodichkova woman. She's really good."

The Teddy Pendergrass School of Communication

If I were an athletic director or the owner of a franchise and I wanted to have a successful team, I'd require that my coaches listen to Teddy Pendergrass before they coached my professional athletes. T.P. exemplifies what most players would love to see a little more in their coaches: someone who will be straight with them. Players hate guessing games. Am I gonna play or not? Are you gonna cut me or not?

I'm the type of person who likes direct communication and when it comes to high caliber athletes, I've found that they prefer this as well. Bush beaters drive me nuts. Just get to the point. And I've only come across two kinds of coaches: those who beat around the bush and those who are graduates of the Teddy Pendergrass School of Communication —they cut to the chase. If you are a person who has trouble speaking your mind or finding the words to tell people how you feel, then I highly recommend a little TP. In his sultry, rhythm and blues cuts, he told women exactly how he felt. Songs like "Turn Off The Lights", "Close The Door" and "I Don't Love You Anymore" are a few examples of his direct communication style. Now, you can't get more direct than that, can ya?

Players I'd Want With Me If I Got Stuck in Say, Amsterdam

In 1985, I was going on my first USA National team trip with the Jones Cup Select team. Our coaches were Theresa Grentz (Illinois) and Chris

Weller (Maryland). And the players included Suzie McConnell (Serio), Debbie Black and Lisa Becker. We'd trained in Piscataway, New Jersey and had spent a few days practicing in Germany. It was time for us to go on the longest part of our trip before the Jones Cup tournament in Taiwan later in the summer. We were heading to Warsaw, Poland for a few games. That's when I got the scare of my life. Theresa came over to us as we were about to walk into the airport. "Gather around everyone, I've gotta tell you something important," she said looking a little too serious for my taste. And if you know Grentz, you know it doesn't take a lot to make her look overly serious.

We all huddled up with the assistant coaches, managers and trainers looking on. "Can everyone hear? Okay, the United States Olympic Committee is conducting an experiment. They wanna see if a team can travel to Europe without supervision." All 12 of us started mumbling. Experiment? No coaches? Grentz came back in. "Now listen up because we don't have a lot of time." Our manager then handed her a pile of papers and passports. "You've got two minutes to decide who you want to take care of all the details while you're traveling. This person will handle everything—travel arrangements, hotels, and all game related stuff. This person will also coach you," she continued.

By this time my face was all contorted and my heart was beating like a drum. This was not what I'd signed up for and I couldn't believe the United States Olympic Committee was fool enough to send a bunch of twentysomethings into the wilderness without at least one real adult. But this was what Grentz was saying. "Okay, now who's it gonna be?" That's when my life passed before my eyes. All the players said, "Fran." And before I could say a word, I had an arm full of passports and Grentz was spouting off about what I'd need to do when we arrived into Warsaw.

I stood there catching flies with my mouth as she talked. I didn't hear anything, not one word she said. Not one syllable. All I had were visions of Nazi soldiers dancing in my head. "We're joking," she said as she burst into laughter. And then I looked around and noticed that Lynn Barry, the

USOC executive who traveled with us, was taking snapshots and had been since Grentz had first started her little practical joke. All the players were laughing and hugging each other. Me, I was leaning on a nearby pole about to barf. "Listen up," Grentz said. "You just picked your captain. I needed to know who you'd trust with your lives. That's the person who should lead you. Let's get going before we miss our plane."

CHAPTER 9

Sex, Lies & Videotapes, and Agents, Managers & Wannabes

Baby Daddies & Groupies

Each time I read about palimony suits filed against NBA players I wonder what is the world coming to? The men, some married, sleeping with any pair of Hanes that walk their way. And women sleeping with men who have wives, 2.5 kids and a Yorkshire Terrier at home. I don't get it. Actually I do get it, I just hate that it's that way.

In a word, groupies are taking over. And their desire to be on the inside is so strong that they will stop at nothing to get what they want. Sometimes it's an autograph. Sometimes it's sex. My brother asked me during my first season in the WNBA if the groupie thing was as bad for the women as it is on the NBA side. I don't think anything can top the things that go on in the NBA—women following them to hotels or showing up at their rooms wearing nothing. Booty calling is old hat in the NBA, I'm told by my friends who play in the league.

Have I had unwanted sexual advances? Yes. Are there scary people out there? Absolutely. I don't think there's anything you can do about groupies. People who want a piece of you because you're a celebrity. People who are just slightly mentally imbalanced. They'll always exist. But I do think all of us have some degree of control over what we attract. I really believe you get what you put out. If the energy you put into the universe welcomes craziness, you'll probably get some crazies in your mix.

So, you've gotta be careful who you hang out with when you're a WNBA star because there are some folks out there with some major issues. Issues that will make them create false stories about you. Issues that have them wearing your game jersey on non-game days. Issues that will make them never wash a sweaty T-shirt you gave them three years. Folks who spend a frightening amount of their disposable income on their favorite players' memorabilia. Folks who follow you after the game to see where you live and then leave little sweet nothings on your doorstep leaving you to wonder if you need to get a body guard. Some players have gotten letters from foreign admirers or prison inmates. Don't get me wrong, there's nothing wrong with a little fanfare, but WNBA athletes have to always be conscious of their personal security.

Just Say No

During the '97 season we were playing the Sting in Charlotte and I'd just come out of the game. I went to the end of the bench, got some water and took my seat. A few minutes later during a television timeout I happened to be staring into space when I noticed that a guy seated courtside directly in front of me was smiling at me. I came out of my trance and offered a smile even though I didn't know who he was. He waved and continued to look over at me. He looked familiar but I don't see things at a distance too well so I still didn't know who he was. But after about two minutes of squinting, I realized that the guy who was flirting with me was one of the NBA's biggest stars, who also happened to be very cute and one of the league's nicest guys. After the game he waited courtside as we headed into the locker room. When I emerged, some 15 minutes later, he was waiting. We spoke briefly and he asked where we were staying, but I didn't tell him. It was clear that he didn't' wanna come to the hotel to discuss the merits of switching on an on-ball screen and roll. Boyfriend was looking for some12-play. That's how stuff that don't need to get started, gets started. That's how rumors and unwanted children are born. And that's just how some NBA players get themselves caught up in a web of women and palimony suits. Some of them just won't say no. So, about two months later, I'm sitting on a plane and I read in a magazine that this same guy who couldn't watch the game for watching me, was engaged to be married.

The Breakfast of Champions

When I was in college in the late '80s, there was heightened interest, lots of research being done on eating disorders—mainly anorexia and bulimia. College women were literally starving themselves to death according to these studies. Why? Because they wanted to be thin—even those women whose normal body structures weren't predisposed to thinness. I've coached hundreds of girls and to my knowledge I only had one player who had an eating disorder and it scared me to death. During practices I'd notice that this girl would always have to leave to go to the restroom. I just thought she had a troublesome bladder or colon. I didn't ask and she never offered a reason. I thought maybe she was just trying to get out of conditioning. That's the kind of thinking coaching can reduce you to if you let it. Either way, I didn't say anything.

Whenever she'd ask if she could be excused, of course I'd say yes. Then one day she missed a few practices and I asked where she was. The players all looked away. So, the next practice I pulled her aside and asked her if everything were okay. She said yes and no. "I'm bulimic," she said. "And I've been really sick." I didn't know what to say. I was shocked and I didn't really know why. Maybe because I'd never had the disease slap me in the face. I'd heard that several athletes in college (men & women) had been bulimic but never anyone I knew personally. She then began to cry. "Please don't kick me off the team," she pleaded. "I'll get help." "Why would I kick you off the team?" I said. "Then I'd have no one to say follow your shot to."

I had a long talk with this player and her parents, who eventually got her the treatment she needed to get well. I've known players in the WNBA who eat candy bars for breakfast and a container of yogurt for dinner. This is not healthy behavior but nobody talks about it. We're scared to approach our friends who are doing these kinds of things. That's why I was so impressed when University of Connecticut star, Shae Ralph, talked openly about her battle with the disease. Thankfully, each year the WNBA brings in professionals to do seminars not only on nutrition—even though that has nothing to do with eating disorders—but also body image and the pressures to perform at the elite level. As taboo as the subject of eating disorders is, when a player lives on candy bars, somebody needs to start talking.

Agents, Managers & Wannabes

Everybody and their cousin was trying to get in on the action in 1997. I mean, everybody. The emergence of the WNBA brought out some shady characters from the woodworks. Folks who wanted to capitalize on the newfound novelty of women's pro basketball. Folks who were sure that they could make a quick buck off of the women. And we had our share of these folk in Houston.

It was the Sunday night after the open tryouts in Houston. Coop asked me if I'd go with her to meet with this agent slash marketing slash public relations type person who wanted to represent her. She wanted to take us to dinner and Coop wanted my impressions. We were supposed to meet at Pappadeaux Seafood Kitchen but she was late and instead an associate of hers met us. We talked until this person, let's call her Opal, showed up. It was an interesting meeting.

We had tons of questions for her. Questions we wanted reasonable answers to. Cynthia wanted to make sure that this person was going to work 24/7 for her because the league had made it abundantly clear that she was not in the WNBA's short or long term marketing plans at the time. And I was there to ask things like what kind of marketing plan did she foresee putting together for Coop. I asked if she'd already thought about logical spokesperson opportunities or causes that might be natural fits for Cynthia based on her passion and interests.

The meeting lasted a few hours and actually went fine. But I'd dealt with enough salespeople during my four-year career at P&G to know a smoke blower when I met one. And this agent slash whatever she was, was giving me smoke-blowing vibes and I told Coop this. But at the same time there weren't that many people who really believed that they could make money off of WNBA players so we didn't feel that there were that many alternatives. Coop signed with her and began working with her but it finally ended in a somewhat bitter divorce. We learned a lot of lessons through this experience. Mainly that sometimes you have to wade through the green, yellow, blue and red M&Ms to get to the brown ones.

"I Don't Like Your Hair..."

I walked out of the locker room after our first game against Phoenix in '97 and was immediately flagged down by this tall, handsome guy who said he wanted, no, needed to speak to me. I was already ticked off because Van had not played me enough minutes and I was in no mood for bull. Here's my card, he said. Call me when you get a sec. About what? I asked.

"I've got some ideas for how to market you. Actually, if you've got a few seconds I could talk to you now." I didn't have anything to do but go back to my apartment, call my friends and bitch about how through I was going to be if Van continued to screw me over with playing time, so I said what the hay. "Sure," I said. "Talk."

He pulled me over to a secluded corner in the hallway and it was all downhill from there. "See, I think there are some unique opportunities with you," he said.

"Like what?"

"Well for starters, you're attractive. You're not a hag like 90% of the women in the WNBA."

"I see."

"And because you're pretty, sponsors will want to hook up with you…but I'd like to see you do your hair the way you did it in the exhibition games…I didn't like it today."

During the Phoenix game I had worn my hair pulled back into a ponytail with a few strands of hair hanging underneath it. It kept it out of my face. The style he liked was when I pulled it back from my face with a nondescript, gray headband. I thought I looked like a milk chocolate Patty Duke when I wore it that way. Not the look I was going for, however. I was so taken off guard by his stupid, Neanderthal comments that I actually started laughing.

"Is that funny?" he asked. "Did I miss something?"

"Yeah, you did. Wait a minute, let me see. I have something for you," I said looking through my bag. He waited patiently as I rummaged through my things. Finally I pulled a quarter and a dime from my duffel. "Here you are. Go call somebody who cares what you think about her hair." With that, I got up and left. I looked back and laughed one more time though, you know, for good measure.

Please Be Kind and Rewind

Here's how it is when you play poorly in the WNBA. You get back home or to the hotel and the coach pulls out the videotape of the game where you had ten turnovers and shot 2 of 14. And you better believe she's gonna use that bloody thing against you until your team plays well enough to make him forget it.

In my 20 something years of basketball, I've never heard one coach say, "Let's watch the videotape of last night's game because I want you to see how good you were." Not once. It's always, "You guys stunk last night and I got the tape to prove it." Then in the tape session they always have the manager or assistant coaches, now known as the videotape engineer or coordinator, keep rewinding the tape to the play where you got broken down off of the dribble and looked like you were playing Matador D. It never fails. And then you're sitting in this room, thankful that all the lights are out so that no one will have to see how embarrassed you are. Or if you're like me, so no one will catch you making faces at the coach for clowning you. Or if you're like Chantel Tremitiere, you don't wanna get caught catching zees. Just kidding, Chan.

CHAPTER 10

Baby Mamas

Carla Pryor-McGhee

You can't tell me that Carla McGhee is not related to Richard Pryor. She's too funny not to be his cousin, half sister or something. Richard Pryor is the funniest guy I've ever heard in my life. Funnier than Chris Rock, Eddie Murphy, Steve Martin, Chris Tucker and Robin Williams put together. He is hilarious. Which is why I know that Carla's gotta be his peeps.

Judge for yourself.

I was taking notes during an Orlando practice right before the 2000 playoffs and it must have been payday or something because Carla McGhee was talking about her paycheck.

"At least we not on the Italians' pay system anymore," she said. Carla has played a lot of years of overseas ball and she apparently had endured some rather untimely paychecks. I'd heard about that kind of stuff happening to American players but I'd never played for a team who didn't pay me on time. But Carla had and she hadn't forgotten about it either.

"Girl, you know I was playing in Sicily, right?" Her teammates nodded, already laughing. That's what you do when Carla starts telling a story because you know that before it's over, something she's gonna say is gonna have you holding your side. She's stretching as she continues her story. "Well, one day I was needing my money and you know it's on payday when they act like they can't speak English, right?" All the players standing around are cracking up. We don't even know where the story's going but we are slapping our knees already. "They come to me with that uh, uh, me no speak-a-English shit. They know they know what the hell I'm talking 'bout." We're crying now because we've all been in a foreign country and had someone who speaks perfectly good English on one day suddenly lose this ability on a day when you need for them to know that the hell you're talking about. Carla continued. "Anyway, so I break it down for this fool. I say, I neeeeeeds my mo-ney. Soldi, dolare. Capish?" We're rolling as she gets closer to landing her plane. "Okay, so you know it's Sicily, right? So, everybody knows the Mafia's all up and through Sicily, so I go to the team manager and I say. "Listen up, Luca, or whatever the hell yo' name is, I neeeeds my money, see...and I don't give a damn who you gotta kill to get it."

ROOM SERVICE

It's about 8:30 on the night before New York takes on Houston in Game One of the 2000 Finals in New York. I'm in Cynthia and Tammy's hotel room and they've already ordered room service because I took too long to get up there. So, when I arrive, I order a burger mainly because I'm hungry and I know it's kinda hard to screw up a burger. Shortly after I hang up with room service, their food arrives and you know how you order something but when you see what your friends get, you want it? That was me.

Tammy had ordered a roasted chicken over a bed of mashed potatoes and it looked better than my burger sounded. So I called room service again. "I'd like to change my order please." The room service technician said, "Too late." That's when I went goofy on him. "That's the wrong answer for a service-oriented business." Coop fell off the bed laughing.

"God, I miss you. Oooh, I miss you. You are the only person I know who would say something like that," she said. Then she repeated it about three times laughing. Meanwhile, the room service guy, uh, food service specialist, is on the phone trying to tell me that I can't change my order because two minutes ago I ordered a burger. I tell him to let me speak to his manager and all of a sudden my chicken is possible. I hang up and think it's handled. That's when the phone rings again. We all look at it. Coop says, "Want me to get it?" Sure, I say, because I love it when she takes care of things, it's funny.

She snatches up the phone. "Hello?" she said. "No, no, no she doesn't want a burger. She wants chicken. No, no, we're not paying for a burger because she doesn't want a burger, she wants chicken. Let me...let me talk to your manager. I don't care...she just ordered it two minutes ago. Are you trying to tell me that you've already *cooked* the burger? That's what I thought. So...so she'd like chicken and that's it. Okay, we straight? Alright now, don't bring no burger up here." She hangs up the phone and I'm cracking up. She takes another bite of her crab cakes and looks at me rolling on the floor. "They don't know who the hell they messin' with, do they?" she said.

That's Just My Baby Mama: The Real Women of the WNBA

When my mother died nearly 20 years ago, I caught a glimpse of what it must be like to be a single parent. Tough. That's why I respect the players in the league who are raising their children by themselves. It's an honor to raise a child. But it's also a challenge in today's time. So, I got nothing but crazy love for the women who balance motherhood and the rigors of the WNBA season. As always, not everyone sees this situation as I do.

I got an email this summer from a woman who said that she didn't think that the networks should continue to do profiles on the mothers in the WNBA. 'Isn't that sending the wrong message?' she asked me. What message might that be? We're not here to judge people. Or crucify them for the choices they've made during their lifetime. And furthermore, we should applaud women who are loving, supportive single parents. Here we go again with that old double standard. When we see single fathers raising their children, we applaud them and never question how their 'single parentness' came about. But when we see a woman raising her child alone, we immediately think that the child was born out of wedlock or that the child was born to a teenage mother.

We should celebrate women who are able to excel in a demanding professional athletic environment and at home with their children. Did this woman think that by highlighting these women that we were encouraging premarital sex? That's not our place anyway. Or did she think that we were saying that men are dispensable? That's not our call either. Our job as broadcasters and producers is to develop compelling stories that illustrate how phenomenal the women of the WNBA are. It's not the network's responsibility to raise your children. That job is all yours.

No Sex In The City...or Any Other Location

The previous story did remind me of a little nugget involving my mother. When I was 16, a month or so before she died, my Mom called me to her room. She was folding laundry when I walked in. "Now," she said looking at me then back at the towels. "You and Sherman are dating, right?" I smiled because that was the first time she'd even acknowledged that I *had* a boyfriend. My mother was real good at that. Nothing was really happening until she said it was.

She continued with what I felt was about to be a real interesting rendition of the Birds and Bees. "Yes, we are," I answered. "Okay, so, I just wanna say one thing," she said. I braced myself. "No sex," she said. I sorta chuckled because it was funny to me. But my mother didn't think it was funny—the subject or her approach to it. "Huh?" I said because I couldn't get anything else out. "I said, *no sex*." And she made her eyes bug out for emphasis.

I looked at my mother and said, "Well, uh, you see, I don't want you to take this the wrong way but if I wanted to have sex, I mean really wanted to, which I don't, but if I did, your telling me not to would not stop me from doing it, Mama."

My mother looked at me like she was possessed and then she said, "Oh, Fran, you just gotta be so grown, don'tcha. Go on, get outta here." I wasn't serving my mother sass, well, yes I was, but what I was trying to communicate to her was that she didn't have to worry about me having sex because I wasn't interested in having sex with Sherman. But I was also trying to get her to face the reality that most teenagers, her daughter included, listen to what their parents have to say but they still have to make their own decisions. And I was no different.

CHAPTER 11

When In Rome: The Life & Times of American Players Overseas

One of the first things I noticed when I got to Italy in 1987 was my teammates' choice of underwear. They wore thongs. During practice and games. Long before Sisqo ever penned his nasty 'lil Thong Song, the women in Cesena were sporting those booty splitting things like nobody's business. I admit, I was intrigued. After all, I had trouble keeping my 100% cotton briefs out of my butt; I didn't know how they managed a thong for 40 minutes of basketball. So, one day I asked Rita, the oldest player on our team, "Hooooow do you wear those things during a game?" She shrugged her shoulders and replied, "Boh." "Boh?" I responded. Boh means a million things to the Italians. It can mean I don't know, who cares? What else is there to say? It's very versatile. So, I continued. "Doesn't it hurt?"

"Non, e molto comfortable." I loved Rita for mixing Italian and English because it was the only way I learned the language at first.

"Comfortable, Rita? Come' comfortable?"

Rita was a woman of many words but this one question didn't seem to warrant much of a conversation. "Boh," she said laughing as she dropped her thong, grabbed her cigarettes and headed into the shower.

Strong Enough For a Man But Made For Some Europeans

It's not that Europeans don't use deodorant, it's just that it doesn't seem to work very well. It was hell standing in a huddle sometimes. I mean, I don't mind a little B.O. (body odor) but 12 women standing in a semicircle smelling like a basket of freshly cut onions, was not my idea of a good time back then. Still isn't. At first I thought they didn't use deodorant at all. But I knew that wasn't true because I'd seen containers in their bags. So, one day while we showered after practice, I watched carefully. I was gonna find the person who was forgetting to put on deodorant and have a little talk with her. I sat on the side watching out of the corner of my eye. That's when I realized that it wasn't the lack of deodorant that was the problem. They were putting it on, it was just getting caught in the 4-inch long hair under their armpits.

Don't Pinch My Cheeks

I had my first real encounter with Italian men at a basketball game. I was inbounding the basketball on the sidelines. In Italy, the fans are often about two feet from the floor. It's a very intimate setting. On this night, as I passed the ball into play someone pinched me on my right cheek. Not the cheek next to my nose and under my eye. My butt! I was so shocked, that I just stood there with my mouth open. The official looked at me wondering why I wasn't throwing the ball in. But I couldn't. I was frozen. I looked around and there was a row of men looking innocent. The referee gave me a five-second violation and awarded the other team the ball. I shook my head and waved my finger at those men and ran onto the floor. They laughed. And after that, I started watching the fans a lot closer.

Can I Get An Extension?

When I was playing ball in Switzerland, the management persuaded me to coach a co-ed juniors team, called the 'minis', on Mondays and Wednesdays. I thought why not? Two days a week, can't be that bad. And plus, they were gonna pay me. This was during my first stint in 1997, right before the inaugural WNBA season. Because of all the drama with the management in Switzerland and everything being so last minute, I didn't have time to get my hair braided by a professional, so I asked Annette, ex-UT teammate, if she'd do it for me. I told her I didn't need anything special, just a few braids to hold me over for two months.

The moment I arrived in Baden I started having hair troubles. The braids *looked* good but they were awfully loose. No sweat, I thought. It's not like someone's gonna be pulling on my hair or anything. So I didn't give it another thought. I put my scrunchie on and went on about my business. There were only 30 minutes left in minis practice and I'd just given the kids a water break so that I could go over my notes for the last part of the workout. That's when it happened.

I looked up from my notepad and two dozen Swiss, Italian and German kids were walking towards me like a herd of cows. Some wore puzzled looks. Others stared at my head like it was revolving or something. I just thought it was a simple case of kids being kids so I said, "Are we ready?" They stared harder. "Sei pronti?" I asked in Italian. They began circling me. "What is going on?" I asked in broken German. That's when the one English-speaking girl emerged from the crowd. She had something behind her back. "What is it?"

"Fran?"

"Yes."

"Is this yours?" she asked as she showed me a single, 8-inch braid. I screamed and grabbed my head.

"Yes, yes it is," I said laughing hysterically. They all started to laugh too. And now they're circling me like they're doing some tribal dance.

"Your hair fell out?"

"Yes, well, no…see, it's not my hair." They frowned as I tried to explain in German, Italian and French why I was short one braid.

"It's not?"

"Well, sorta, I bought it. Yeah it's mine. Now, let's do lay-ups." They all paused. "Uh, Gabriela," I called out. "The braid, please."

They Hail You Then They Nail You

My original plan was to go play in Baden, Switzerland for about five years. It was the perfect off season plan because the competition was tough enough to keep me sharp but the practice schedule was light enough to keep me from burning out before I headed back to the WNBA in May. In Baden, at first they treated me like the queen I am. They paid me on time. They arranged a contract at a wonderful restaurant in town so that I didn't have to cook dinner every night. They secured a membership to a fitness center so I could lift weights or work on agility drills when we couldn't practice. In short, it was the perfect marriage. Until Thanksgiving Day 1997.

Part of my weekly ritual was to have a massage. On this day, the therapist crossed my personal boundaries and touched me in a way that I felt was inappropriate. It didn't help that this individual was also a member of our staff and related to our coach. A million thoughts went through my mind. I didn't know if it was my imagination or if he'd done it on purpose. All I know is that I was very upset. I felt violated. I walked down to the corner and called my friend, Claudia and asked her to meet me downtown. When she got there, I was standing in the rain crying uncontrollably at the bus stop.

We went to her apartment and talked for hours to try to figure out what I wanted to do. I was distraught, confused and very angry. Angry that people can be so ignorant. Angry that sexually inappropriate behavior happens every day and the perpetrators often go unpunished because people don't tell anyone. A million thoughts went through my mind, hours after the incident. How was I going to tell my coach that her relative had offended me? Would I be able to sit in the same room with the offender and not beat the hell out of him? I didn't know the answers to any of my questions. All I knew was that I was not going to be able to go to practice and see this person every day for another five months. No way. So I called the coach and asked to meet with her.

She came over and I broke the news to her. She was very sensitive to my feelings and encouraged me to come forth. The next day we met again but this time her relative was present. I explained again what had happened and of course, he denied everything. I told them both, "I don't care whether you believe me or not, I know what happened and so does he." I told the management of the team and they said that they wanted to conduct a formal interview and wanted me to stay until it was completed, which if you know anything about Europe, this could have meant months. I was not going to sit around while they took their time to look into the matter. I told them that they needed to make this a priority or else I was going home the very next day. They said that the earliest they could get an attorney to do the deposition was on Monday.

Ironically we had a game against the team we were tied for first with on Saturday. They asked me if I'd play and then added, 'the team shouldn't have to suffer.' They just wanted us to beat Bellinzona. So, I went to the game and didn't tell anyone a thing. Only a few people knew about the incident: the coach, Claudia, the management and me. Everything appeared to be normal except that I hadn't eaten in almost two days. None of the players had a clue and everything went according to plan. Except that we lost to Bellinzona and moved into 2nd place.

On Monday they took my deposition with Claudia in the room. I told them everything that had happened and they said that they would need to hear 'his side' before they could go forward. But wouldn't you know, that before they got to hear his side, he had a heart attack, further postponing matters. So there I am. Thousands of miles away from home. No family. No friends who knew me and knew that I'd never make something like this up. I was scared to death. And to make matters worse, folks were starting to show their true colors.

The management team that had treated me like royalty was now treating me like a foreigner and that hurt. People were saying that I was homesick and that I just wanted to go home, which was stupid because when Americans want to go home, they go. I know so many players who one day, decided they didn't like their situation and just packed their grip and vanished like a fart in the wind. No one ever knew what happened to them. They were there one day and gone the next.

A week passed and still no closure with the management. So, I decided that it was time for me to go home. I arranged to meet with the entire team the next day. When we all got together in the back of a restaurant, two days before I left, I found out that they'd already heard about the incident and many of them were quite angry.

About 15 minutes into the meeting, I learned that their anger had more to do with me breaking up the team than it did anything else. Some of them didn't believe that this man would do what I was accusing him of. They said that it had to be a mistake. They even went as far as to say that I'd made the whole thing up to get to go home early for Christmas.

I sat and listened to them tell me that I was ruining their lives, tearing down the fabric of the team and destroying their chance at a championship. I couldn't believe what I was hearing. It was classic. And it reminded me of all the horrible stories that I've heard about people who come forth when they've been abused. People rarely support the person who's been abused. They almost always come to the rescue of the abuser. That's exactly how abusers get to keep on abusing—because society protects them. Society says 'when someone accuses you of a heinous act, we won't believe them because you're an upstanding member of our community and you of all people would never hurt anyone'. I got news for you. Those are the folks you have to sometimes watch out for.

It was in that meeting that I knew that there was no turning back for me. My days in Baden were numbered. I went home and confirmed my airline reservations. There was no way I could play on a team with people who didn't support me or who weren't even willing to consider that this guy had behaved inappropriately. That was the day I knew that I was an outsider. When I was scoring 45 points, I could do no wrong. They all wanted to take me home to meet their mamas and daddies. But the moment I shattered the looking glass around their fantasy world, they nailed my butt to the wall.

Two days later, December 3, Claudia and I took a taxi to Zurich. She was the only person who believed and supported me. I know how difficult it was for her to be loyal to me, the foreigner she'd known for less than a year. The management wouldn't even provide me with a ride to the airport the next morning. It had snowed so overnight that we were afraid that even a taxi wouldn't be able to drive to Zurich.

I stepped outside of my apartment complex for the last time, and breathed the crisp, cold mountain air. I'd never seen a more magnificent sight. Too bad it was on my way out.

Got a light?

People think that I'm lying when I tell them that the Italians on my team smoked...often during the halftimes of games. But it's true. Three or four of my Italian teammates smoked and it tripped me out. One time during a pre-season game our coach, Paolo, was delivering the pregame speech and I heard a lighter flicking. I looked around and

Stefania, who we called Ugo, was puffing away. I looked at Alessandra, my interpreter. "What is she doing?" Ale laughed. "Exactly what you see." She didn't speak very good English either but she was much better at it than anyone on the team. "Smoking?" Ale nodded yes while laughing harder, probably at the squint of disbelief on my mug. "Smoking," she managed to get out. "Smoking? Who *smokes* before a basketball game, Alessandra?" I asked, now fanning the circles Ugo had blown my way. "Fran," she laughed even harder. "Your face. It's very funny. You should see it."

CHAPTER 12

Rings 'n Things: Inside The Comets Dynasty

The Comets Mystique

People look at the Houston Comets and think, how do they do it? They really only have three great players, they say. How can three players beat an entire *team*? I laugh because it makes me remember that folks said the same thing about another great team out of Chicago for a long time.

First, these are not just any ol' three players. These are three women whose weaknesses are so minute that they're difficult to exploit. If you stop one of them, you'll still have to contend with the other two. Rarely will all three have a bad game on the same night. When you play Houston, you have to forget about your ego, you cannot stop Cynthia Cooper in straight up, one-on-one coverage. You will never shut Sheryl Swoopes down because her points come from a variety of sources. And Tina Thompson is too complex to defend. She can shoot over smaller defenders and she's quicker than most power forwards who guard her.

I watched the Comets play all season long and each time I saw a team attempt to defend these players one-on-one, I'd put my head down. I knew where that strategy would take them. Back to the drawing board. I had the distinct privilege and displeasure of trying to guard all three of these players during the first season in practice. And then in the second season as a Utah Starzz. And both times were equally challenging.

But I've studied these three players, the first two seasons as a competitor, the second two as an analyst. And I've found that there are three ways to stop the Comets. One is to be completely focused on the defensive assignment of limiting The Big Three's touches. Two, double team them individually and make them give up the ball to teammates who aren't used to carrying the offensive load. And three, have a team that matches their talent, athleticism and mental will.

When Houston took the floor against the Orlando Miracle on June 28, 1999 in the Compact Center I witnessed one of the best coaching jobs I'd ever seen against the Comets. Carolyn Peck, who'd led Purdue to its first ever national championship in March of that year, was now at the helm of the Miracle and was showing why she was one of the greatest young coaching minds in the game.

Her Miracle team was on task. Completely unflinching in their mission: make the supporting cast accountable. The Miracle had aced the most important part on the Hoopology IQ test. They'd checked their egos at the door because it has no place on the court when you're playing a monster team with more offensive weapons than the Gladiators.

Orlando was one of the most athletic and gifted teams in the league that year and it would have been easy for them to get caught up in showing the Comets just how talented they were. Instead, they were completely harmonized in their pursuit of defeating Houston. They harassed and hounded the Comets for the entire 40 minutes. And they did exactly what they set out to do. They made the players surrounding Coop, Swoopes and Tina beat them. They couldn't. The Comets are just not the Comets without The Big Three, period. And at least one team in the league finally figured that out and did something about it.

The Clash of the Titans

The hype was unreal. Los Angeles had beaten Houston, not once, not twice but three times in 60 days. Just about everyone outside of the Houston city limits had nailed the coffin shut on the Comets 2000 championship hopes. They were all riding the Sparks bandwagon. And why not? The Sparks had opened up an industrial sized can of whup ass on nearly every team in the league. They were the team to beat, even according to Cynthia Cooper.

Coach Michael Cooper had prepared his team for greatness and they appeared to be ready to finally live up to their billing. But sometimes fans forget that the game is played on the hardwood, not in the newspaper. The Sparks knew that and so did the Comets. For the first time in the league's short existence, Houston was the underdog. They knew it and surprisingly, they didn't mind being in that position, as foreign as it was. For the first time in four years, the Sparks and the Comets had switched places. The Sparks were Goliath and the Comets, David.

As I watched the regular season series between these two teams, I kept thinking that Los Angeles needed to lose at least one game to Houston. And the worst thing they could have done was the very thing they're known most for: sweeping Houston during the regular season. Why was it bad for them to do that? Because by doing so they became the team that was *supposed* to win and that's a tough place to be in. In fact, Houston's the only team in the league that truly knows what that feels like. When the Sparks became the favorite in the Western Conference finals series versus the Comets, it was stand and deliver time for a team that really didn't know how to win in crunch time. Beating Houston during the regular season was fine and dandy and it made for great media brouhaha. But beating Houston when it counted the most was an unbelievable amount of pressure for a relatively young team.

Los Angeles was the only team in the league that had an athlete and a potential scorer at every single position. Michael Cooper said that at the end of the '99 season that he gave all of his players challenges to think about. For Tameka Dixon, his 4th year guard out of Kansas and '97 second team All WNBA, it was simple: drop a few pounds and show me what you got. She took care of the first part of Cooper's charge and her return gave Los Angeles back its best off the dribble player and one of the league's most lethal starting fives.

Leslie and Milton was the toughest high-low tandem in the league. As tough as Charlotte's Rhonda Mapp and Vicky Bullett used to be before Bullett was traded to Washington in 2000. In their offense, when one of them goes high to the free throw line or beyond and the other stays low, it usually spells trouble for smaller and slower defenders. When Leslie or Milton can't get by on quickness, they simply jump and shoot right over the outstretched hands of most centers (except Large Marge of Utah).

Leslie is the best center in the game and she showed it by putting up double-doubles nearly every night. But I thought Los Angeles' X factor in the millenium season was Mwadi "The Skywalker" Mabika. The woman who jumps so high when she shoots that defenders are left staring at the soles of her feet. Wadi has an incredible upside and she'll only continue to get better primarily because she hasn't been playing the game that long. She's versatile, strong and powerful. One of her greatest values to the Sparks is that she can guard quickness *or* size at the small forward spot—a rarity in the WNBA.

Bad Girls

Everyone thinks the Sparks are the bad girls in the WNBA. Like the Bad Boys of the late '80s, the Detroit Pistons, the Sparks have earned the reputation of taking cheap shots, giving that extra elbow, or shoving people for no reason at all. All in the name of the Lord according to some detractors. When DeLisha and Lisa were running around saluting during the 1999 season they made a lot of people mad. Fans and even some players in the league felt like they were taunting. Lisa and DeLisha said that they were praising God. Just giving Jesus the glory when they saluted after great plays.

I think folks were just mad because Los Angeles was beating everybody down. Some of them just couldn't get with Leslie. They didn't like her. Thought she played dirty. I guess I understand this a little. They see her on the court, throwing bows and swatting shots like they're mosquitoes at your family reunion. I've even been tangled up with Lisa on the court and her elbows are like thumbtacks. But having played with above average players all of my life, I understand Lisa's angst. She gets her share of hacks that the officials never call. So, she's just getting folks back when she puts her elbow in their throats. It ain't personal. It's bitness.

And let's talk about Sunshine by day, D'Nasty by night, for a second. DeLisha is not running for office out there on the court. You won't see her gripping and grinning and trying to make friends between plays. That chile is just plain mean. She's got a streak in her that you want on your team. But when you play against that girl, look out. She's coming atcha like gangbusters.

But Lisa and D combined have nothing on Sue Wicks. Sue's got more tricks than that silly rabbit. That's what playing ten years overseas will do for ya. Wicks is old school and these youngstahs could never outwit an old schooler. Sue knows the precise place on your jersey to pull so that the officials don't call a foul. She knows how to interlock her elbow with her opponent on a rebound so that they can't reach up when the ball eventually comes off of the rim. Wicks has mastered the art of running down court so close to her opponents that she's almost setting a screen while impeding their path to an open lane.

And don't get me started on T-Spoon. During the inaugural season Spoon and I went for a loose ball that I was going to get to first. But just as I was about to make my move for the rock, Spoon grabbed my shoelaces. So it was like I was standing in quicksand. I was so stunned that all I could do was laugh. I was so tickled that I couldn't even get myself together for the next play. The Liberty got the ball and Spoon winked at me. I coulda killed her.

I'm The MF Here

I'm the muthafucka here. The words flowed from her mouth like the gospel according to Coop. Cynthia Cooper had something to prove and she was not going to let anybody get in her way.

It was the first week of training camp of the 1997 season and Sheryl Swoopes had already declared herself ineligible for the season because she was pregnant. Coop and I were shooting around after practice. Just shooting the breeze about the team, the upcoming season and her latest woes with her then steady Italian beau, Gian Luca.

Coop understood her place in the Comets regime. She understood it well. First comes Swoopes, then comes Coop. At least that's how the league would have had it. And actually, Coop was assigned to Houston because Sheryl was going to miss the inaugural season to have Jordan. The WNBA wanted the Comets to have a marquee player with Sheryl out. But they had no idea that Cynthia was as good as she was. No idea.

Call it fate, call it destiny, but the stars aligned and Cynthia was right where she wanted to be: at the center of the cosmos. During her college and national team years, she'd played second fiddle to great players but it had been a long time since Coop had been a backup singer. And when she got to Houston and found out that she'd fallen into a situation that meant that she'd get to sing lead instead, she was happier than a three-year-old with a paint set.

As I said, we'd started to talk about the upcoming season and where she saw herself fitting in. That's where the muthafucka comment came in. And that's one thing you learn about Coop early on, she doesn't say things she doesn't mean. So, I figured what the hay…what did I know? Maybe she *was* the muthafucka. So, I kept rebounding her swishes.

That was four seasons ago and I guess Coop was right. She was all that and the whole picnic basket. The first, second, third *and* fourth season. But as the Comets began the third season the tide had somewhat changed. That spring, Coop's mom, Mary, had succumbed to breast cancer after a two-year fight and her best friend, Kim Perrot, the guard who had passed her the ball in the Comets' offense for two seasons, announced that she had a rare form of lung cancer. All of sudden Coop was talking about family and life instead of basketball.

When I spoke to her by phone one day shortly after her mom died, she sounded much different than she had that first summer. Somehow basketball had fallen into its proper place. It was now just something she did. No longer all of who she was. As her mom and Kim's conditions worsened, playing ball became harder and harder. She looked and sounded like a deflated balloon. She became a withering flower and understandably so. I was amazed that she kept going. That she didn't just crumble under the pressure. I asked myself, how does she do it? And of course the answer is that she didn't know how *not* to do it. That's not how she's built.

I was no longer looking at the same person who had marched into the clinic where we were having our physicals during the inaugural season. The woman who announced that she was a good vocalist and then proceeded to totally destroy Erika Badu's *Lifetime.* I had to check several times during the phone conversation to make sure I was talking to the same *muthafucka.* She assured me it was she who had inked a deal. And I assured her that she still couldn't sing. And then she reminded me that it was she who had just signed a record deal with Virgin Records, not I.

An Affair To Remember

A summer in New York is not nearly as bad as Phoenix in July but it's still pretty wretched with all of those people around. It was the day before the inaugural All-Star game and the league had put together the mother of parties. Every single person connected with the game seemed to be lodging at the Sheraton New Yorker because I swear you couldn't move an inch without smelling someone's breath.

Because of the compact summer schedule, the first All-Star game had to take place on a weekday, to most people's chagrin. And even if there is always something to do in the City most people I know prefer to do the Apple on the weekend.

The first order of business on Tuesday night, the eve of the game, was a dinner cruise at Pier 81. A long list of invited-only guests stood waiting for the rope to drop and the drinking to begin. Aboard the cruise would be the players and their agents. Coaches, women's basketball dignitaries and tons of drooling members of the media.

It was fun. A buffet style meal with lots of choices.

At the game the next day it was a media circus. The highlight of the entertainment was going to be bad girl, Whitney Houston, who was singing the national anthem. When the slinky songstress walked out onto center court at Madison Square Garden, right before tip-off, the crowd erupted like a volcano. She wore what resembled a silk warm up suit, remarkably similar to the Houston Comets' sweats. She sported that infectious smile and plenty of attitude. Then Whitney proceeded to rip our nation's theme song to itty-bitty pieces. Giving new meaning to what so proudly we hail and prompting most of us to pat our feet and say 'oh, say can you *sing!*"

A sellout crowd in any other city somehow never quite measures up to the grit and glamour of the one in the Gahden. The sidelines were laced with celebrities such as New York Liberty faithfuls, Gregory Hines and Stephen Baldwin, who high-fived and shouted from tip-off to the final buzzer. Tara Banks got her boogie on with some young girls during halftime. Tom Brokaw shot from his seat on numerous plays. Even Spike Lee had to pull in the reigns on his little girl, who seemed determined to get out on the court and show Teresa Weatherspoon how to really do a behind the back pass.

The Best Little Scorehouse in Texas

I'm thinking about filing for restitution from Sheryl Swoopes.

Over ten years ago, when I was an eager but lowly graduate assistant coach at The University of Texas at Austin, my boss, head coach Jody Conradt, gave me a simple enough charge. Get Swoopes to come and play her college ball here. As you know by now, Swoopes did *not* graduate from my alma mater. But she did attend UT. Confused? Here's the story of how the 2000 WNBA MVP, Defensive Player of the Year and league scoring champion almost ruined my life as a college coach.

It started when Conradt brought me into her office for a private meeting about a special player. She said she'd never wanted a player as much as she wanted Swoopes. After I reminded her that she'd said the same thing about me and some of my teammates, she recanted. "Not lately," she lied laughing.

I remember thinking, who's this Swoopes person and how did she get such a great basketball last name? Conradt gave me the quick rundown on Sheryl's prep career and then dumped a box of videotapes in my lap. "Here's her phone number. Call her but I have to warn you, she's pretty quiet." I would later learn that that was the understatement of the year.

I got home and stuck the first tape into my VCR and immediately understood why my normally low-key boss and former coach had bubbled over like a boiling pot when she spoke of Swoopes. She was angel hair thin and faster than a speeding bullet. And I was amazed that her

svelte body even made it through the 32 minutes of a high school basketball game without getting pummeled.

As I looked at her run past the other players, I wondered how she'd
make it at the college level with *that* buck-o-five body? I was sure that
the more muscular, brawny collegians would squash her like a fly at a
picnic. Then it dawned on me that the key to being crushed was being
caught. That was it. Nobody was ever going to catch up with her to lay a
body on her. Her agile, speedy and athletic frame weaved in and out of
traffic like a cop in heavy pursuit of someone who'd run a red light.

Conradt was right, Swoopes was painfully shy. And in those first few
conversations I found myself polishing my nails or balancing my check-
book as we sat on the phone in silence. I'd ask a question and she'd
answer. I'd ask another one, she'd answer. And this went on for oh, 30
minutes.

"How was your day?"

"Fine."

"What did ya'll do in practice?"

"Just a bunch of drills."

Finally I'd say, "Well, okay, I'll talk to you tomorrow."

"Okay, talk to ya then," she'd say.

I'd hang up thinking, 'Get her to *come* here? Hell, I'd love to just have
a conversation with her!'

The next day I went to Conradt and plopped down on a chair in her
office. "Are you sure we want this person?" She looked perplexed. I continued. "She, she doesn't even *talk*...at all!" I said.

Conradt laughed. "This is how recruiting is. They're babies...you've
gotta warm them up. She'll open up to you, that's why I gave her to you.
I think she'll really like you."

My mouth hung open and my eyes bugged. How was some kid out in
West Texas who I'd never met and who'd said all of three words to me,
gonna eventually 'really like me'?

"Keep working on her," Conradt replied. "I give you the ones we really want."

"Yeah, right, Coach," I said. I was born at night but it wasn't last night. "If you say so, but I'm telling you, she'd better be worth every minute I spend missing Knots Landing."

After that, my daily ritual became going to class, then to practice, to the library for study groups and then home to work on Project Swoopes. A breakthrough finally came. We talked for ten continuous minutes. I went to Conradt the next day all excited. "She talked! She talked!"

"Told you she'd talk to you," was all she said. "Is she coming?" she wanted to know. "We're getting there," I said. "She doesn't really like to talk about all of that." But secretly I was getting closer to getting a commitment from the girl whose 2-minute pauses I'd come to have genuine affection for.

Time passed and Swoopes and I were talking on the phone multiple times a week for hours on end. Mainly about nothing. That's what 17-year olds talk about—nothing. And I have to admit, at 23 years old I'd gotten pretty damn good at it. The national signing date was approaching and it was time for me to put my money where my mouth had been for the previous six months. The signing period is full of insecurity and anxiety. Coaches bank their whole season on signing a blue chip athlete. While scores of fickle, often psycho teenagers make their living stringing coaches along all fall only to sign with another school in the spring.

And as the college recruiting wars waged on, I began to understand why so many college coaches aged prematurely. It was during Project Swoopes that I decided that coaching *college* basketball, because of the recruiting, was not my calling. I knew myself well enough then to know that I would have no patience for a Fifteen-year old whose parents had let her believe that the world and my basketball program could ever revolve around her.

As we headed into the week of the signing day, I called Sheryl. "You coming here, right?" She giggled and said yes. "Okay," I said. "Don't make me have to come out there and hurt you." She giggled some more. I was serious.

The signing day finally came and Swoopes inked with Texas, a major coup. In the prior ten years, we'd gotten all the top Texas talent and by getting a player of Swoopes' caliber we were destined for multiple Final Fours. Plus, we'd once again beaten out arch Southwest Conference (now Big 12) rival Texas Tech by stealing a player who played her high school ball so close to that university.

That was the spring of 1989 but when Swoopes got to campus in August, I could tell something was not right. She seemed really unhappy. She was distant and despondent. She didn't really hang out with her teammates. We talked to her and found out that she was incredibly homesick. She'd never really been away from home and Austin, which could easily swallow her tiny hometown whole, was a long way from Brownfield where she'd grown up.

A week later, she transferred to South Plains Junior College—in Brownfield—because at the time a player would have to sit out one year if they went to another Division I institution; two seasons if they transferred to a college in the same conference.

Two years later though, irony would raise its ugly little head, and Swoopes, who'd by then broken tons of scoring records at the junior college level, would sign with Texas Tech. In 1993, two years after she became a Red Raider, they would win their first national championship with Swoopes exploding for 43 points in the title game.

So, how ironic is it that when the WNBA was born that my prize recruit and I would be playing on the same team, playing the same position with lockers right next to each other? Pretty ironic, let me tell you. No, we never talked about the recruiting thing. Some wounds are best left unopened. But I seriously thought about mentioning it to her in Hawaii when I interviewed her during Team USA's blowout of the USA Select team. Who knows? Maybe we could have had a moment. You know, like old times.

Changing of the Guard

A Comets player was shooting a free throw at a decisive moment in one of their last regular season home games. It was one of those games that should not have been close but it was for some reason. I sat in a trance staring at the other end of the floor. In my usual spot—third seat from the left—at the media table near the visitor's bench in the Compaq Center. Coop, who was in the game, though not shooting the freethrow, walked over directly in front of me about 30 yards and made her hand in the form of a phone.

"Call me," she mouthed. I nodded in acknowledgement. That's strange, I thought. She'd never done that before. I thought it odd but didn't really think much about it. Sometimes I didn't go to the locker room for interviews after the game. So maybe she thought she wouldn't get to talk to me after the game. Anyway, I drove back home that night wondering what had prompted Cynthia to ask me to call her *during* a game. She'd never asked me to call her during a game. So, a day or two passed and then my phone rang.

"I guess you already know this," the depressed voice on the other end said.

"Know what?"

"Cooper's retiring. It's in today's Houston Chronicle."

"So that's what she wanted to talk to me about," I said under my breath.

"Huh?"

"Oh, nothing," I said aloud to this avid Comethead. "What did it say...I mean, why?...did she say why?"

"Something about it being time, but I think that's bullshit. What's going on?"

I'd made it a habit to discourage people from asking me for the 'scoop'. If Coop had gone on the record to say that her retirement was because it was time, then that's what she wanted the public to know. Did I believe it? Sure, I believed it. But I also knew that it was only part of the reason. In a perfect world, would she have retired after just four seasons in the league? No. She'd planned to play at least a few more. But I also know from experience that external factors sometimes speed up that 'it's time' thing. Sometimes things get so whacked that you wanna say 'later for this'. And that's where Cynthia was.

Her announcement rocked the women's basketball world. And we all held our collective breaths. Emails from dejected fans poured into my mailbox. Folks wanting some kind of insight into this seemingly erratic move by the player who had redefined the off guard position for the past three years. Power went out all over the world because of people were hanging out for hours on the Internet message boards. Some people were sad, others were mad. Some begged her to stay. Some sang "Hit The Road, Jack".

When I began to hear from various sources about what was going on in the Houston Comets camp, I knew that Coop would not hang around much longer. So, when she made it official, I went on the record as saying that I believed her. Later that day I called Coop on her cell phone. "What the hell's goin' on, girl?"

"I'm tired, Fran," she said in a barely audible tone. "It's over."

"Just like that?"

"Just like that."

"You *are* tired," I said. I knew how much basketball had meant to Coop for the last 17 years. I'd watch her go from a role player on USA National teams in the mid-'80s, playing behind Teresa Edwards for three summers straight. I'd watched her blossom into a superstar on Italian soil. And I knew that the thought of going back to being a role player after being the 'woman' for 14 years was not going to go over well with her. And I didn't blame her one bit. But I also didn't think she was being asked to take a back seat to anyone. To me, it's all perception. And perception, for most of us, is reality.

And since Coop perceived that Chancellor was asking her to assume a lesser role in the Comets' regime, then that's what she acted on. It was painful. And it got ugly.

My first summer with Cynthia Cooper was on the 1986 World Championship/Goodwill Games team. We had gone through trials in Colorado Springs together and had made the final cut, which meant that we'd go to a training camp where further trimming would be done before we left for Moscow, Russia, in June. About 20 finalists assembled in Raleigh, North Carolina for the first leg of training camp. In case you don't know this by now, these teams generally make up the nucleus of the Olympic team every four years. So, expectations of us were extremely high.

The spring before the tryouts we'd beaten USC enroute to our first NCAA championship. Excuse me, did I say we'd beaten them? I'm sorry, we shellacked their asses. All World Cheryl Miller had fouled out after not playing very well. But not Coop. Coop had been sensational. And she was the one we'd been most concerned with heading into the game. It's always that player who doesn't get as much publicity that you have to watch out for. They're the ones with that necessary hunger. They're always motivated. And they're always dangerous.

It was during that '86 summer that Coop started driving us all crazy singing and rapping. Folks would ask me to ask her not to sing. She'll listen to you, they'd say. And I'd tell them that no one was going to tell her not to sing. I could ask. I could even plead. Offer incentives and money, but she was still gonna serenade anybody who was within, oh, 30 miles. That was just her way.

If you've read her autobiography, *She Got Game*, then you know that those USA national tours did not provide her with enough opportunities to shine. Part of it was the system's fault, part of it hers. There was no question that Coop was talented. But her mouth often turned people off. And unless you cared about her, as I did, you just wanted to put a muzzle over that mouth of hers. Sometimes I wanted to do it myself. But coaches are funny. If your personality turns them off, they're not as likely to give you a chance on the court no matter how good you are. It's like their way of controlling you. If I can't make her shut up at least I can bench her. If I can't stop her from voicing her opinions (that's me), then at least I can introduce that butt of hers to some Pine Time. It's wacky, but it's true. And some of the coaches we had during those summers, just couldn't get past Coop's verbal flamboyance.

No player has gotten more headlines, praise and/or criticism. And no player has gotten more mileage out of her WNBA career than Coop. Granted, there are lots of things to like and not like about all of us. To the public, athletes are like those plastic figurines on a birthday cake—a display piece for people to stare at endlessly. Something for people to pick apart, play with and discard when they no longer get enjoyment out of it. But Cynthia understands this game. Not basketball, but the *game*. She knows that one day you could be the Catch of the Day and in less than 24 hours, you're leftovers. Yeah, she knows about this sorta thing all too well. Which is one reason she came to the WNBA with one goal: to get it while the getting was good. No more, no less.

And whether you like her personally is irrelevant to what she's meant to this game.

Her in and out, swivel dribble move (catch it if you can) may not be the quickest in the league but it's utterly unstoppable. During the '99 campaign I gave her the nickname Drive by Diva because her baseline penetration continued to leave defenders reaching for their prescription strength Tylenol. Her ability to split defenders and shoot with either hand still leaves coaches shaking their heads and wringing their hands. And if you're guarding her and decide to respect the drive, she won't hesitate to promptly administer a facial from the great beyond. It didn't just start in the WNBA, although no one really knows this because ten years ago the best players could only make headlines on foreign soil. Coop's basketball legend actually began in college.

Go back, if you will, about 14 years. The 1986 Final Four championship game was being played on CBS. It featured the best player in America at the time, Cheryl Miller, against the best team in the land, the 33-0 Texas Longhorns. We knew Miller's talent and zest for the game were off the charts, but the player we were most concerned about heading into our first title game, was #44. The rapping 5'10" guard with the Gheri Curl who you always heard before you saw. Cynthia Cooper was the one our coaching staff told us to keep a close eye on.

After graduation, Coop, like most of us, headed for Europe or Japan to continue her playing career. And it was in Parma, Italy, that she became the Prima Dona of pallacanestra. In Parma, Coop was given the freedom to become. The go ahead to evolve into the player she was destined to be. At USC she had played in the shadows of Miller and twins Pam and Paula McGee. During the college offseasons we labored together on ultra talented USA National Teams. Back then Coop was an eager member of the team's supporting cast, a role though, that she was anxious to step out of once those grueling tours to places like Russia and Yugoslavia were over.

When my Italian team met up with hers in our first of two meetings in the fall of 1987, I knew Coop was about to explode. She had matured as a player and the offensive freedom the Italians gave her truly made her a Michelangelo of hoops in no time. We talked about how great it would be to have a league in the states. And I wondered to myself if the world would ever get a chance to see how great she had become.

She boldly took the Italian league to frontiers it hadn't planned on going. She led the league in scoring numerous times, won MVP honors and once scored 63 points on some poor team. And in a move that I know was motivated by wanting to stay in the Italian media, she learned to speak the language fluently. All we needed was Coop on Italian. Mamma mia! It was not uncommon for me to turn the television to Rai Uno, an immensely popular Italian station, and see Coop's mug working some reporter's last nerve in Italian. They ate it up. As if this woman needed any encouragement.

I don't think any group of people is better at making you feel like a queen than the Italians. Instantly, she became an icon. It didn't matter that she wasn't Italian or even that she was African American. The Italians love a champion and they don't care what package they come in. Cynthia may have learned to be the center of attention at home in Watts, as her mother has said on many occasions, but she perfected the skill on the basketball court in Italy.

Her friends are few. Unlike her critics, they know that she's also one of the most giving, loving, sensitive human beings on the planet. Not that you'll ever see any of this. You probably won't. But it's there. I've talked to and interviewed lots of athletes and have found most people to be fairly fake. In private, Cynthia's not superficial. It would be impossible with the life she's had. She knows pain as intimately as anyone. She knows struggle too. Full of herself? Without a doubt. But there are worst things to be. Like a liar, a cheat or a serial Internet Bulletin Board basher. Few can deny what she's done for her sport in four short years. Four time WNBA finals MVP. Two-time regular season MVP. League leading scorer two years straight. Olympian. WNBA scoring leader.

She didn't create the raise the roof gesture and she wasn't the first one to do it on our team in '97, but nobody really paid much attention until she started doing it. She drove millions of fans and critics to ponder the meaning of the waving hand gesture she made after she sank a basket.

Toward the end of the season, I had a long conversation with Coop and found myself feeling particularly nostalgic as she talked about walking away from the game that's given her and WNBA fans so much joy.

FH:How can you just untie the sneakers and walk away from ballin', when it's given you everything you ever dreamed of...especially when you still have so much to give to it?
CC:Because it's time. Time for me to move on. I've given the city of Houston and the Comets my all and it's time for me to go.

FH:A lot of people have criticized you, saying that you're selfish, that you just can't stand to see someone else reap the glory. Is that true?
CC:I have nothing to prove. People are going to say whatever they want, it's human nature. It's not that I'm selfish, I just don't feel that I should have to take a supportive role. I feel that I've proven myself. I've been asked to be in the background and that doesn't suit me. I'm not happy in that role. That's not who I am, it's not who I've been in a very, very long time. Have I accepted it? Yes. But accepting it doesn't mean I have to like it.

FH:So, why not go be the forefront player somewhere else, on another team...why give it up completely just because you feel that Houston's not the place for you anymore?

CC:I'm tired, Fran. Mentally, I've been through so much. I don't wanna have to start over somewhere else. There are other non basketball-related opportunities before me—and I'm excited about those. I can walk away with my head held high, I've had a fabulous career. Yes, I've still got a lot of game left but I wanted to start and end my basketball career right here in Houston.

And somehow, Cynthia Cooper in any other uniform, just doesn't feel right either, does it?

Ode to Lil Kim

I met Kim Perrot several years before we became teammates in Houston in the summer of 1997. But I'll never forget our reunion meeting. It was Mother's Day and St. Thomas Gymnasium was lined, I mean, wall to wall, with hundreds of players who wanted to be a Houston Comet and make it in the WNBA as much as I did. The trials were scheduled for both Saturday and Sunday, but when I'd spoken to Van Chancellor the week before tryouts, he'd told me that he wouldn't dream of asking me to come on Saturday because it was going to be a meat market. He said I'd earned the right to come to the last two practices of the last day and that would be good enough for him.

Keep in mind that the last time I'd seen Van Chancellor was when my Texas team had beaten him, Alisa Scott and Jen Gillom in the '86 Midwest Regional Finals on our way to an undefeated NCAA title. He'd later remind me that we cost him his one trip to the Final Four. I remember thinking that either he was letting me come to trials on the last day because he thought I was really good, therefore, he wouldn't need to see a whole lot or else he thought I was really trash and didn't wanna have me there stinking up his practices for two whole days.

So, it's Sunday and I walk into tryouts and Kim's the first person I see. We were cordial at best with each other. I noticed her because she was the speediest person in the gym but I also thought she dribbled too damn much! I thought to myself, 'If me and girlfriend get to play on the same team, I'm gonna have to let her know.' Well, it didn't take Van long to see something in me and Kim, so he called me, Coop (Cynthia) and Kim to the sidelines at the end of the first session. And in his Southern dialect he said, "I'm liking what I'm seeing…I want Perrot (which of course he pronounced as Per-ROW) at the 1, Cooper (which he pronounced Cupper) at the 2 and Harris (hard to screw that one up) at the 3. This could be the Comets' starting perimeter team, he went on to say.

So, off we go to face our scrimmage opponent, knowing that whoever it was, they were going to get sufficiently creamed. And I was right. Kim was sensational. And most of us were mesmerized with her athleticism and quickness. But I was about to discover that Kim had something that I liked even more: grit. After one scrimmage in which she had missed me on several wide open passes because she'd turned the ball over for, you guessed it, dribbling too damn much, I walked over to her.

Now, I'm 6'0 and Kim was 5'5 on a good day. "Hey," I said. "You need to give it (ball) up a little sooner." Kim looked up at me and smirked. "You just keep gettin' open, you'll get the ball." I swear I wanted to laugh so bad when she said that. I thought, who's this little pipsqueak talking like she's about 6-foot-7? But I loved her from that day on. And we quickly became good friends. We played together for the rest of the try-outs and I knew that she was gonna either drive Van crazy with her sometimes erratic and reckless play or he was gonna love her to pieces for what she would do to demoralize ballhandlers throughout the league. Turns out it was both depending on which day of the week it was and how many turnovers she'd had in the last game or practice.

The effect that Kim Perrot had on our team could never adequately be penned or described. Her courage and tenacity are what I remember most. And she loved a challenge. One practice Van took Kim off of the red team and put me in her spot. He charged me with bringing the ball up the floor against full court pressure. No problem, I thought. Until I saw that Kim was going to be my defender. I was doing just fine at first because I could hold her off with my size. But just before I crossed half court, she swiped the ball right from me and blazed down for a layup. Practice ended promptly and Kim walked over to me with this expansive grin. "Fran Harris, don't try to bring the ball up against me, girl." And every time I see a guard bring the ball up court in the Compaq Center in Houston, I think of Kim. Every single time. Sometimes I cry, but most of the time I just smile and think about that day in training camp when she affirmed that I'd never be half the point guard she was.

As August 19th, the anniversary of Kim's death approaches, it's hard for me to believe that the woman who always called me by my first and last names, is gone. You just don't think about people your age dying. Or you try not to. It's hard to sit in the Compaq Center without seeing her running around picking every WNBA guard's pocket who thinks there gonna rob her team of another championship. It's hard not to hear her and Van jaw about which of them is the better dominoes player.

I've got some great Kim memories, on and off the court. In '97 R&B artist Joe recorded a hit song called "The Things Your Man Won't Do" and Kim loved this song. I mean loved it. Each time it came on the radio she'd start bobbing her head and saying, "Yeaaaaaah, turn that up. That's the jam there, Fran Harris." And if I agreed she'd laugh and say, "Whatchu know about that? You don't nothing about that, girl."

When she didn't believe something you'd said, she'd turn up her lips and say, 'Yeah, right' about ten times in a row while you were talking. You couldn't even finish telling your story because you were laughing too hard at her facial expression with her lips all contorted. When she'd call us into the huddle on the court she'd get this really high pitched tone that dogs would have responded to. She'd say, 'Let's go, ya'll. We're not playing our type of game. We gotta pick up our D. Defense on 3. 1-2-3. Defense!'

But my favorite Kim memory has to do with the raising the roof gesture. Van didn't mind us celebrating after a good play or basket as long as we could get back into our defensive setup quickly. This one game, we were in a full court press and Kim had stolen the ball before the ball-handler got to half court. She took it down for a layup. Then she slammed the ball down on the floor in the middle of our basket and proceeded to raise the roof so fast, it looked like she had been put into fast forward mode on a VCR. It was hilarious. I mean I can still see her doing it. She *had* to get that celebratory gesture in. Boy, we teased her about that one all season long.

It Takes Money, Honey

My fondest memory of the championship game versus New York in 1997 was actually not on the floor but on the bench next to Yolanda Moore. Yo, Swoopes, and I were cheering and cutting up during the whole game because we hadn't gotten to play, and we had to find some way to entertain ourselves. We had taken the lead but New York had started to cut the deficit. We were saying the usual things teammates say to teammates who are losing their fight out on the court, "Let's go, ya'll". New York continued to claw and cut into our lead. That's when Yo looked over at me with those Bambi eyes and said, "See, now they fuckin' with my money!" I died laughing. We laughed for five straight minutes about that one. And then we wiped our eyes and cheered our little hearts out. After all, we had a $10,000 bonus check that we were sure already had our names written on it.

Why New York No Longer Loves Rebecca Lobo and Why They Love Becky Hammond

During the first year in the league, Rebecca Lobo was the toast of the town. Little girls, especially white ones, loved Lobo. And with good reason. She's nice, congenial and a good basketball player. But in New York, good is never good enough. The WNBA had hailed Lobo as the Second Coming and by golly that's what the fans at Madison Square Garden expected out of Lobo. The first year, they tried to make Lobo into something she was not: a superstar at the pro level. It was unfair to Lobo. She was never going to be able to live up to those lofty expectations. So, what happened? The fans at MSG started booing her and the media ripped her to shreds. But why? Lobo didn't ask to be lifted up as the league's savior. She was 23 or 24 years old. Hell, she hadn't even peaked as a player. She hadn't played overseas. Barely got to play in the '96 Olympic Games, but she was supposed to lead the WNBA to the Promised Land? Go figure. Now they love Becky Hammond and I totally get it. Becky's one of the nicest, most wholesome-looking women in the WNBA. Becky represents the underdog in all of us. She's the little guy that you pull for because she plays hard and has fun. And fans appreciate that in a player. Because I'm a shooter, there aren't many things more exciting to watch than a great shooter, and Becky's becoming one of the league's top threats. So, the fans in the Garden adore her. Today. But look out, Becky. That could all change in the twinkle of an eye. Ask Rebecca.

Why Houston Loves Tina Thompson

When the lights go low and the spotlight comes on and the public address announcer says, "#7, Tiii-naaaah Thomp-sooooooooon", the fans in the Compaq Center go absolutely berserk. Tina gets a louder ovation than Swoopes or Cooper. Few players in the league get the kind of appreciation Tina gets in Houston. They believe she's one of the most underrated players in the league. But they're wrong. Yep, you heard me right. Tina's not underrated. People *know* how good Tina is. Even the folks who put Natalie Williams on the first team instead of her. I don't care what anybody says, Tina Thompson made first team All WNBA

2000. She may not have been *awarded* the honor but she earned it. She says that it didn't bother her but I think it did. Knowing Tina, it'll just fire her up for next season.

In fact, there are a few things that you don't ever wanna do to Tina. One is park too close to her Mercedes Benz. Two, ask her not to wear her lipstick in games. And three, point out on national television what she needs to work on as a basketball player.

It was the second week of the 2000 season and Tina Thompson was obviously quite fired up about something when I walked up to her locker for a post game interview following their June 6 game versus the Sacramento Monarchs. Because before I could say boo, she sprang from her stool and got in my face with this expansive but somehow intimidating grin.

"What's that you said about me Fran Harris?"

Tina Thompson and Kim Perrot are the only two people in the world who call me Fran Harris as if it were one word. I couldn't imagine what she could have been referring to and I reminded myself that she was at least three inches taller than I am. Nevertheless, I poked out my little chest and went for it.

"I have no idea what you're talking about, Tina Thompson," I said. "But I'm sure I meant it."

"Something about the way to stop me is to make me put the ball on the floor, was that it?" she asked.

"Yeah, so?"

I'd just sat through the SAC game marveling at how adept she had become at dribble penetration. So, I knew I was about to get an earful.

"So, how you like me now?" she asked in a way that let me know that perhaps her feelings had been hurt by the comments but also in that cocky way that athletes talk when they know they've at least temporarily, silenced their critics.

"I like ya," I answered laughing. "These days I'm liking yo' game a lot actually." Apparently so is everyone else in the WNBA basketball and media community as she's starting to move farther out of the shadows of The Big Two.

Perhaps the most remarkable aspect of Thompson's improvement is that for the first time in her short professional career she has consciously worked to improve her game. Although extremely talented, before the 1999 season, she spent most of her offseasons flying back and forth from Los Angeles to Houston because she was so homesick. And a lot of times after practice in '97, instead of staying to get in extra shooting, Tina would head to the Galleria and work that mall like nobody's business.

But after coming out of the blocks strong in the inaugural season, landing a spot on the All WNBA first team for two years straight in '97 & 98, Thompson admits that even she was less than impressed with her performance in the 1999 season. "There was just a lot going on—not to make any excuses—but it was difficult to focus on basketball," she said.

Not many people know it but Thompson was very fond of Kim Perrot. In fact, she was the first person on our team in 1997 to call Perrot the nickname Pee Wee. Kim didn't allow anyone else to call her by that name. But when Tina said it, it was just fine. Kim's illness took its toll on Tina from the jump and I don't think she ever recovered. Her game suffered tremendously and I never saw her get into a rhythm in '99.

"I was miserable last year. And on top of that I wasn't playing well, which made it worse," she's said on numerous occasions. But now that all seems like a distant memory to the 2000 All Star MVP. An honor that Thompson was genuinely surprised to receive.

On a team that showcases two of the world's most explosive scorers in Cynthia Cooper and Sheryl Swoopes, Tina has had to bide her time. Setting more picks for Swoopes and Coop than she'd care to number herself. But her patience has paid off, and she has been refreshingly humble about her accolades even though she's already one of the most decorated young players in the league. She leads the Houston Comets in rebounding with seven per game. Her 44% 3-point shooting accuracy is the best on the team. And her 17 points per game, ties with Cooper behind Swoopes, the Comets' leading scorer at 21 ppg.

All of this for a woman who wants to pursue a career in criminal justice and who told me that she wasn't even sure she was going to be drafted in the WNBA that first year. But she was. And for Houston Comets fans, the fact that the top pick of the '97 draft is only 25, means lots of hoop years left—even though last fall she said that her own retirement might not be that far away.

"Yeah right," I said. "Retirement my butt…you ain't but 12."

"Fran Harris," she said. "I'm not kidding…and you know how I am when I make up my mind about something."

Don't I, though.

CHAPTER 13

Hot Cocoa For My Soul: Things In and Around Basketball That Help Me Keep Life in Perspective

Hold On, I'm Coming

In 2000, some players were so unhappy with the salaries the league offered them that they chose to sit out rather than play for nothing. Leading that group was Jennifer Azzi, who played with the Detroit Shock in '99. Azzi came out of retirement after her agent negotiated a bigger compensation package that included a trade to Utah and a personal services contract designed to provide her with extra income opportunities in the community. Cindy Brown, who would have been playing with Azzi in Utah in the 2000 season decided that she wanted a bigger hunk of cheddar from the WNBA and when they said no, she did too. Ditto for Andrea Congreaves who was a starter in Orlando last year.

Other WNBA players simply held out in training camp to see if they could get a better deal. Tammy Jackson was one of those players. And I don't blame her. Tammy has made a significant contribution to women's basketball, most recently on three of the Comets' four championship teams. She deserves more respect than she's gotten these past four years in the salary department.

I don't know where the Comets would have been in 1997, 1999 and this past season without Tammy Jackson. I jokingly told her after they beat Los Angeles in the Western Conference Finals that she should propose a Tammy Jackson Rule to the Comets management team. Under this rule, she'd get to just hang out during the regular season. Practice if she wants. Go on the road if she feels up to it. And then have Van call her on or about July 21. In that conversation he'd say something like this. "Jackson, the playoffs are coming and we need you to get off the golf course and get back to Houston. Make sure you're in shape, we're gonna need you in about two weeks to deliver those ungodly (that's his favorite word) performances you've been known to give us in late August."

Tammy thought it was a decent proposal especially since it meant she could skip training camp and still get some glory at the end of the season. I think Van would go for this idea. He told Tammy at the beginning of the season that she didn't have to worry about a thing. To practice if she felt like it. If she didn't, no biggie. He told her to make her health a priority because he was gonna need her down the stretch. Van ain't crazy. He knows a good thing when it knocks him over the head. And I liked that he was taking care of my girl. At least somebody was.

What is most amazing about Tammy is that she's the only player I know who can keep herself mentally in the game to the point that she can be awesome in the playoffs even after riding the pine for most of the regular season. Van's right this time. That's just ungodly.

You Are Getting Verrrry Sleepy...and Goofy...and Cranky

If you've ever paid close attention to the players on the bench, you've noticed that there's a definite protocol over there. There are certain things that must happen on the bench whether you're at home or on the road. For example, you've gotta rag on somebody who's on the floor.

Don't matter if she's wearing the same uniform as you, you've gotta dog somebody out before the night's over. It's just a rule. One of those things that we understand as the caretakers of the bench.

For instance, if a player's sporting a new hair do that's not working for her, you might hear somebody say, "Girl, who got a hol' of huh head?" The whole bench laughs. Even that player's best friend. That friend might say something like, "Ya'll ain't right. And don't talk about my friend." But she still laughs. It's just the way it is over there. Another thing you might hear is, "Is the ball coated with a film of fire? 'Cuz girl- friend didn't let it sit on her fingers for two seconds before she let it fly!" The bench cracks up again. The person who said this is also often the first person off the bench to tell that same ball hog, 'good shot, baby'. That's just how it is. Another thing that happens involves a coach who walks down to the end of the bench to complain about what's happen- ing on the floor.

Well, you're sitting on the bench and you're thinking, "Why is she telling *me* what a bad shot that was, I didn't shoot it and furthermore, I ain't even in the game" or "Why does he keep yelling about nobody being on the baseline for helpside…either put me in the game so I can do something about it or shut the hell up." Of course, most of us never actually said any of these things but we sure thought them. And when the coach walks back to the front of the bench, the bench players almost always roll their eyes and crack on the coach. It's not personal, it's just the way things flow from the best seat in the house.

A Little Known Fact...

A coach told me something a long time ago that proved prophetic. "You wanna know the reason you were able to score so many points during your career here?" Because I'm automatic," I thought. "Nope," I actually said. "Because your teammates loved you. If they didn't like you, there's no way you would have been the leading scorer on this team three years in a row." I pondered the wisdom in that statement for years. And when I got to Italy to play in my first professional basketball season, I understood what this coach had meant. Part of the reason I'd had such a great season in Italy in '87 was because my teammates liked and respected me. They didn't mind that I took most of the shots in the offense because I treated them with respect and shared the ball (and any glory I received) with them. Now, had I disrespected them, not learned to speak Italian and acted like a prima dona, things would have been different, no doubt about it.

So, my coach was right, and I'd seen this work on at least one other occasion during my career at Texas. Remember my friend Annette who got me the hook up with the agent to go overseas? The one who braided my hair before I went to Switzerland? That Annette. She was a phenomenal post player who stood only 5'11—five feet of which were the skinniest legs this side of the Mississippi. Nette's greatest asset was that she could run all day long, she played hard and she had springs in those kiwi-sized calves. But more importantly, we adored Annette. Every single player on that team loved them some Annette.

She was always upbeat and she loved, absolutely craved practice, a fact that made you look bad if you decided to slack. Anyway, whenever I'd get the ball on the wing, if Nette were on my low post box, I'd look for her. If I were leading a break, I'd look for those lanky legs and that big mouth saying, "I gotcha left, Real (one of her nicknames for me)." And when we graduated in 1986 she finished as the all time leading scorer at UT—male or female—with nearly 3,000 points. Now that's love.

Very Superstitious

Stevie Wonder wrote a song in the '70s called "Superstition". Its words were prophetic for athletes all over the world. *When you believe in things that you don't understand, you suffer.* And he was on point. Athletes are quirky. All of us. And we have superstitions that are just plain nutty. In college, one of my teammates wore the same sports bra in every single game. That thing was so ratty by the end of the season, I was surprised it didn't fall apart. Thankfully, it didn't have a whole lot to support or it would not have lasted from November to March. Janeth Arcain steps onto the court with her left foot first. Tina Thompson wears the same shade of lipstick every single game. Teresa Weatherspoon wears 11 cornrows. I've never seen Sophia Witherspoon without a piece of gum in her mouth during a game. And after the movie *Flashdance* came out in the '80s, I listened to that title track, "What A Feeling", before every game that season. Just plain nutty.

I had a college teammate, C.J., who would never 'split a pole'. In other words, if you were walking with her and the two of you approached a telephone pole, she'd insist that both of you walk past it on the same side. So, of course, I made it a point to split it every time we walked to class together. Just to drive her crazy.

So, you say, what's so crazy about superstitions? Think about it. If superstitions were so powerful, you'd never perform poorly when you carried out your ritual, right? Right. Nothing bad would ever happen, right? Ah, but there's the flaw in superstitions. Nothing can guarantee you 100% success. Not lipstick, not a fly soundtrack and not a hairdo. Some nights you're just gonna shoot 23%. Some days you're gonna be a step slow. That's the nature of sport. That's why we have winners and losers. We're human and humans are not perfect. But superstitions aren't all bad, are they? Not unless you're a rabbit and you're tired of being hunted so some crazy person can cut your foot off to make them shoot free throws better.

Coaches Say The Darndest Things

He asked my best friend if I were pregnant. Why else would I be nearly fainting in the middle of a two-hour practice? All the other players simply leaned over in exhaustion. Holding their shorts. Grasping and gasping for that one last breath before he would blow the whistle for us to take off running again. I lay plastered to the wall as my eleven teammates took off like wild horses. I could barely hold myself up. Thank goodness for doorknobs. I couldn't run another suicide. I was sure I would die if I took another step. What was wrong with this guy? Didn't he know that this was the first time I had ever done any kind of conditioning?

He whistled and I took off in slow motion. "Go, Harris. Let's go," he yelled in my direction.

I wanted to cry but the tears wouldn't come. Only a pitiful, shrieking sound, as I made my way to the other end of the court while my agile and athletic teammates zoomed past me to make it to the end line before the buzzer sounded. I fell to the floor. Splat! No more. Not one more. The gym fell silent. The only thing I could hear was the sound of my heart beating like a drum. A few seconds later one of my teammates came over to attempt to peel me off the floor. "C'mon, Fran, you can do it."

"No, I can't...go on. Just leave me here. Tell my mama I love huh and I'm sorry I changed those 3s to 2s in the third grade."

I looked in the direction of our coach but everything was fuzzy. Like he was standing there but there were 12 of him. I think my coach just had pity on me or else he was scared that he had killed me, because he ended practice and told my teammates to take me downstairs to the locker room. It was then that I found out that he'd asked my buddy, Angela, if I were pregnant. Pregnant? Me? I wasn't going near a penis! I was too scared of getting pregnant.

For one full week, I went through the identical exercise. Run and fall out. Run and fall out. It had stopped fazing my teammates. They just kept running. Stepping over me when appropriate like a car driving over a speed bump. Coach Blair would just stand on the sidelines and shake his head in disgust or pity—I stopped being able to distinguish after a day or so. Finally, he approached me directly. His face red with frustration. His eyebrows wrinkled with worry. When he heard about my bloodline, he had bragged to all the coaches in the district that he had the next great ball player on his team. "Harris? You gon' make it?"

Both of my older brothers had gone to my high school. Both had been superstars. So, I was expected to be this great player. Another All-State Harris. Only I didn't know the first thing about greatness outside of the classroom. I didn't know the first thing about pushing myself physically beyond imagination. I couldn't even run a sprint without nearly fainting. But something happened to me the day he looked at me and asked me that question. It dawned on me that although he was asking me a question, he felt he already knew the answer. I could tell he had given up on me. *Harris, you gon' make it?* Something clicked inside me.

I smiled and looked away. I didn't know how to admit failure. I had never really been faced with anything as hard as basketball practice. I could spell pertinacity by the time I was seven years old. I could tell you all about the Pythagorean Theorem by the time I was 12 years old. But at 15, I couldn't make it through a two-hour workout without puking. What was wrong with me? I gotta tell you, I wondered myself.

I looked him dead in the eye and through my dizziness and fatigue, I stood straight up and said, "Yeah…yeah, I am."

What if…

I've never been to jail but sometimes I wonder what might have happened had I made certain choices in my life when I was younger. When I was 17 years old and about to make the all-important decision about where to attend college, a funny thing happened to me. A Midwest college coach had been recruiting me and I liked her and her staff a great deal. Had they been closer to Texas I might have gone there.

As the recruiting process started to wind down I had some decisions to make. Which schools would I visit? Did I want to start or go somewhere where we'd have a chance to make it to the NCAA tournament? Did I want to be a part of a rebuilding process or did I want an established program? It was a lot for a 17-year old to deal with.One of the things that helped me narrow my choices was the organization that governed women's sports in 1982. Under the AIAW, Association of Intercollegiate Athletics for Women recruiting rules, a prospective athlete had to pay for her transportation to and from a recruiting trip. This was before the NCAA days when an athlete could get five paid visits to any college in the United States.

Anyway, this head coach was very sly. She had her assistant coach do the shady work. They said that they were really interested in having me come and play for them and I told them I might like that too but that there was just one problem: how was I going to get all the way to Missouri? I wasn't driving and I didn't have the money to fly.

Her reply stunned me. "Just get here and don't worry about it." I wasn't sure I was hearing this person right so I got very quiet on the phone. "Did you hear me?" she asked. "No, no I didn't," I said.

"I said, if you can find a way to get here, we'll take care of everything," she said.

I played it off and quickly told this coach that I had already made up my mind. I was going to Texas. I got off the phone and tried to make sense of what had just happened. And I was scared. Had this coach just offered me money and reimbursement once I arrived on her campus? She had.

I later played on a national team with a player who had gone to that same university and when I mentioned the recruiting incident, she smiled and said, "Girl, you should've come...they take care of you there." Incidentally, this university has yet to make it to the Final Four, and that coach is no longer running the program.

Making the Grade

I was a model student until the second six-week grading period of my third grade year. That's when I went a little wild. Wild was not a good thing in the Harris household. There were things that just were not allowed: dishes in the sink, bad manners and sub-par grades.

Bad grades were high on my mother's list of no-nos. I was supposed to bring home only 1's (A's). An occasional 2 was fine but twos were not to get the idea that they were welcomed at 1028. This one six-week period I'd let my mouth runneth over during class and hadn't listened very well to my teacher, Ms. Haynes. She was a stern, spectacled woman who wore her glasses too low on her nose so that she could look out over the top of them and scare you. Anyway, my excessive conversation had resulted in some less than stellar marks on this sixth week report card.

I already knew that my report card was not going to look like the previous six weeks had. So, I braced myself when Ms. Haynes passed them out. She shot me a disapproving look and said, "Your mother's not going to like that one bit Frances Harris." There goes that first-last name thing.

Ms. Haynes was right. Mama wasn't gonna be down for the quantity of squiggly numbers on my report card. Two 1's, Two 2's, and Two 3's. I was in deep doo doo and there was no denying it. I tried to figure out how I could avoid getting into trouble when I got home. I sat all the way through lunch trying to devise a strategy for avoiding a whuping when I walked through that door. I decided that I needed an extra day to think it all through. Fortunately, this was still during the days of hand-written grades on a 3X5 card.

I took my report card home that day but I didn't dare show it to my mother. Boy, that was the scariest day of my life! I kept thinking, what if she finds it and then thinks that I was trying to hide it from her? Above all, my mother hated being lied to. She despised deception. Almost as much as she did 2's and 3's on a report card. So, I was also trying to avoid lying to her since it was like the absolute worst thing you could do in my house.

To avoid committing the ultimate sin, I hid my report card in my book bag and prayed that it would be safe until I could come up with a way to deceive my mother. The next morning I woke up with a plan. I'd take the report card to school. Then I'd steal a few moments during the day to doctor it. I'd make the 3's into 2's and although I wouldn't win any awards at home for the 2's, I'd still be more likely to not get my butt tapped.

Since I couldn't remember what color the marks were, I found two pens—one black, one blue—and sneaked them into my book bag. My mother had not stopped driving me to school even though we lived only three blocks away because I guess she didn't want anyone abducting me. Sometimes I got to walk home from school because I guess she felt safer. There tended to be crowds of kids walking my way at that time of day.

That morning in the car I tried to avoid any eye contact with her because I knew she had that radar thing that mothers have. And I knew if she took one look at me, she'd know something was up. But I also knew that if I didn't say anything during that five-minute drive to school that she'd know something was up. So, I made very small talk and then leaned over and kissed her. "I love you. See ya later." Phew! I was in the clear until 3:00 that afternoon when I'd have to face the music…or the belt.

Later that day at school I took my black pen and I looped a line from the bottom of one of the threes so that it connected with that little bridge in the number 3. Doing this would make it look like a fancy 2. I had to do this twice cuz I had two of those bad boys on there. There. All done, I thought. Now, I have a respectable report card, full of nothing but 1's and 2's.

The school bell rang and my heart got heavy. I'd have to show the report card today, I couldn't put it off any longer or she'd become suspicious. So, I walked into the kitchen and there was my mother sitting at the dinner table talking to my brother, Larry. Good, I thought. She'd be less likely to blow her stack because she was already in a good mood. That's when I whipped that puppy out of my book, handed it to her and held my breath. I stood there for what felt like an eternity as she surveyed my report card in complete silence.

Finally she spoke. "Fraaaannnn?" I think she was giving me time to fess up but I didn't say anything. "This looks like it's been changed. Did you change these grades, girl?" I shook my head no. And I was so cute, how could you not believe me? "Did you? I knoooowww you didn't change this from a 3 to a 2?" I nodded no again. "Cuz if you did you're gonna be in big trouble, little girl."

That's when I learned a little something about negotiating. Sometimes you just gotta keep your mouth shut and let the other person talk. So, I held my ground and didn't say a word. "You hear me talking to you?" I had to answer.

"I didn't change anything. If you don't believe me, you can ask Ms. Haynes." What? I couldn't believe those words had come out of my mouth but they turned out to be my ace in the hole. By saying that she could call my teacher I was doing that psychology thing and I didn't even know it. My mom just looked at me real suspicious like. Then she signed the back of my report card while keeping her eyes on me. She slid it across the table in my direction and rolled her eyes. "I just might do that, Ms. Pris."

That was just like my mom to have the last word. And it was always a word that left you wondering if the lie you'd just told would come back to bite you on the butt. Fortunately, she never called my bluff and I never brought another 2 into my house.

Hey Now, You're an All-Star

Remember when your 1st grade teacher used to wear you out with that old adage, 'Your attitude determines your altitude?' My fifth grade teacher, Carneda Mulkey, used to work my nerves with this saying. Whenever I would act like I didn't care about my studies, she'd say, "Frances Harris (cuz you know they called you by your given names back then), your attitude determines your altitude, young lady."

It took me a whole six weeks to figure out what Ms. Mulkey was talking about, but I knew that whenever she said it that it was time for me to straighten up and fly right. That was another thing all the teachers used to say that we didn't understand. Straighten up and fly right? My mother liked that one too.

The things adults say to confuse 9-year olds. Be patient, I'm going somewhere with this little story. Yes, here we go. Brandy Reed's rumored bad attitude almost cost her a well-deserved spot on the 2000 All-Star team. In case you were sleeping during the All-Star break, the Western Conference coaches did not originally choose Reed (through votes), I think because she's rumored to have an awful attitude. And had the All-Star game not been played in Phoenix, Brandy would've just been out of luck. Which would have been too bad because Brandy's got ridiculous skills.

But fate is the Great Equalizer because it just so happens that Coop was still nursing an ankle injury and the West team needed a replacement. And I'm sure that the threat of a boycott and daylong protest outside of America West Arena by the Phoenix Mercury fans had nothing to do with Reed getting on that team. Nah, probably not.

A Class Act

Some airlines have a reputation for being downright rude but others really do work at being exceptional. During the 2000 WNBA season I had several unfortunate—sexist and racist incidents occur on a certain airline. The first one went like this. I am the second person to board the plane. As I head to my seat, 3A, I notice that there are no blankets in the overhead, so I place my bag on the floor in front of me at 2A and reach for blankets in the second row overhead. That's when it happened. "Uh, please don't take those blankets from up here, there are plenty back there." It only took 1.5 milliseconds for my head to spin around like Linda Blair in the Exorcist. I looked at this tiny, fiftysomething Anglo woman and I said, "I am *up here.*"

People are just nuts, that's what I always say. Who in their right mind would say something like that? So, I wrote the airline a very long note, outlining all of the things that had happened to me on my summer travels, telling them in great detail about all of the racist and sexist comments their flight attendants had made to me in 90 days. A week and a half later I received a letter from a top executive apologizing; promising to share my letter with all employees and to address the issues company wide. They also upgraded me to gold status.

A lot of people thought I should try to sue this airline because I have to admit, the attendants who offended me were awfully stupid. But I think people sue too much. They're always looking to get somebody into court. I think our society has forsaken the art of dealing civilly with one another. And no one wants justice more than I do, but there are lots of ways to get it. Now, had any of these people tried to deny me rights on an aircraft as that fool did back in the '50s with Rosa Parks, then yes, I would have taken action. But there's a big difference between profiling and discrimination.

Why Some Businesses Will Never Get Into My Wallet

One night a good friend, who happens to be white, and I walked into a local hot spot. I walked up to the podium where customers check in and place their names on a waiting list. My friend walked over to the window about ten feet away. The host, who was also white, came over to the podium, looked at me and then at my friend. To her he said, "May I help you, Ms?" My friend turned around and we looked at each other with puzzled expressions. I looked back at the guy.

I blurted out. "Do you not see me standing here? Am I invisible? See, cuz, it looks like I'm standing here." I looked at my friend who's about to pounce on this guy. I continue going at him.

"Do-you-see-me-standing-here? Maybe I'm just not here to people standing behind the podium. Yeah, that's gotta be it" And I went on like this for another two minutes, rambling about how invisible I must have been. The guy turned redder than a tomato and then tried to come up with some lame excuse about why he ignored me, saying that he thought we were together. "Then if you thought that, why didn't you just speak to me? I'm the one standing right in front of you."

"Well, uh, uh, I just…," he said.

"Save it. We will never eat here again."

We walked out of that place and I have never been back. That was over two years ago. And I don't care if they do have the best pancakes in town, Kerbey Lane Café on South Lamar will never get another cent from me.

The Future of the WNBA

Remember these names. Lennox, Brown, Thomas, Frese and Wolters. No, it's not the WNBA's new legal counsel team but I certainly wouldn't take this quintet lightly. They're the new faces in the league and were among the leading candidates for Rookie of the Year honors. They also distanced themselves from their classmates slowly but surely and established themselves as the ballers to watch as this league matures.

When we looked at the crop of seniors coming out in 2000, the perception was that it was weak, diluted and disappointing. A lot of WNBA coaches even gave up picks in this year's draft to improve their chances of having a shot at next year's seniors, Tennessee's Tamika Catchings and Semeka Randall, Notre Dame's Ruth Riley and Coco and Kelly Miller, the twins from Georgia.

This year's WNBA rookie class was so sick of hearing about how soft their class is that they took it personally and delivered big time performances against big names and teams. "We keep hearing how the 2K class wasn't that strong," said Minnesota Lynx guard Betty Lennox. "Our attitude is to go out and show them just how good we are."

True, Lennox and former Louisiana Tech teammate, now Detroit Shock guard Tamicha Jackson believed in taking 30 shots apiece back in college, but these two speedsters can flat out play the game. Lennox stared at off guard for the Lynx and her 14.7 scoring average ranked 7th at one point during the season. Shock head coach Nancy Lieberman-Cline loved Jackson's winning attitude. "T.J. is incredible and she's such an intelligent player. I'd love to see her mix a little more John Stockton with her Allen Iverson," Lieberman-Cline told me before her team beat the Cleveland Rockers toward the end of the season. Edwina Brown, Jackson's partner in crime in the backcourt, had an up and down season but will be a terrific pro within the next five years.

Even though the Portland Fire had been anything but hot during the 2000 season, they do have a promising future. The buzz is that Michigan grad, Stacy Thomas, is on track to be one of the league's top defensive specialists. Thomas, a lean 5'10", earned a starting position and was often given the task of guarding the opposing team's top offensive threat. Her teammate, Lynn Pride (Kansas), played sporadically during the season but her coach, Linda Hargrove, wants her to improve defensively. No surprise, most college grads don't come into the league with exceptional defensive skills.

Utah's Stacy Frese may one day have a big end of the season payday. She ranked among the league's leaders in free throw percentage with a 95%. A slight 5'6, Frese logged lots of minutes with the Utah Starzz as a rookie and I look for her to win some shooting awards before her WNBA career ends.

I know, I know. Kara Wolters is not a rookie but technically she should be considered one. And I also know that there are still a lot of Kara Wolters detractors out there. I was one of them. But I've been born again and I reminded myself of how important it is for a player, any player, to get into the right system. Indiana Fever interim head coach Anne Donovan understands big women. The 6'8 Olympian and Old Dominion All American has seen her share of double teams and she knows the abuse they take from smaller players, officials and the press, particularly when they don't dominate immediately. Anne also knows how to develop big people, which is why Wolters flourished under her tutelage. Wolters was a sweet and gentle 6'7 wallflower in Houston last summer but this season became one of the Fever's first offensive options. Okay, so she didn't get the 2000 Rookie of the Year hardware but she and Tangela Smith should have tied for the league's Most Improved honor.

If You Were Born Post 1970, We're Taking You Back In Time

My proposal to the league is simple. Anyone who's twentysomething should be required to take a trip back in the women's basketball time capsule. The days when 50 folks in the stands meant somebody's family was in town. The days when the media stuck the results of your upset victory over your archrival, way in the back of the sports pages. Wait, that's still going on, isn't it?

I want these youngstahs to go back to the short shorts days. The Afros, hiphuggers and bellbottom days. The days when 99% of women's basketball teams wore Converse sneakers because they were the only company interested in women's basketball. Back to the days when there was one, count it, one televised game for the entire season and it was on Easter Sunday. It was the national championship game featuring one of these four teams: Old Dominion, Louisiana Tech, Delta State or Immaculata. That's where I wanna take these youngstahs. Let them see from whence we've come.

Who's Got Next? Expansion: Less is more

Each year there's more parity in the WNBA. But heading into the 2001 season it may be more difficult to achieve this equal state because there will be no expansion draft. In the previous three years, the league added two to four teams, a process that required existing franchises to 'give up' some of the players on its current roster. In theory, this meant that the foundation for expansion teams like Seattle and Indiana would be stocked with talented, experienced, players. Although the league wanted teams to be able to maintain some roster consistency, in reality this system was flawed from the very beginning. Why? Because in the 2000 expansion draft for instance, existing franchises could 'protect' up to five players. Protection meant that no team could 'touch' or draft them. So losing a bench player or two for teams like Houston meant that they'd still have the nucleus of a team that had won three straight championships.

This meant that instead of being able to pick up a star player on whom a new expansion coach could build his or her team, they were restricted to drafting reserve players who may or may not have logged many minutes. Essentially, an expansion team would have a difficult time being competitive in its first season in the WNBA primarily because it's not easy to bring in a new coach and all new players and expect them to hit the ground running on all cylinders. The Orlando Miracle is an exception as they almost made it to the playoffs in their inaugural season in 1999. But remember, this was also the first season that American Basketball League (ABL) players were available and head coach Carolyn Peck was able to snag the likes of veteran Shannon Johnson who'd led the Columbus Quest to two ABL championships.

Wisely, the league has put the breaks on expansion for a few years. Teams can now grow into themselves and fans will now be given a chance to get to know the players on their teams and also build some loyalty without the fear of their favorite personalities being shipped off to another team the following season.

EPILOGUE

As I write this, I am on my flight from Honolulu. I was a sideline reporter for ESPN for Team USA's last exhibition game in the States before they headed over to Australia for the Olympic Games. When I got home, a friend of mine pointed out how great it was that the game against the USA Select Team had been televised on ESPN2. I didn't understand. The game was a blowout. That's when she reminded me of the huge gap that exists between our Olympic caliber athletes and collegians.

Critics of the WNBA have long moaned about the WNBA being a mere showcase of college-level talent. I disagree. And the 91-57 shellacking by Team USA proves just that. Yes, the WNBA has its share of mediocre talent, but it is without question the place where our elite athletes shine. The Jones Cup Team/USA Select Team would beat a bunch of college-aged players but they never had a chance against the likes of Leslie, Griffith, Edwards, Staley and Swoopes. Never.

During this game, I introduced a piece at the halftime on Lisa Leslie. And as I wrote the introduction right before the game, it dawned on me just how fortunate Lisa's generation is. They were born at the right time. They will get to start and finish their basketball careers on their home soil. And what's even better is that my children will grow up during a time when there's always been a WNBA. Sweet.

AFTERWORD

It's official. The WNBA grew up this year and established itself as a real professional sport. We saw real rivalries take shape in both conferences. We saw home crowds (besides New York) boo opposing teams. We watched the first major retirement announcement rock the foundation of the league. We saw one superstar emerge from the shadow of another. We saw a young, eager and ultra talented team fold under the gun because they didn't know how to win when they were *supposed* to. We saw the league's most dominant team prove that they were mere mortals like the rest of the WNBA.

While the WNBA has come a long way since the inaugural '97 season, we've still got a ways to go. Let's look at the progress.

Salaries. In Year One, the league minimum was $5000. In '99, everyone makes five figures. We still haven't had our $1 million dollar salary woman yet, but I've got a feeling that it's not too far away.

Players. In the beginning, we were supposed to accept that Rebecca Lobo and Lisa Leslie were the best women's basketball had to offer. Today, players like Sacramento's Yolanda Griffith, Los Angeles' Tameka Dixon and Houston's Tina Thompson step on the court and prove that they're money without the hype of the WNBA's marketing machine.

Television Exposure. In the beginning, you sorta felt like the eventual champions had been pre-ordained by the number of televised games they had on the schedule. In 1997, each weekend the national broadcasting slate was full of the New York Liberty and the Los Angeles Sparks. Today, the wealth is spread out a bit more evenly with expansion teams getting a little of the love on occasion. The next steps are to get better time slots and upgraded pre and post game shows.

Fanfare. League projections for average attendance in '97 hovered somewhere around 4,000. Women's basketball fanatics shattered that goal and poured into arenas to the tune of 10,000 a night. And although attendance dropped slightly this season, attendance is quite healthy for such a young league. In '97 a team would walk into a visiting arena and receive a standing ovation. When the Los Angeles Sparks ran onto center court at the Compaq Center in Houston last Thursday, they were not served milk and cookies, instead they were booed for a good two minutes.

East Rivalries. The race to the eastern conference championships was tight until the bitter end. While Cleveland, Orlando and New York battled for 1st place, Detroit and Washington duked it out for the fourth and final playoff spot. The Mystics eventually won, but Nancy Lieberman-Cline did an excellent job of getting her completely revamped Detroit team into playoff form after losing five players to the Olympics and expansion.

West Rivalries. No one thought that the Los Angeles Sparks would sweep the Houston Comets during the regular season. Not even the Sparks. But former Los Angeles Laker Michael Cooper planted two seeds on the opening day of training camp. He told them that they would be the best team in the league if they could channel their efforts to defense. However, during the conference finals, when regular season records mean nothing, the talent-laden Sparks didn't have the leadership and mental toughness to beat the playoff-experienced Comets.

Turnarounds. After finishing a pitiful 7-25 and being hailed as the WNBA's worst team in 1999, the Cleveland rockers drafted Ann Wauters, one of Europe's top young players and advanced to the Eastern

Conference Finals before falling to the Liberty despite losing its top scorer a year ago, Eva Nemcova to a knee injury.

Mortality. It was a question I got every single week. Can Houston win a 4th championship and if so, is one dominant team good for the league? This year's road to the Finals for the Comets was by far its most remarkable. Cynthia Cooper, the league's best player for the last three years has announced her plans to retire. The Comets may have had their share of internal turmoil but let's not forget that they also exemplified all that is good about team sports. They've produced three of the league's four Most Valuable Players. And they've turned non-believers into fans from coast to coast, evidenced by the record crowds that pile into arenas when the Comets brought their show to town.

Changing of the guards. Sheryl Swoopes' ascent to the league's upper echelon hasn't been as easy as most people think. After missing the inaugural season to give birth to her son, Jordan, she returned to a Comets team that was already well on its way to its first championship. The following year was spent reestablishing herself on a team who already had not one, but two superstars in Cynthia Cooper and Tina Thompson. In 1999, Swoopes finally stepped out of Cooper's shadow, tallying the highest number of All-Star votes and coming very close to beating Yo Griffith for the MVP award. But it was the 2000 season when Swoopes forgot about honors and just decided to play the game. The results? MVP, Defensive Player of the Year and the second consecutive season with the most All Star votes.

ABOUT THE AUTHOR

Fran Harris was a member of the Houston's Comets first WNBA championship team in 1997. She was also the leading scorer on the 1986 national championship 34-0 team at The University of Texas at Austin. A women's basketball analyst since 1988, she joined the Lifetime Television WNBA broadcast team in 1998. Her debut novel, *Houston By Morning,* a story set in the world of agents, broadcasters, players, media and coaches in the WNBA, has a Winter 2001 release date. She wrote, produced and directed her first short film, A Rose Is Still A Rose, in October 2000 and is completing a stage and screenplay about women in the clergy. She writes a syndicated column, *Raising Good Sports,* which encourages healthy youth athletic experiences. She resides in Texas.

For more information on Fran, please visit www.franharris.com

Celebrate The Moments of Your Life